THE TROUBLED PARTNERSHIP

HENRY A. KISSINGER, Professor of Government at Harvard University, is a faculty member of the Center for International Affairs as well as Director of the Defense Studies Program at Harvard. From 1955 to 1958 he was Director of Nuclear Weapons and Foreign Policy Studies for the Council on Foreign Relations, also serving for two years of that time as Director of the Special Studies Project for the Rockefeller Brothers Fund, organizing the studies and writing several of the reports. Throughout the years Professor Kissinger has been consultant to various government boards and agencies including the National Security Council, the United States Arms Control and Disarmament Agency, and the Weapons Systems Evaluation Group of the Joint Chiefs of Staff.

Professor Kissinger has written for many publications, including *Foreign Affairs, Harper's,* and *The Reporter.* He is the author of *Nuclear Weapons and Foreign Policy,* for which he received the Woodrow Wilson Prize in 1958 for the best book in the fields of government, politics and international affairs, *The Necessity for Choice,* and *A World Restored.*

THE TROUBLED PARTNERSHIP

A Re-appraisal of
the Atlantic Alliance by
HENRY A. KISSINGER

GREENWOOD PRESS, PUBLISHERS
WESTPORT, CONNECTICUT

Library of Congress Cataloging in Publication Data

Kissinger, Henry, 1923-
    The troubled partnership.

    Reprint. Originally published: Garden City, N.Y. :
Anchor Books, 1966, c1965.
    Bibliography: p.
    Includes index.
    1. Europe--Foreign relations--United States.
2. United States--Foreign relations--Europe. 3. North
Atlantic Treaty Organization. I. Title.
[D1065.U5K54 1982]   327.4073   82-15533
ISBN 0-313-23219-9 (lib. bdg.)

THE TROUBLED PARTNERSHIP was originally published in hard covers by McGraw-Hill Book Company for the Council on Foreign Relations, Inc. The Council on Foreign Relations is a nonprofit institution devoted to the study of the international aspects of American political, economic and strategic problems. It takes no stand, expressed or implied, on American policy.

The authors of books published under the auspices of the Council are responsible for their statements of fact and expressions of opinion. The Council is responsible only for determining that they should be presented to the public.

Reprinted by arrangement with McGraw-Hill Book Company

Reprinted in 1982 by Greenwood Press
A division of Congressional Information Service, Inc.
88 Post Road West, Westport, Connecticut 06881

Printed in the United States of America

P

In order to keep this title in print and available to the academic community, this edition was produced using digital reprint technology in a relatively short print run. This would not have been attainable using traditional methods. Although the cover has been changed from its original appearance, the text remains the same and all materials and methods used still conform to the highest book-making standards.

For Elizabeth and David

PREFACE

This book grew out of a series of three lectures delivered at the Council on Foreign Relations in March, 1964, under the sponsorship of its Atlantic Policy Studies. It was written at the Center for International Affairs, Harvard University. This Center was created in 1958 to foster the study of basic world problems by scholars from various disciplines and senior officials from the United States and abroad.

In writing this book I have benefited from the advice and assistance of many friends and colleagues. Caryl Haskins and Harold van B. Cleveland, Director of the Atlantic Studies Project, have read the entire manuscript and made many extremely valuable suggestions. Stephen Graubard was very helpful with the chapters dealing with political issues. Tom Schelling's incisive and brilliant advice contributed greatly to the chapters on strategy.

I am indebted to my colleagues on the Steering Committee of the Atlantic Policy Studies of the Council on Foreign Relations for many stimulating discussions. These studies deal with major problems of the Atlantic area and are financed by the Ford Foundation. The members of this Committee are: Charles M. Spofford, Chairman; Hamilton Fish Armstrong, Gabriel Hauge, Klaus Knorr,

Ben T. Moore, Alfred C. Neal, James A. Perkins, Eugene V. Rostow; and David W. MacEachron, Secretary. John J. McCloy, Grayson Kirk, Henry M. Wriston, Frank Altschul and George S. Franklin, Jr., are members *ex officio*.

I feel especially grateful to the Carnegie Corporation and its President, John Gardner. For many years a grant from the Carnegie Corporation has facilitated my research, including research for this book. John Gardner's wise counsel has shaped my thinking in many tangible and intangible ways.

Portions of this book have appeared in *Foreign Affairs*. Like every other contributor to this distinguished journal, I have benefited enormously from the patience, skill and encouragement of its editors, Hamilton Fish Armstrong and Philip Quigg.

Stephanie Jones copyedited the entire manuscript at several stages. It owes whatever readability it may have to her sensitive editorial hand. Peter Rodman was an enormously able research assistant.

Constant rewriting and tight deadlines have imposed a great burden on those who helped get the manuscript ready for the printer. Joan Blanchard, Margie Lynch, Therese Blazhys and Georgia Sherman have typed, proofread, checked footnotes and made themselves generally useful with good humor and great efficiency.

In many parts of this book I have been more detailed in my criticisms of American attitudes or policies than of those of our Allies. This is not because I believe that we are primarily to blame for existing difficulties. Many of the most creative acts of Atlantic policy have been American in inspiration. But past achievement does not guarantee, it may even inhibit, adaptation to new conditions. Because we are the strongest nation of the Atlantic Alliance, our acts have greater consequences, for good or ill, than those of other Allies. This is why I have stressed the changes in our policies and in our attitudes which seem necessary rather than dwell on our accomplishments.

In recent years, the subject of Atlantic relationships has produced strong passions. To my regret, I find myself in disagreement with some men, including colleagues, whose views I respect very much and who have contributed greatly to building close Atlantic ties. I have tried to sum up their views fairly, though, of course, no summary can do full justice to them.

Needless to say, I alone am responsible for the contents and conclusions of the book.

Henry A. Kissinger

CONTENTS

PART ONE

Introduction

Chapter One

THE STRUCTURAL PROBLEMS
IN THE ATLANTIC ALLIANCE

The most constructive American foreign policy since the end of World War II has been the development of Atlantic relationships. Through a series of far-sighted and bold measures starting with the Greek-Turkish aid program and the Marshall Plan, the United States helped Europe recover from the economic dislocations of six years of war. When the Communist coup in Czechoslovakia and the Berlin blockade raised fears about Soviet aggressiveness, the United States organized the Atlantic Alliance to insure the security of Europe. Every administration since then has promoted European recovery, Atlantic cooperation and joint defense. As a result, Europe has become more prosperous than ever and it feels safe from invasion. Significant steps toward European integration have been taken, such as the Coal and Steel Community, EURATOM (an agency for the joint development of the peaceful uses of atomic energy) and, above all, the Common Market. Until President de Gaulle's veto of Britain's entry into the Common Market on January 14, 1963, a form of European political union seemed the logical next step. According to the expectation of most American leaders, an ever more intimate Atlantic association would have followed. This was expressed in President Kennedy's Grand Design for a partnership between a united Europe and the United States.

In recent years this promise has been flawed by increasingly sharp disputes among the Allies. The absence of agreement on major policies is striking. On the Continent, the fear of a bilateral United States-Soviet arrangement is pervasive. The United States-British view with respect to disarmament is rejected by France and greeted with distrust and fear by the Federal Republic. The United States finds little support in Europe for its Asian or Latin American policies. The attempt to establish a common trade policy with the Communist world has been generally ineffective. For over a decade, the Western Allies have been unable to agree on a common attitude toward the former colonial areas. Progress toward European political unity has been slowed. Britain has been excluded from the Common Market. Basic issues of strategic doctrine have gone unresolved. The issue of nuclear control threatens to divide the Alliance.

Of course, in an alliance of sovereign states, a measure of disagreement is to be expected. What makes current disputes so complex is that they really involve basic assumptions about the nature of Atlantic relationships, the future of Europe and the relative influence of the various partners. For the first time since the war there exists an open challenge not just to the technical implementation of American plans but to the validity of American conceptions. Our strategic conceptions no longer go unquestioned; our preferences concerning the organization of Europe and the most efficient Atlantic relationship are being contested.

Many blame this on the somewhat out-of-scale figure of President de Gaulle. There is no question that the intransigent tactics of the French President have severely strained the pattern of Allied relationships which emerged after the war. But no one man could have disrupted the Alliance by himself. Fundamental changes have been taking place in the relative weights of Europe and the United States, in the nature of alliances and in the character of strategy. Allied relationships would have had to be adapted to new conditions, no matter who governed in Paris—or in Washington, for that matter.

The Atlantic Alliance has been brought face to face with two questions not unlike those with which each Western society has had to deal in its domestic affairs: How much unity do we want? How much pluralism can we stand? Too formalistic a conception of unity risks destroying the sense of responsibility of our Allies. Too absolute an insistence on national particularity must lead to a fragmentation of any common effort.

The impact of particular statesmen aside, the Atlantic Alliance is beset by two kinds of problems: those produced by structural conditions, with which policymakers must learn to live, and those caused by acts of policy. This chapter will deal with the structural problems of the Atlantic Alliance.

THE CHANGED NATURE OF ATLANTIC RELATIONSHIPS

Perhaps the deepest danger we face is that, as with all great achievements, nostalgia for the patterns of action that were appropriate when America was predominant and Europe impotent may become an obstacle to the creativity needed to deal with an entirely new situation. Those Americans who deserve the greatest credit for promoting the recovery of Europe and forging existing Atlantic ties are finding it most difficult to adjust to conditions in which American leadership is no longer unquestioned. The fact of a challenge to American pre-eminence is almost as irritating to them as its content. They suffer from the distortion of perspective produced when, in the late forties, the end of America's isolation coincided with

the temporary loss of Europe's ability to play an effective
international role or to protect itself against foreign dan-
ger. They remember a Europe torn by World War II.
Every European country—with the exception of Great
Britain—had known defeat at one time or another during
that conflict. Every country—again with the exception of
Great Britain—had been the victim of foreign occupation.
Societies were shattered. Europe was dependent on the
United States for its material well-being, domestic cohe-
sion and safety from invasion.

United States-European relationships took on their
present cast during this period. Faced with a ravaged
Europe, the United States came to deal with its Allies
paternalistically. This has involved a certain self-righteousness and impatience with criticism. American policymakers often act as if disagreement with their views is due
to ignorance which must be overcome by extensive briefings and insistent reiteration. They are less inclined to inquire whether there may be some merit in an opposing
view than in overwhelming it with floods of emissaries,
official and semi-official. As a result, the United States
and Europe have too often conducted their dialogue over
the technical implementation of a blueprint manufac-
tured in America.

In part, this American attitude was both the cause and
the product of some bad habits developed by Europe during the period of unchallengeable American dominance.
Throughout much of the postwar period, the policy of our
European Allies has consisted essentially in influencing
American decisions rather than developing conceptions of
their own. This, in turn, produced querulousness and insecurity. At times, our Allies have seemed more eager to
extract American reassurance than to encourage a consistent United States policy. Excessive suspicion has been
coupled with formal pliancy. For a decade, European
statesmen showed their disagreement by stalling on agreed
measures rather than by developing alternatives. This has
led to a negativism characterized by a greater awareness

of risks than of opportunities and by a general fear of any departure from the status quo.

The period of American hegemony came to an end in the late fifties and early sixties under the impact of four events in which United States policy had played a major role: European economic recovery; European integration; decolonization; and the Cuban missile crisis and its aftermath. Each of these events illustrates that results cannot always be judged by the intentions of those whose policies start a historical process, even less by their pronouncements.

The United States promoted European recovery in a constructive and far-sighted spirit. We saw Europe as a potential partner eventually sharing with us the burdens and responsibilities of world leadership. Most pronouncements of American purposes reflected our expectation that after its recovery Europe would no longer require American economic assistance but would continue to pursue parallel, if not identical, policies.

This was, however, always unlikely. With the growth of European economic vigor, Europe's traditional political dynamism was bound to return. The trend was given impetus by the existence of an intact younger generation—the first since the carnage of World War I—eager to assert its own view of the world.

The process of European economic integration magnified Europe's new-found assertiveness. The orthodox American view was that the Common Market should be "outward-looking," by which we meant that its economic strength would buttress all free peoples without discrimination. However, it is the essence of a common market that it will maintain *some* tariff barriers against the outside world, and, as internal barriers are lower than external ones, a measure of discrimination will be unavoidable. Moreover, these external barriers can be reduced only as the result of governmental negotiations. And, obviously, the stronger the economic unit, the more formidable its bargaining power.

The increasing economic strength of the European Common Market was bound to complicate economic negotiations with Europe—a fact not to be eliminated by epithets like "inward-looking," which American policy-makers tend to use to oppose policies they consider unfavorable to American interests. The internal logic of the Common Market produces its own necessities. It is no accident that in most economic negotiations—whether they concerned Britain's entry into the Common Market or the so-called Kennedy Round of negotiations designed to adjust tariffs between the Common Market and the United States—the position of the Common Market Commission has been close to that of France despite profound differences about the political organization of Europe. The economic interests of the Common Market often coincide with the political goal of France to assert a more independent role for Europe.

The process of decolonization has also contributed to Europe's new vigor. Freed from overseas commitments, many European countries for the first time in a generation are able to develop a specifically European role for themselves. Ironically, the end of Europe's colonial empires has led to a reversal of the traditional postwar attitudes of the United States and Europe toward many underdeveloped countries. Some European leaders are now repeating the American argument of the fifties: that the larger interests of the free world are sometimes served by allowing for differing, occasionally even competing, Western approaches to the emerging nations.

This attitude, too, was inevitable, even though it bears the marks of De Gaulle's high-handed tactics. Having shed their colonial possessions, often under American pressure, our European Allies have a psychological block against running major risks on behalf of areas from which they have been so recently ejected. As a result of decolonization, our European Allies have ceased to think of themselves as world powers. They possess neither the resources nor the domestic framework for distant enterprises. No European government, with the possible exception of the United Kingdom, is likely to be convinced that its security is jeopardized by events in another part of the globe.

United States spokesmen often exhort our Allies to play a more active global role with the argument that their resources are now adequate for such a task.[1] But the problem is more complicated. The availability of resources does not guarantee an interest in assuming worldwide responsibilities as is demonstrated by United States policy prior to World War II.

The same is true today for almost all our European Allies. Each of them has an interest in preserving the peace. But this general concern will not produce meaningful support for such United States policies as the defense of Southeast Asia. If our Allies give assistance, it will be token in nature, and the motive will be to obtain a veto over United States actions. The thrust of their recommendations will be to avoid a direct showdown and even the semblance of risk. In other words, we are now the only member of NATO with world-wide interests, and this produces unavoidable differences in perspective.

Finally, relations with the Communist world have changed dramatically since the Cuban missile crisis. Most of our European Allies have reached the conclusion that the two main nuclear powers will avoid a direct military confrontation for an indefinite period. This conviction has been strengthened by the hope of some, and the suspicion of others, that bilateral United States-Soviet dealings are under way. Such an atmosphere of detente removes the previous urgency for Allied cohesion. As the Soviet threat appears to recede, the scope for largely national action widens proportionately. As the impression grows that bilateral Soviet-United States negotiations are proceeding, Third Force tendencies in Europe are stimulated. The

[1] See, for example, George W. Ball, "NATO and World Responsibility," *The Atlantic Community Quarterly,* Vol. 2, No. 2 (Summer 1964), p. 215.

issue is not whether the United States would make a "deal" contrary to the interests of its Allies. It is rather that in an alliance of sovereign states each country will think that it is a better judge of its own requirements than any partner, however close. No ally will be prepared to let another negotiate about what it considers its vital interests.

As the detente develops, the need to transform the Alliance from its present defensive concept into a political arrangement defining itself by some positive goals will grow ever more urgent. Defense against a military threat will soon lose its force as a political bond. Negotiations with the East will prove corrosive unless they go hand in hand with the creation of common political purposes and the institutions to embody them. The need, in short, is to go from alliance to community.

Thus major changes have occurred in U.S.-European relations that have not been caused by any individual, though they may have been exploited by willful men. On both sides of the Atlantic the persistence of old attitudes in new circumstances has contributed to the impasse. Adjusting to a loss of pre-eminence is always a difficult process. Grown accustomed to finding its views unchallenged, the dominant ally tends to identify its policies with the general interest. This conviction is reinforced by a network of connections with individuals who have helped develop the existing pattern and who consider it natural. The desire of the erstwhile protégés for autonomy appears as distrust; the quest for independence seems indistinguishable from self-will. Why should a country want freedom of action when, by definition, its interests cannot diverge from those of the dominant partner?

By the same token, countries striving to alter a relationship of tutelage will be tempted to emphasize the burdensome aspects of the existing relationship and to neglect its benefits. They will not credit the motives of the senior partner and look for hegemonial designs in sincere efforts to achieve a consensus.

In the process, both sides emphasize form over substance. On one side, the method of integration becomes a good in itself; on the other, a posture of autonomy is sought for its own sake. Wisdom and restraint would be severely tested in the best of circumstances. But the circumstances have not been fortuitous. The change in relationships within the Atlantic area has had to be carried out at a moment when the whole concept of alliances is in a state of transition, and it has been overshadowed by the dread specter of nuclear warfare.

THE CHANGE IN THE NATURE OF ALLIANCES

During the last decade, an important change has taken place in the nature of alliances. In the past, alliances have been created for three basic reasons: (1) To provide an accretion of power. With conventional weapons, overwhelming power could generally be assembled only by way of coalition. The wider the alliance, the greater its power to resist aggression. (2) To leave no doubt about the alignment of forces. It has often been argued that had Germany known at the beginning of both world wars that the United States—or even England—would join the war, aggression would have been averted. (3) To transform a tacit interest in mutual assistance into a formal obligation.

To be sure, even before the advent of nuclear weapons, there was some inconsistency among these requirements: The attempt to combine the maximum number of states for joint action occasionally conflicted with the desire to leave no doubt about the collective motivation. The wider the alliance, the more various were the motives animating it and the more intense and direct had to be a threat to produce a united response.

This difficulty has been compounded in the nuclear age. Nuclear war requires tight command of all weapons, which is to some degree inconsistent with a coalition of sovereign states. Moreover, the enormous risks of nuclear warfare affect the credibility of traditional pledges of mutual assistance. In the past, alliances held together because it was believed that the *immediate* risk of conflict was less than the *ultimate* danger of facing a preponderant enemy alone. But when nuclear war hazards the lives of tens of millions, some allies may consider the outbreak of a war the worst contingency and, in times of crisis, act accordingly.

As a result, many of the theories of nuclear control now current within the Western Alliance have a tendency either to turn NATO into a unilateral United States guarantee or to call into question the utility of the Alliance altogether. American strategic thought verges on the first extreme; some French theorists have hinted at the second.

As for the United States, official spokesmen have consistently emphasized that the European contribution to the over-all nuclear strength of the Alliance is negligible. European nuclear forces have been described as "provocative," "prone to obsolescence" and "weak." [2] For a time during the Kennedy Administration, some high officials held the view that the Allies might be induced to ask the President to serve as the Executive Agent of the Alliance on nuclear matters. Since then, the United States has made various proposals for nuclear sharing; the common feature of these has been the retention of the United States veto over the use of nuclear weapons.

However sensible such schemes may appear from the point of view of division of labor, they would perpetuate American hegemony in nuclear matters. Allies seem to be considered necessary not so much to increase over-all strength as to provide the ability to apply power discriminately. Allies are useful because they permit resistance to aggression by means less cataclysmic than all-out war.[3] In such a structure, American decisions must

[2] For the classic indictment of Europe's national nuclear forces, see Secretary McNamara's speech at Ann Arbor, Michigan, June 16, 1962, *Department of State Bulletin* (hereafter referred to as *DOSB*), Vol. XLVII, No. 1202 (July 9, 1962), pp. 64–69.

[3] For a discussion of American strategic doctrine, see Chapter 4.

continue to be paramount. The nuclear weapons of the Alliance have to remain under central control, which in effect means American control. The predominant United States theory is a sophisticated elaboration of the situation of the late forties and early fifties. It is designed to make our hegemony more bearable, not to alter it.

According to the opposing view, alliances have lost their significance altogether. A French theorist, General Gallois, has argued, for example, that nuclear weapons have made alliances obsolete.[4] Faced with the risk of total destruction, no nation will jeopardize its survival for another. Hence, he maintains, each country must have its own nuclear arsenal to defend itself against direct attack, while leaving all other countries to their fate.

This formula would mark the end of collective security and would likely lead to international chaos. In the face of the growing nuclear arsenals of the major protagonists, it would be idle to deny that the threat of nuclear retaliation has lost some of its credibility. The Gallois theory would, however, transform a degree of uncertainty into a guarantee that the United States would *not* come to the assistance of its Allies, thus greatly simplifying an aggressor's calculation.

Moreover, in order to protect itself in this new situation, each country would need to develop not only a nuclear arsenal of its own but also foolproof procedures for assuring the Soviets that a given nuclear blow did not originate from its territory. If Gallois is right, and no ally is willing to risk nuclear devastation for another, it will also want to avoid being forced into nuclear war by its partners. Thus it will have a high incentive to devise methods to protect itself against attacks based on misinformation. The Gallois theory would lead to a multiplication of national nuclear forces side by side with the development of methods of surrender or guarantees of non-involvement.

[4] Pierre M. Gallois, "U.S. Strategy and the Defense of Europe," *Orbis*, Vol. VII, No. 2 (Summer 1963), pp. 226–249.

When views such as these carry influence on both sides of the Atlantic, it is no accident that much of the debate on nuclear matters within NATO turns on the issue of confidence. The United States tends to ask those of its allies possessing nuclear arsenals: If you trust us, why do you need nuclear weapons of your own? The allies reply: If you trust us, why are you so concerned about our possession of nuclear weapons? Since the answer must inevitably emphasize contingencies in which either the goals of the Allies or their strategy would be incompatible, the debate on nuclear control within NATO has been inherently divisive.

The preponderance of nuclear power in the hands of the United States poses one set of problems; the range of modern weapons raises another. In the past, a threatened country had the choice either of resisting or of surrendering. If it resisted, it had to be prepared to accept the consequences in terms of physical damage and loss of life. A distant ally could generally be helpful only if it was able to bring its strength to bear in the area of conflict.

Modern weapons have changed this. What each member country wants from the Atlantic Alliance is the assurance that an attack on it will be considered a *casus belli*. It strives for deterrence by adding the strength of a distant ally to its power. But, equally, each state has an incentive to reduce damage to itself to a minimum should deterrence fail. For the first time the range of modern weapons provides the technical possibility of combining these objectives. In 1914 Belgium could not base its defense on a strategy that transferred to Britain the primary risks of devastation. In the age of intercontinental rockets this is technically feasible.

Part of the strategic dispute within the Alliance, therefore, involves jockeying to determine · which geographic area will be the theater of war if deterrence fails (though this obviously cannot be made explicit). A conventional war confined to Europe must appear in a different light to Americans than to Europeans, on whose territory such a war would be fought. A nuclear exchange which spares their territory may seem to Europeans a more attractive strategy and the threat of nuclear retaliation a more effective deterrent. Although the interests of the Alliance may be indivisible in an ultimate sense, this does not guarantee that there will not be sharply clashing perceptions about methods to reach common objectives.

Thus the deepest problem before the Alliance is that the pressures of the new technology run counter to traditional notions of national sovereignty. The risks of nuclear warfare may be too great to be combined reliably with what has heretofore been considered a key attribute of sovereignty: the unilateral right of a sovereign state to alter its strategic or political views. The destructiveness and range of modern weapons have a tendency to produce both extreme nationalism and neutralism. A wise alliance policy must take care that in dealing with one of these dangers it does not produce the other.

The nature of alliances has changed in yet another way. In the past, one of the reasons for joining an alliance was to impose an additional obligation for assistance in time of need. Were each country's national interests completely unambiguous, it would know precisely on whose assistance it could count; a formal commitment would be unnecessary. Both the aggressor and the defender would understand what they would confront and could act accordingly. Wars would not be caused by a misunderstanding of intentions. They would occur only if the protagonists calculated the existing power relationships differently.

Traditionally, however, the national interest has not been unambiguous. Often the aggressor did not know which countries would ultimately be lined up against it; Germany in 1914 was genuinely surprised by the British reaction to the invasion of Belgium. Occasionally the defenders could not be certain of their potential support—for example, Great Britain and France had no assurance of U.S. assistance at the beginning of both world wars. A formal understanding, tacit or explicit, has often been the determining factor in the decision to go to war. In the decade prior to World War I, the staff talks between Britain and France which led to the transfer of the French fleet to the Mediterranean were one of the key factors in Britain's decision to enter the conflict in August 1914. (Thus the talks achieved one objective of traditional alliances: to commit Britain to the defense of France. They failed in another: to make the opposing alignment clear to the potential aggressor.)

In the contemporary period, ideology and technology have combined to produce a global confrontation. This, in turn, has rendered the national interest of the major antagonists less ambiguous. Neither the United States nor the Soviet Union can permit a major advance by its opponent whether the area in which it occurs is formally protected by an alliance or not. Neutral India was no less assured of American assistance when Communist China attacked than allied Pakistan would have been in similar circumstances. In these conditions, the distinction between allies and neutrals is likely to diminish. A country gains little from being allied and risks little by being neutral.

This inevitably results in the weakening of allied cohesion, producing what some have described as polycentrism. But polycentrism does not reflect so much the emergence of new centers of physical power as the attempt by allies to establish new centers of decision.

The gap in military strength between the United States and its European Allies has in fact widened, not narrowed, in the past decade. What *has* changed is the use to which the power can be put. On the one hand, the enormous risks of nuclear warfare call into question traditional pledges of formal assistance. On the other hand, those issues with respect to which nuclear threats *are* credible are so clear-cut as not to seem to require formal reinforcement. Polycentrism is on the rise not because the world has ceased to be bipolar, but because with respect to nuclear weapons it essentially remains so. President de Gaulle is convinced that those circumstances in which the United States might be prepared to resort to its nuclear weapons cannot be fundamentally affected by his actions. In other words, the United States commitment need not be purchased by being conciliatory and cannot be jeopardized by intransigence—within very wide limits at least.

Thus President de Gaulle sees little risk and considerable potential gain in political independence. In a curious way, it is possible for him to add American power to his own. Measures contradictory to those of the United States are thus in a sense supported by the American nuclear umbrella—a fact that adds to the irony of the situation and to the annoyance of some American policymakers. Although traditionally a state's diplomatic influence corresponded roughly to its military strength, this is no longer inevitably the case. Influence can now be achieved by using another country's protection even for policies not in accord with the ally's preferences.

The frequent insistence of United States officials and commentators that in the nuclear age an isolated strategy is no longer possible misses the central point: Precisely because an isolated strategy is indeed impossible, allies have unprecedented scope for the pursuit of their own objectives. And the more the detente—real or imaginary—proceeds, the more momentum these tendencies will gather. We live in a curious world where neutrals enjoy most of the protection of allies and allies aspire to have the same freedom of action as do neutrals.

THE NATURE OF THE STRATEGIC DEBATE

The nature of power has never been easy to assess. But in the nuclear age this problem is complicated by the enormous destructiveness of weapons and the rapid change of technology. A basic discontinuity has developed when a statesman is compelled to risk millions of lives instead of thousands, when his decision no longer involves the loss of a province but the survival of society itself. Even if the classic principles of strategy are not entirely outmoded, the statesman will inevitably be reluctant to put them to the test.

This situation reflects the basic paradox of the nuclear age: Power has never been greater; it has also never been less useful. In the past, the major problem for strategists was to assemble superior strength; in the contemporary period the problem more frequently is how to make the available power relevant to objectives likely to be in dispute. Yet no matter what spectrum of power the major contenders may have at their disposal, the fear of escalation is inescapable. Though states have an unprecedented capacity to devastate their opponent, their threats to do so have only a limited credibility. This is because the ability to destroy is not related to the ability to disarm—so that using one's nuclear arsenal indiscriminately against a major opponent guarantees only self-destruction.

This dilemma creates potent pressures against the very concept of strategy. War, it is said, has become unthinkable, and diplomacy is therefore asked to take over. But if nuclear war has become the last resort of desperate men, this has not made the conduct of diplomacy any easier. In the past, unsuccessful negotiations never returned matters to their starting point; they called other pressures into play. But many of these pressures are no longer available, and thus diplomacy, too, has become less flexible. Where no penalty for noncompliance exists —no *ultima ratio*—there is no incentive to reach agreement. As statesmen have become increasingly reluctant to resort to war, negotiations have become more and more ritualistic. Even when tension persists, the Alliance may well remain uncertain and divided about the conclusions to be drawn from this situation. Though pacifism is not a novel attitude, the pressures within the Alliance against the need for any effective military policy are likely to mount.

This problem is made more acute because the primary purpose of modern weapons is deterrence. But deterrence is as much a psychological as a military problem. It depends on the aggressor's assessment of risks, not the defender's. A threat meant as a bluff but taken seriously is more useful for purposes of deterrence than a "genuine" threat interpreted as a bluff.

Moreover, if deterrence is successful, aggression does *not* take place. It is impossible, however, to demonstrate why something has *not* occurred. It can never be proved, for example, whether peace has been maintained because NATO pursues an optimum strategy or a marginally effective one. Finally, the more effective deterrence is, the more credible becomes the argument that perhaps the Communists never intended to attack in the first place. An effective NATO deterrent strategy may thus have built-in pressures to strengthen the arguments of the quasi-neutralists.

Even when the necessity for a military policy is not challenged, serious disputes are produced by the novelty of modern weapons. Never before in history has so much depended on weapons so new, so untested, so "abstract." Nuclear weapons have been used in wartime only against Japan, which did not possess means of retaliation. No one knows how governments or peoples will react to a nuclear explosion under conditions where both sides possess vast arsenals.

Then, too, modern weapons systems are relatively untested. During the debate over the Nuclear Test Ban Treaty, a great deal of attention was focused on the adequacy of nuclear warheads. In fact, the other components of modern weapons systems contain many more factors of uncertainty. The estimated "hardness" of Minuteman silos depends entirely on theoretical studies. Of the thousands of missiles in our arsenal, relatively few of each category have been tested under operational conditions. There is little experience with salvo firing. Air-defense systems are designed without any definite knowledge of the nature of the offense. A high proportion of the phenomena discovered in nuclear testing has been unexpected.

The novelty of modern weapons is compounded by the difficulty of forming a plausible conception for their use. How does one threaten with solid-fuel missiles? As these are always in an extreme state of readiness, how does one demonstrate an increase in preparedness which has historically served as a warning? From a technical point of view, it is highly probable that missiles can perform most of the functions heretofore assigned to airplanes. The shift from airplanes to missiles described by former Deputy Secretary of Defense Roswell Gilpatric makes a great deal of sense technically.[5] But has adequate attention been given to the kind of diplomacy which results—particularly in crisis situations—when the retaliatory threat depends entirely on solid-fuel missiles in underground silos? During the Cuban missile crisis, dispersing SAC planes to civilian airports proved an effective warning. What will be an equivalent move when our strategic forces are composed entirely of missiles?

The intricacy of these problems has had a demoralizing effect on Allied relationships. An ever-widening gap has appeared between the sophistication of United States technical studies and the capacity of Allied leaders to absorb them—a gap that makes meaningful consultation increasingly difficult. It is unlikely that even the most conscientious Allied leader can devote as many hours to a given problem as the American experts have had months to study it. And few of our Allies have the technical possibility to develop expertise of their own. Thus, side by side with the restoration of European economic and political vigor, the military predominance of the United States continues. Differences in perspective are unavoidable when one partner possesses not only an effective monop-

[5] Roswell Gilpatric, "Our Defense Needs: The Long View," *Foreign Affairs*, Vol. 42, No. 3 (April 1964), p. 373.

oly of power but also a monopoly of expertise. The American tendency to treat psychological and political problems as if they were primarily technical compounds the difficulty. As leader of the Alliance, the United States cannot rest on the theoretical adequacy of its views. It is also responsible for the answer to questions as these: Do the Allies understand American strategic doctrine? Do they believe it? Does it encourage confidence or a sense of impotence? A too complicated strategy can lead to the paralysis of will of those who may ultimately have to implement it.

Moreover, the United States has been slow to admit to itself that real differences of interest between us and our Allies are possible. Our penchant for treating the Atlantic area as if it were a single unit runs counter to the fact that the Alliance is still composed of sovereign states. If NATO were, in fact, one political entity, it could concentrate on the most efficient form of over-all defense. In that case, exposing a part of the Alliance's territory to the fluctuations of a local conflict could seem a small price to avoid the devastation of general war.

But as long as the Alliance is based on sovereign states, they will not acquiesce in a strategy which appears to them to spell the end of their national existence. If NATO forces withdraw as little as 100 miles on the central front, the Federal Republic would have lost the greater part of its territory. What might be tolerable for a single state becomes unacceptable to a coalition. It is therefore not enough to say that the United States will take the defense of Europe as seriously as that of Alaska. Precisely because Alaska is not sovereign, it can be defended by a strategy which might prove unacceptable to our European Allies.

The reluctance to face this conflict of interests has produced what the French call a "dialogue among the deaf." The United States is concerned primarily with the most efficient organization of the common resources for defense against attack from the East. For many Europeans, assembling an adequate defensive force is not enough if, in the process, their historical position is destroyed. American proposals tend toward a rationalization of efforts for an objective so much taken for granted that it requires no debate. Many Europeans opposing American conceptions are not content with acting simply as advisors in an American decision-making process; instead, they strive for a structure in which they have autonomous responsibility. They want their agreement to represent an act of will, not an organizational necessity.

This is why in many countries the leaders and groups traditionally most committed to national defense have developed views on strategy that challenge American concepts, while some of those most ready to accept U.S. strategic hegemony have in the past been the least interested in making a serious defense effort. Acquiescence in American strategic hegemony can have two meanings: It can either represent a sincere commitment to Atlantic partnership or disguise a neutralist wish to abdicate responsibility. Many who applaud our views may do so for reasons that will not prove very comforting in the long run. The American nuclear umbrella, now sometimes exploited by President de Gaulle for his own purposes, can also be used—and more dangerously for the West—to support policies amounting to neutralism.

The United States may, therefore, have to make a choice between the technical and the political side of Atlantic policy, between the requirements of conducting a nuclear war and the imperatives of a vital Alliance diplomacy. From a technical point of view, there is undoubtedly great merit to the American insistence on central command and control of military operations. But, from a psychological point of view, unless centralization of strategy is coupled with an effective sharing of political decisions—far beyond anything so far envisaged—the practical consequence could be a growing sense of irresponsibility among our Allies.

DIFFERENCES IN HISTORICAL
PERSPECTIVE AND ACTUAL STRENGTH

Some of the strains on Atlantic relationships have resulted from factors outside anybody's control. Many reflect the growth in Europe of the very strength and self-confidence which American policy has attempted to promote since the end of World War II. Others have been caused by the nature of modern weapons whose destructiveness is not really compatible with insistence on undiluted sovereignty.

But perhaps the deepest cause of misunderstandings—and the reason that structural problems have proved so intense—is a difference in historical perspective. Americans live in an environment uniquely suited to a technological approach to policymaking. As a result, our society has been characterized by a conviction that any problem will yield if subjected to a sufficient dose of expertise. With such an approach, problems tend to appear as discrete issues without any inner relationship. It is thought that they can be solved "on their merits" as they arise. It is rarely understood that a "solution" to a problem may mortgage the future—especially as there is sufficient optimism to assume that, even should this prove to be the case, it will still be possible to overcome the new problem when it materializes.

When applied to foreign policy, such an approach tends to treat division of labor as its own justification. Allies are considered factors in a security arrangement. Their utility is measured in terms of their contribution to a common effort. Criteria are often determined abstractly with each nation assigned a specific role with little regard to its history or domestic structure. There is a great proclivity toward abstract models. Means sometimes become exalted as ends.

But Europeans live on a continent covered with ruins testifying to the fallibility of human foresight. In European history, the recognition of a problem has often defined a dilemma rather than pointed to a solution. The margin of survival of European countries has been more precarious than that of the United States. Each country—with the possible exception of Great Britain—has known national catastrophe as America has not. European reasoning is thus likely to be more complicated and less confident than ours. Our European Allies think of themselves not simply as components of security schemes but as expressions of a historical experience. Policies that neglect their sense of identity may destroy the psychological basis of any common effort.

This difference in perspective is crucial to understanding some of the strains in Atlantic relationships. Americans tend to be impatient with what seems to them Europe's almost morbid obsession with the past, while Europeans sometimes complain about a lack of sensitivity and compassion on the part of Americans. In the fall of 1963, our newspapers were filled with derisive comments about French maneuvers then taking place. These maneuvers were based on the assumption that an aggressor was attacking through Germany. France's allies had surrendered. As the aggressor's armies were approaching her borders, France resorted to her nuclear weapons.

It is, of course, easy to ridicule this scenario by contrasting the small size of the French bomber force with the magnitude of the disaster envisaged. But the crucial issue is not technical. It arises from the fact that France has undergone shattering historical experiences with which Americans find it difficult to identify. The French maneuvers recalled importantly—though perhaps too rigidly—France's traumatic experience of 1940, when foreign armies attacked all along the Western front and France's Allies collapsed. The British Fighter Command remained in England. The fact that this critical decision was wise does not affect the basic psychological point.

Moreover, the French disaster came at the end of two decades in which France almost single-handedly shouldered the responsibility for the defense of Europe while her erstwhile Allies withdrew into isolation or offered strictures about France's obsession with security. The nightmare that some day France might again stand alone goes far deeper than the obstinate ill-will of a single individual.

A comparable problem exists in Germany. Washington has at times shown signs of impatience toward the German leaders and their frequent need for reassurance. Secretary Rusk has been reported more than once to be restless with what he has called the "pledging sessions" which the Germans seem so often to demand. However, insecurity is endemic in the German situation. A divided country with frontiers that correspond to no historical experience, a society that has lived through two disastrous defeats and four domestic upheavals in forty years cannot know inward security. The need to belong to something, to rescue some predictability out of chaos, is overwhelming. To subject such a country to constant changes of policy—as we have done—is to undermine its stability. The memories of our Allies should be factors as real in the discussions of our policymakers as the analysis of weapons systems.

The importance of this difference in historical perspective is compounded by the continuing disparity in strength between the two sides of the Atlantic. While Europe has recovered remarkably, it is important not to draw too sweeping conclusions from its new-found vigor. Europe *has* gained in economic strength over the past decade and a half. It can and should play an increasingly responsible role. But for the foreseeable future we are likely to be by far the stronger partner.

It is important to be clear about this because it requires that the United States show unusual tact and steadiness. Many of our Allies have been guilty of unilateral actions far more flagrant than ours. But when we act unilaterally, disarray in the Alliance is almost inevitable. Sudden, drastic and, above all, unilateral changes in United States strategic doctrine—whatever their merit—create a sense of impotence and are resisted as much for symbolic as for substantive reasons. Actions without adequate consultation, either in diplomacy or in troop deployment, increase European pressures for more autonomy. Bilateral dealings with the Soviets, from which our Allies are excluded or about which they are informed only at the last moment, are bound to magnify Third Force tendencies. When our Allies oppose such practices, it is not necessarily because they disagree with our view but because they are afraid of creating a precedent for unilateral changes in other policies. (Even statements of substantive disagreement may be a smoke screen for deeper concerns.) Moreover, many Allied leaders who have staked their prestige on United States policies can suffer serious domestic setbacks if we change them unilaterally.

All of this causes the voice of Europe to reach us in extremely distorted form. President de Gaulle sharpens all disputes and even creates them in pursuit of his policy of independence. But some other leaders do not give full expression to their disquiet because they do not want to undermine further the solidarity on which their security is thought to depend. Whereas France exaggerates her disagreements, some other countries obscure theirs. Thus the dialogue with Europe is often conducted on false issues, while real issues—such as the future of Germany, or arms control, or the role of tactical nuclear weapons—are swept under the rug in order not to magnify the existing discord.

American policy toward Europe must therefore take account of two contradictory trends: Europe's economic and psychological recovery and the tenuousness of this assertiveness. Many United States policies are geared only to the first of these tendencies. The assumption seems to be that European vitality will be permanent and that the only obstacle to Atlantic cohesion is an excessive estimate by the Europeans of their power.

However, De Gaulle's policy may have produced an illusion of European strength and self-confidence which is more a reflection of his personality than of underlying factors. If one moves from Europe in the abstract to an examination of the individual European countries, it becomes apparent how precarious Europe's stability really is. On the Iberian peninsula, stability may not survive two aged dictators. Italy's center-left coalition is tenuous; its capacity for major policy initiatives is limited. A post-De Gaulle France may be rent by internal schisms. Germany suffers from the absence of traditions and the pressures produced by a divided country. The vigor so noticeable in Europe today is very close in time to nihilism; European self-confidence is still shaky. Little would be gained by replacing a nationalism of insufficient strength by a neutralism which exalts impotence. To avoid both dangers and to create a new and more vital structure is the challenge before the Atlantic Alliance.

In the redefinition of Allied relationships a great deal depends on America's sense of proportion. Any new act of construction involves stress. The danger is that an attempt may be made to solve new problems by applying outmoded concepts. There is a great deal of talk about "unity," "community" or "indivisible interests." But the issue before the West is precisely to give these terms concrete meaning. Invoking the need for unity will not change the fact that American and European interests outside of Europe are not identical. Disparagement of national sovereignty emphasizes a contradiction in United States policy which exalts nationalism as the most reliable bulwark against Communist domination everywhere except in Western Europe, where the concept originated. Proclaiming indivisible interests does not explain how Allied cohesion can be maintained in negotiations with a suddenly multifaceted Communism. Slogans about integration do not answer the question of how national sovereignty can be related to the need for community in the era of nuclear weapons. In moving from alliance to community the United States will not long be able to

evade the issue of how much of its own freedom of action
it is prepared to give up.

All the realities of human aspirations and of a technology of global impact require a close association of the nations bordering the North Atlantic. But Western history
is full of tragedies, where a basic community of interests
has been submerged by subsidiary rivalries or insufficient
understanding. Ancient Greece foundered on this dilemma. Western Europe nearly tore itself apart before
it discovered its underlying unity. And now the nations
bordering the North Atlantic face the perennial problem
of the West: Whether they can generate sufficient purpose
to achieve community without first experiencing disaster.

PART TWO

The Political Issues

Chapter Two

THE PROTAGONISTS:
THE UNITED STATES
AND FRANCE

THE UNITED STATES VIEW
OF THE ATLANTIC COMMUNITY:
THE GRAND DESIGN

Problems that may be structural in origin ultimately emerge as policy issues. Thus within the Atlantic Alliance disagreements about the future organization of NATO and the relative roles of its members have multiplied. The chief protagonists have been the United States and France. Now debating the wisdom of negotiating with the Soviets, now contesting the role of nuclear weapons, always disputing the future organization of Europe and the structure of the Alliance, the two countries have sometimes acted as if each had a psychological need to use the other as a foil.

Each side has developed elaborate theories concerning the evil designs of its opponent. French spokesmen have charged that a primary goal of the United States policy is to keep its hands free for some super-Yalta—a strictly bilateral settlement between the United States and the

Soviet Union. American commentators have dismissed French policy as reflecting nothing but outdated nationalism and the illusion of grandeur of a bitter man who cannot forget past slights, real or fancied. French critics have accused the United States of seeking to maintain its dominant position by disguising its aspirations behind high-sounding words about an Atlantic community whose practical consequence will be to dissolve Europe's identity. Leading Americans have replied by emphasizing the futility of seeking to base policy on past glory, and they have accused De Gaulle of trying to identify European unity with French hegemony.

The ironical aspect of the dispute is that both protagonists profess the same objectives. France and the United States avow the goal of European unity. Both insist that their policy will lead to closer Atlantic cooperation. Each side argues that its policy will cause the Communist dictatorships to become more tractable in the long run and thus return the Soviet Union to the community of nations.

It could be thought, then, that the dispute is primarily one of tactics. In fact, the controversy goes deeper. At issue are two conflicting conceptions of international order, two different views of the historical process, two variant visions of the future. What gives the controversy its tragic quality is that each approach might have succeeded but for the existence of the other. Each side has the power to prevent the other from realizing its objective. Neither can achieve its own without the cooperation of its opponent—France even less than the United States. Any discussion of Atlantic policy must therefore begin by tracing the conflicting views of the United States and France.

American policy toward Europe in the postwar period has been remarkably consistent. Greatly influenced by such wise Europeans as Jean Monnet and Robert Schuman, in fact often following their lead, four postwar American administrations have supported movements toward European integration. In the early days of the Marshall Plan, the United States urged that a European organization allocate American economic aid among the individual European countries. It strongly pressed for the European Defense Community which would have brought about an integrated European army. When the French Parliament hesitated to ratify that treaty—to which, of course, the United States was not a party—Secretary Dulles threatened an "agonizing reappraisal" of American foreign policy.

In the end the treaty was not ratified; yet, American policy did not change. The United States welcomed the formation of the Common Market as a step toward European political union. It threw its considerable prestige against British efforts to dilute the Common Market by turning it into a free trade area. As late as 1962, Under Secretary of State Ball warned against the danger of treating the Common Market simply as an economic enterprise and opposed the efforts of the Scandinavian countries and Austria to enter it without making a commitment to political unity. The United States strongly supported the view that Britain could be induced to join Europe only if European economic integration grew so successful that Britain would have no alternative.

European political unity was considered by American policymakers as a prerequisite to the formation of an Atlantic community. On July 4, 1962, President Kennedy proclaimed his Declaration of Interdependence between the United States and a united Europe. A politically and economically integrated Europe would become an equal partner with the United States and share with us the burdens and obligations of world leadership.[1] To its fervent enthusiasts, in Europe as well as in the United States, such a partnership seemed realizable by only one method: a politically unified Europe in close association with the

[1] John F. Kennedy, "The Goal of an Atlantic Partnership," July 4, 1962, *DOSB*, Vol. XLVII, No. 1204 (July 23, 1962), pp. 131–133.

United States. Similarly, a single solution was offered for
the achievement of European unity: supranational federal
institutions controlled by a European Parliament.

Four arguments were generally advanced on behalf of
a federal Europe: to end Europe's internecine wars, to
provide a counterweight to the U.S.S.R., to bind Germany
indissolubly to the West and to provide an adequate partner for the United States.[2] American pronouncements
always equated a united Europe with supranational institutions. Anything less was not considered to be unity.

Prominent among the factors producing the preference
for supranational institutions was the conviction that the
American experience was directly applicable to Europe.
"The United States of America, with its balance of power
and Federal-State division, is the unique political experi-
ment in federation, about which we are proud and self-
conscious," said Deputy Assistant Secretary of State J.
Robert Schaetzel. "We believe that our system works. It
is a natural human reaction to believe that it might also
work for other people."[3] A similar note was struck by
President Kennedy in 1962:

The debate now raging in Europe echoes on a grand scale
the debates which took place in this country between
1783 and 1789. Small states are sometimes fearful of big
ones. Big states are suspicious for historical reasons of
one another. Some statesmen cling to traditional forms—
others clamor for new ones. And every eye is on the

[2] See for example, Douglas MacArthur II, Ambassador to Belgium, "The New Europe—Its Challenge and Its Opportunities for
the United States," address to Young Presidents' Organization, Inc.,
Phoenix, Arizona, April 9, 1962, *DOSB,* Vol. XLVI, No. 1192
(April 30, 1962), p. 711.

[3] J. Robert Schaetzel, "The United States and the Common
Market," speech to 1962 Summer Institute of the Mount Allison
University, Sackville, New Brunswick, Canada, August 18, 1962,
DOSB, Vol. XLVII, No. 1210 (September 3, 1962), p. 351. See
also Christian Herter, *Toward an Atlantic Community* (New York
and Evanston: Harper & Row for the Council on Foreign Relations,
1963), pp. 55–56.

hostile powers who are never far away. All this reminds us of our own organic deliberations.[4]

The incentive to urge the American model was especially great because the nation-state, according to American spokesmen, had become obsolete. Walt Rostow, Chairman of the Policy Planning Council of the State Department, argued:

. . . the major historic lesson of the Second World War; namely, that in the world of the second half of the 20th century the individual nation-states of Europe could only execute effectively a major role on the world scene if they were to unite. The arena of world affairs had widened out to embrace the whole of the planet; and the technology of effective power had outstripped the scale of the old states of Europe.[5]

There is no evidence that any serious consideration was given to whether a partnership among equals was really likely to operate as smoothly or mechanically as official pronouncements suggested. Occasionally the question was posed hypothetically only to be rejected. McGeorge Bundy explained the dominant view as follows: ". . . in the end our confidence in Europe rests on deeper and more solid political grounds. These peoples are our cousins by history and culture, by language and religion."[6] Unfortunately, Europe's record of internecine wars suggests that cultural affinity does not guarantee the absence of political rivalry.

The notion that there was a harmony of interests between the United States and Europe remained unques-

[4] John F. Kennedy, "Trade and the Atlantic Partnership," remarks to Conference on Trade Policy at Washington, D.C., May 17, 1962, *DOSB*, Vol. XLVI, No. 1197 (June 4, 1962), p. 907.

[5] W. W. Rostow, "The Atlantic Community: An American View," speech to Belgo-American Association, Brussels, May 9, 1963, *DOSB*, Vol. XLVIII, No. 1249 (June 3, 1963), p. 856.

[6] McGeorge Bundy, "Policy for the Western Alliance—Berlin and After," speech to Economic Club of Chicago, December 6, 1961, *DOSB*, Vol. XLVI, No. 1185 (March 12, 1962), p. 423.

tioned. Dean Rusk was expressing the conviction of three postwar administrations when he said:

In 1947 the American Government decided that it would link the recovery of Europe to efforts at European unification. We chose quite consciously not to play a balance-of-power game with the nations of Europe but to build toward a strong partnership in the affairs of the West.[7]

As the years went by one particular form of European organization came to be identified with the substantive policy which a united Europe was likely to carry out. In the American view, an "integrated" Europe would be "outward-looking"; a less cohesive Europe would be parochial. A supranational Europe would become a partner to the United States; a Europe organized differently would remain a burden or perhaps turn into a rival. In short, an integrated Europe was essential to complete the Grand Design. This was expressed by Under Secretary of State Ball:

As we have felt the increasing weight of the burdens and responsibilities of leadership—increased geometrically by the existence of a real and present danger from Communist ambitions—we have wished, sometimes wistfully, for a closer and stronger Atlantic partnership. Yet a strong partnership must almost by definition mean a collaboration of equals. When one partner possesses over 50 percent of the resources of an enterprise and the balance is distributed among 16 or 17 others, the relationship is unlikely to work very well. And so long as Europe remained fragmented, so long as it consisted merely of nations small by modern standards, the potentials for true partnership were always limited.[8]

[7] Dean Rusk, "Some Issues of Contemporary History," speech to the American Historical Association, Washington, D.C., December 30, 1961, *DOSB*, Vol. XLVI, No. 1177 (January 15, 1962), p. 86.

[8] George Ball, "Toward an Atlantic Partnership," speech to the World Affairs Council of Philadelphia, February 6, 1962, *DOSB*, Vol. XLVI, No. 1184 (March 5, 1962), p. 366.

This too was the theme of President Kennedy in his speech at the Paulskirche in Frankfurt in 1963:

> It is only a fully cohesive Europe that can protect us all against fragmentation of the alliance. Only such a Europe will permit full reciprocity of treatment across the ocean, in facing the Atlantic agenda. With only such a Europe can we have a full give-and-take between equals, an equal sharing of responsibilities, and an equal level of sacrifice.[9]

Partnership presupposed equality of strength; the United States would concede to a strong and integrated Europe responsibilities which it was withholding from a coalition of nation-states. Thus Presidents Kennedy and Johnson, as well as Secretary Rusk, have hinted that the United States was prepared to grant to a united Europe the nuclear autonomy which it had resisted conceding to individual allies—even though many of the arguments made against the national nuclear forces would seem to apply as strongly to a European nuclear force.

Although United States spokesmen extolled the virtues of partnership with a united Europe, they were rather vague about its nature. George McGhee, then Under Secretary of State, spoke of a "tightly integrated Europe" and a "somewhat looser Atlantic association." He described common tasks in aiding underdeveloped nations and in defending the frontiers of freedom, but he did not spell out the content of these objectives or how the partnership was going to function in practice. There was an implication that the partnership would apply to a sharing of the burdens but that the goals would remain those set by the United States during its period of dominance—not, indeed, because we wished to perpetuate our hegemony but because a decade and a half of unchallenged leadership had accustomed American leaders to believe that their views inevitably reflected the general interest.

[9] John F. Kennedy, address at the Paulskirche, Frankfurt, Germany, June 25, 1963, *DOSB*, Vol. XLIX, No. 1256 (July 22, 1963), p. 122.

The American view, for all its idealism, contained some inconsistencies. In the emerging areas the nation-state was treated as natural, and in Eastern Europe great hope was placed in nationalism as a counterweight to Communism. But in Western Europe, where the concept of nationalism had originated, American policy decried the nation-state as outdated and backward.

Moreover, American claims regarding the general applicability of our federal institutions have ignored those factors which made the American experience unique. The American federal union was formed on a new continent by states sharing a common historical experience. The American colonies had fought together to achieve their freedom. They were roughly of the same size. They had no tradition of sovereignty in the conduct of foreign relations. Their peoples were of similar cultural background and spoke the same language.

The situation in Europe differs fundamentally. Every European state is the product of many centuries of a history in which a sense of national identity was often linked to what distinguished a nation from its neighbors. Independence for many countries required a long process of struggle against the domination of other European states. In other words, the nations of Europe were formed in a manner which emphasized their uniqueness. In Europe, moreover, the conduct of foreign policy and the assumption of responsibility for national defense have been considered among the key attributes of sovereignty. An attempt to abolish the European nation-states, or to reduce their role drastically, represents a much more profound wrench with the past than the establishment of the United States of America did two centuries earlier.

The present-day attitudes of the European states toward the supranational forms of unity are as different as their histories. Smaller countries with a habit of dependence find supranational institutions easier to accept than do those which were once major powers. Italy, where the nation-state was never really consolidated, and the

Federal Republic of Germany, whose sense of identity was smashed in the war, are less reluctant to be amalgamated in a supranational entity than France or Britain, the countries in Europe with the longest history as great powers.

The relative weakness of the nation-state in Europe in the postwar period was due partly to Europe's economic weakness and its fear of invasion from the East. But economic recovery has tended to reduce Europe's receptivity to America's political maxims. This has coincided with the belief that the Soviet threat was ending—a development also fostered by American policy.

These factors might have been counterbalanced had Europe wished to play the global role envisaged for it by the Grand Design. But the process of decolonization has sharply reduced Europe's interest in extra-European affairs. And for a European role, the nation-state is not so obsolete as is sometimes alleged. If European countries are willing to confine their foreign policy to Europe, those joint efforts required by modern conditions are mostly technical or economic in nature. These may be left to experts—perhaps even supranational commissions of experts. But they do not require the supranational political institutions favored by the United States.

Finally, the assumption that economic integration would inevitably lead to political unity and that institutions in the economic field could be transplanted into the political arena has been proved overoptimistic. In the economic field, problems are primarily technical. Within each European government, there has been a well-established tradition of entrusting these matters either to the automatic operation of a market economy or to a group of experts. On the other hand, foreign policy by its very nature involves issues of prestige and power, which are much less suitable for compromise.[10]

But whatever the structure, origin or degree of European integration—whether it was the Europe of De

[10] For an elaboration of these points, see Chapter 8.

Gaulle or the Europe of Monnet—one question could not
be postponed indefinitely: What kind of policy would a
united Europe pursue? The assumption that a united Europe and the United States would inevitably conduct parallel policies and have similar views about appropriate
tactics runs counter to historical experience. A separate
identity has usually been established by opposition to
a dominant power: The European sense of identity is unlikely to be an exception to this general rule—its motive
could well be to insist on a specifically European view of
the world.

This is all the more true because a *European* sense of
identity can no longer be nourished by fear of the
U.S.S.R. Even if the reality of a military threat were accepted—as it is not—it would provide an incentive for
American military protection and thus lead to pressures
for Atlantic, not European, integration. In short, a united
Europe is likely to insist on a specifically European view
of world affairs—which is another way of saying that it
will challenge American hegemony in Atlantic policy.
This may well be a price worth paying for European
unity; but American policy has suffered from an unwillingness to recognize that there is a price to be paid.

Had it not been for General de Gaulle, these problems
might have remained dormant for many years. But his
emergence as President of France precipitated a fundamental change in the United States-European dialogue.
Deliberately, often cynically, exploiting the ambiguities
and ambivalences of the American conception, President
de Gaulle has proclaimed a completely different view of
Atlantic partnership and European unity. This has produced a bitter, often personal, reaction among those who
had considered the previous formula as the only possible
one. But outraged pride is not a good guide to policymaking. European-American relations will never again be the
same as they were before De Gaulle's press conference of
January 14, 1963, which excluded Britain from the Common Market and marked a watershed in European-Amer-

ican relations. Waiting for his disappearance is not a policy but an evasion. It is therefore essential to assess his policies without rancor.

THE ILLUSIONIST: DE GAULLE'S CHALLENGE TO THE GRAND DESIGN

If an international system could be designed with geometrical symmetry, the primary concern of allies would be the requirements of the common undertaking. Their efforts would be regulated by criteria of over-all efficiency and on the basis of a division of labor. But such a perfect symmetry is the illusion of utopians—or of island powers. Historically aloof and geographically isolated, such nations consider that the main function of foreign policy is to remedy the peril that has caused them to commit themselves to a joint enterprise. Secure in their identity, they expect their allies to find fulfillment in being components of an over-all design. Such was the attitude of Great Britain toward the Continent during the Napoleonic wars.

This, too, has been the tendency of the United States since it assumed major international responsibilities after World War II. Security for the United States has involved the defense of geographically remote areas based on coordinating the efforts of many threatened countries. We therefore have expected our Allies to fit themselves into an over-all strategy essentially devised in Washington. States have been judged according to their contribution to a Grand Design, with relatively little concern for their history or tradition. Attempts by our Allies to adjust their positions relative to each other have been considered outdated nationalism.

However, a society rarely draws its inspiration from serving as a contributor to an over-all division of labor; more usually its cohesiveness reflects a sense of shared historical experience and the conviction that it represents a more or less unique set of values. An alliance cannot be vital unless it conforms, at least to some extent, to the image which the states composing it have of themselves. The test of any coalition is its ability to relate the common effort to the values, aspirations and national peculiarities of the individual allies.

This is a particular problem for a country which, like France, has experienced almost uninterrupted dislocations for decades. A society which has suffered severe shocks cannot find fulfillment in the Grand Design of others without risking its identity. Before it can decide what it wishes to become, it has to rediscover what it is. Far from being based on an excessive estimate of France's strength, De Gaulle's policy reflects, above all, a deep awareness of the suffering of his people over the span of more than a generation.

Few countries have known the travail which France has suffered since it lost much of its young generation in World War I. Victorious in 1918, France knew better than any of its allies how close to defeat it had been. Inchoately, the survivors of that catastrophe realized that France could not stand another trial like the one just surmounted. Deprived of its youth, fearful of its defeated antagonist, feeling misunderstood by its allies, France experienced in the interwar period an almost uninterrupted succession of frustrations. Domestically, the Third Republic witnessed mounting governmental instability. In foreign policy, France was torn between its premonitions and its sense of impotence. Nothing could have expressed France's feeling of insecurity better than the fact that it began to build the Maginot Line at a moment when its army was the largest in Europe and Germany's was limited by treaty to 100,000 men. What made the action all the more poignant was that the Treaty of Versailles had specifically prohibited Germany from stationing military forces in the Rhineland—the territory which had to be crossed before an attack on France could be launched. In other words, at the height of its victory France felt so unsure of itself that it did not think itself able to prevent a flagrant breach of the peace treaty by its disarmed enemy and constructed a defensive line inside its borders for that contingency.

As if paralyzed by seeing her fears come true, France stood by while Germany rearmed and proceeded to abrogate one after another of the restrictions put on it by the Treaty of Versailles. The French collapse of 1940 was as much moral as military. Even though France emerged among the victors of World War II, its leaders were aware, despite all the rhetoric and perhaps because of it, that France had been saved largely through the efforts of others.

Once more, peace brought no respite. Instead, the Fourth Republic experienced the same governmental instability as the Third, and in addition it had to go through the searing process of decolonization. Humiliated in 1940, the French army had barely been reconstituted when it was obliged to engage in nearly two decades of frustrating colonial wars each of which ended in defeat.

President de Gaulle's brutal tactics sometimes give the impression that a powerful, self-confident France has been a permanent feature of the postwar landscape. It is all but forgotten that between 1958 and 1962 France was on the verge of civil war three times. So well has De Gaulle succeeded in his *tour de force* that his critics act as if the only problem for Europe were to moderate excesses of French assertiveness—a notion which would have been inconceivable five years ago. But less than a decade has passed since a wise French author could write:

. . . the pretension to indifference . . . is never completely absent. It attracts like nostalgia. . . . At the very moment when we are torn out of our solitude, we go on dreaming of it; . . . we want to stand by the wayside and watch the traffic go by. . . . Our victory in 1918 cost us too dearly. Since then we have wanted to recoup; the result is we have lost everything. Strictly speaking the French nation no longer exists. She is disintegrating at this moment. She proved unable to secure her lands against invasion because she was no longer strong enough to do so alone, and because her allies were not able to come to her aid quickly enough to prevent occupations. This is why France has had such a strong inclination to declare herself neutral. Then no one would have had the right to enter her. . . . We are living like a ruined landlord unwilling to seem bankrupt. . . . We have not been so unhappy in France for a hundred years; our literature has not been so sad; and only because during this time we have experienced hardly anything but deceptions: the Republic in difficulties, socialism bankrupt, our wealth gone, our wars badly conducted.[11]

This spiritual malaise must be understood as the essential background for President de Gaulle's policy. A certain egocentricity on our part causes us to see many of his actions as being motivated primarily by a desire to annoy or to humiliate us. In fact, his central concern is likely to be quite different. For the greater part of his career, he has had to be an illusionist. In the face of all evidence to the contrary, he has striven to restore France's greatness by his passionate belief in it. At first he was the leader of an insignificant faction of Frenchmen casting their lot with the Allies. His primary task, as he saw it, was to reestablish the identity and the integrity of France. Churchill and Roosevelt could concentrate on the tangible goal of military victory. To De Gaulle, the war had an intangible purpose. Victory was empty if it did not also restore the position, indeed the soul, of France. Churchill and Roosevelt understandably considered this quest peripheral to their central objective and treated De Gaulle's insistence as an irritating interruption of more important problems.

The conflict between the pragmatic and the intangible that started during the war has continued to this day. The United States, blessed with stable government, its sense of identity enhanced by its war experience, could pursue

[11] Brice Parain, "Against the Spirit of Neutrality," *Confluence,* Vol. 4, No. 4 (January 1956), pp. 370–379.

single-mindedly whatever technical schemes its bureaucracy thought up at any given moment. To De Gaulle, governing a country wracked by a generation of conflict and
decades of frustration, the mode of reaching a goal has
been as important as the objective itself. He judges the
merit of a policy not only by technical criteria but also by
its contribution to France's sense of identity.

Though De Gaulle often acts as if opposition to United
States policy were a goal in itself, his deeper objective is
pedagogical: to teach his people and perhaps his continent
attitudes of independence and self-reliance. The *"folie de
grandeur"* of which De Gaulle is so often accused is a pe-
culiar kind, for it is tied to a profound awareness of the
suffering and disappointments of his country. In 1960 this
caused him to speak as follows:

Once upon a time there was an old country all hemmed in
by habits and circumspection. At one time the richest, the
mightiest people among those in the center of the world
stage, after great misfortunes it came, as it were, to withdraw within itself. While other peoples were growing
around it, it remained immobile. In an era when the
power of States depended upon their industrial might, the
great sources of power were stingily meted out to it. It
had little coal. It had no petroleum. Furthermore, its population was no longer growing as, in some years, it numbered fewer births than deaths. In the doubt and the
bitterness which it came to have about itself as a result of
this situation, political, social and religious struggles did
not cease to divide it. Finally, after two world wars had
decimated, ruined and torn it, many in the world were
wondering whether it would succeed in getting back on its
feet.[12]

De Gaulle has chosen to revitalize France by an act of
faith powerful enough to override a seemingly contrary

[12] Charles de Gaulle, address on June 14, 1960, *Major Addresses, Statements, and Press Conferences of General Charles de
Gaulle, May 19, 1958–January 31, 1964* (hereafter referred to as
Major Addresses), French Embassy, Press and Information Division, New York, 1964, p. 79.

reality. In his view, an almost mystical communion has existed since the war between himself as the embodiment of the general interest and the French people. Thus, during the revolt in Algiers in 1960, De Gaulle could say: "Finally, I speak to France. Well, my dear country, my old country, here we are together, once again, facing a harsh test."[13] The effort to achieve greatness required that France regain—wherever possible—the right of independent decision. France could agree with the decisions of others: but it had to make clear that this represented a voluntary act and not the abdication of the impotent.

This is why De Gaulle never tires of insisting on his imperturbability in the face of Soviet threats or American criticisms. During the height of the Berlin crisis of 1960, he spoke as follows:

But however resounding these commotions may be, obviously they could not succeed in upsetting or intimidating France. We are today strong enough, stable enough, sufficiently self-assured not to allow ourselves to be impressed by word battles or gesticulation.[14]

In De Gaulle's concept, a great nation moves at its own pace; its objectives are dictated by its interests. Its sense of purpose enables it to become the master of events instead of their prisoner.

Consequently the dispute between France and the United States centers, in part, around the philosophical issue of how nations cooperate. Washington urges a structure which makes separate action physically impossible by assigning each partner a portion of the over-all task. Paris insists that a consensus is meaningful only if each partner has a real choice. Therefore, each ally must—at least theoretically—be able to act autonomously. Washington, postulating a community of interests, relies on consultation as the principal means for solving disagreements. In its

[13] Address on January 29, 1960, *Major Addresses*, p. 74.
[14] Press Conference on September 5, 1960, *Major Addresses*, p. 84.

view, influence is proportionate to a nation's contribution to a common effort, somewhat like share-owning in a stock company. Paris insists that influence depends not only on the existence of consultative machinery but also on what options are available in case of disagreement.

Where United States spokesmen stress the concept of partnership, De Gaulle tends to emphasize the idea of equilibrium. Many United States officials assert that all disputes can be settled by talking things over in a "community spirit." To De Gaulle, sound relationships depend less on a personal attitude than on a balance of pressures and the understanding of the relation of forces. If these are correctly calculated, negotiations can be successful. If not, goodwill cannot serve as a substitute. Philosophic convictions thus combine with personality to produce De Gaulle's aloof and uncompromising diplomatic style:

Man "limited by his nature" is "infinite in his desires." The world is thus full of opposing forces. Of course, human wisdom has often succeeded in preventing these rivalries from degenerating into murderous conflicts. But the competition of efforts is the condition of life. Our country finds itself confronted today with this law of the species, as it has been for two thousand years.[15]

The art of statesmanship is to understand the nature of the world and the trend of history. A great leader is not so much clever as lucid and clear-sighted. Grandeur is not simply physical power but strength reinforced by moral purpose. Nor does competition inevitably involve physical conflict. On the contrary, a wise assessment of mutual interests should produce harmony:

Yes, international life, like life in general, is a battle. The battle which our country is waging tends to unite and not to divide, to honor and not to debase, to liberate and not to dominate. Thus it is faithful to its mission, which always was and which remains human and universal.[16]

[15] Address on May 31, 1960, *Major Addresses,* p. 75.
[16] *Ibid.,* p. 78.

De Gaulle's nationalism is in the tradition of Mazzini, who thought that nations which achieved their independence would respect the dignity of others. His diplomacy is in the style of Bismarck, who strove ruthlessly to achieve what he considered Prussia's rightful place, but who then tried to preserve the new equilibrium through prudence, restraint and moderation. His policy is bound to clash with ours because he is operating in a different time-frame.

The United States as the leader of the Alliance inevitably concentrates on solving immediate problems. De Gaulle is more concerned with the period ten or fifteen years hence. Precisely because he is sure that the United States will protect Europe in the immediate future, he wants to use this respite to establish insurance for the far future. He is looking ahead to a time when present leaders will have disappeared and American attention may be focused on other continents. Protestations of American good faith are therefore in a sense beside the point as is the rhetorical challenge that De Gaulle describe the circumstances in which the American guarantee might fail. De Gaulle need not be able to describe the circumstances which might arise when the convictions of existing leaders are no longer relevant in order to wish to reserve some measure of control over the destiny of his country or his continent. However arrogant his style, De Gaulle's approach to history is relatively humble. He is the leader of a country grown cautious by many enthusiasms shattered; turned skeptical from many dreams proved fragile; a country to which the unforeseen is the most elemental fact of history. American leaders while personally humble are much more confident that they can chart the future. What cannot be described concretely has little reality for them. Involved, ultimately, are differing conceptions of truth. The United States, with its technical, pragmatic approach, often has analytical truth on its side. De Gaulle, with his consciousness of the trials of France for the past generation, is frequently closer to the historical truth.

Though most American leaders tend to ascribe Allied tensions to the obstinacy of one man, the structure of present disputes is not novel. During World War II, many senior American leaders committed to assumptions about Soviet good faith and a world-wide system of collective security reacted with considerable hostility to Churchill's attempt to insure the future by some physical safeguards. Churchill's views about the postwar European balance of power were then considered short-sighted and a symptom of old-fashioned nationalism. However, a subtler style, the prestige of Great Britain's heroic wartime effort and a common language prevented the conflict from being so explicit. In our impatience to realize Grand Designs we are often reluctant to admit that a statesman must concern himself with the worst—and not only the best—foreseeable contingency.

Whatever the deeper reasons for the disagreements, De Gaulle's belief in the continued role of the nation-state was bound to come into conflict with the American conviction of its obsolescence. The problem is not that De Gaulle wishes to reactivate Europe's traditional national rivalries as so many of his American critics allege. On the contrary, he affirms the goal of unity for Europe as passionately as his detractors. But where the American and European "integrationists" insist that European unity requires that the role of the nation-state be diminished, De Gaulle argues that unity depends on the vitality of the traditional European states. To De Gaulle, the states are the only legitimate source of power; only they can act responsibly:

. . . it is true that the nation is a human and sentimental element, whereas Europe can be built on the basis of active, authoritative and responsible elements. What elements? The States, of course; for, in this respect, it is only the States that are valid, legitimate and capable of achievement. I have already said, and I repeat, that at the present time there cannot be any other Europe than a Europe of

States, apart, of course, from myths, stories and pa-
rades.[17]

The States are, in truth, certainly very different from one
another, each of which has its own spirit, its own history,
its own language, its own misfortunes, glories, and ambitions; but these States are the only entities that have the
right to order and the authority to act.[18]

Thus De Gaulle's proposals for European unity invariably envisage a confederation of states rather than supranational institutions. In his press conference of September
5, 1960, he called for regular consultation between the
European governments, for specialized subordinate agencies and for an assembly composed of delegates from the
national parliaments. He urged a European referendum
"so as to give this launching of Europe the character of
popular support and initiative that is indispensable."[19]

This affirmation of the need for European unity has
been repeated regularly:

. . . France . . . must help to build Western Europe into
an organized union of States, so that gradually there may
be established on both sides of the Rhine, of the Alps and
perhaps of the Channel, the most powerful, prosperous
and influential political, economic, cultural and military
complex in the world.[20]

. . . Western Europe must form itself politically. Moreover, if it did not succeed in doing so, the Economic Community itself could not in the long run become stronger or
even continue to exist. In other words, Europe must have
institutions that will lead it to form a political union, just
as it is already a union in the economic sphere.[21]

. . . Western Europe appears likely to constitute a major

[17] Press Conference on May 15, 1962, *Major Addresses*, p. 176.
[18] Press Conference on September 5, 1960, *Major Addresses*,
pp. 92–93.
[19] *Ibid.*, p. 93.
[20] Address on February 5, 1962, *Major Addresses*, p. 159.
[21] Press Conference on May 15, 1962, *Major Addresses*, p. 174.

entity full of merit and resources, capable of living its own life, indeed not in opposition to the New World, but right alongside it.[22]

Most of these ideas were incorporated in the Fouchet Plan for European integration proposed by France in 1961 to its partners in the Common Market.

It is often argued that these proposals are a subterfuge for a design to establish French hegemony in Europe—the mirror image of the French claim that American conceptions camouflage our thirst for domination. It is impossible, of course, to be certain about De Gaulle's "real" designs. However, if French hegemony is his aim, he has chosen a curious road toward it. If a united Europe makes its decisions on the basis of a unanimous vote of its member states—as De Gaulle has proposed—it can be dominated, if at all, by moral leadership alone. France could achieve pre-eminence only if French leaders succeeded in identifying themselves with the main currents of opinion in Europe. The other states are not likely to be so blind to their interests or so unsure of themselves as to refrain from casting their veto if they disagree with French policy.

American hostility to this line of thinking reflects in part our preference for federal institutions, in part our ambivalence on the issue of European unity. The United States, while advocating European unity, has recoiled before some of its consequences. It is uneasy when European states establish closer relations with each other than they do with the United States. Especially in the military field the United States has discouraged the emergence of a European point of view and has dealt with its partners either bilaterally or through integrated commands where we are likely to be dominant. De Gaulle, by contrast, considers defense a principal attribute of autonomy. He therefore resists establishing organic links between the United States and individual European countries which

[22] Charles de Gaulle, Press Conference on July 23, 1964, *Speeches and Press Conferences*, No. 208, French Embassy, Press and Information Division, New York, p. 4.

would tie the defense of Europe to American weapons
or American conceptions. In his view, Europe should concert its own policy and then deal with the United States
as a unit.

This is why De Gaulle has opposed the Nassau Agreement, which tied the British nuclear program to that of the
United States, and the proposed NATO multilateral force.
Both programs, in his view, would make Europe completely dependent on the United States. Whatever influence Europe could exercise would depend on its ability
to sway essentially American decisions. Europeans would
be lobbyists and not partners. De Gaulle considers such a
role demeaning for a great power, and he is convinced
that it will destroy the moral substance of the "integrated"
partner:

France had been materially and morally destroyed by the
collapse of 1940 and by the capitulation of the Vichy
people. . . .

That is why, with regard to the United States—rich, active
and powerful—she found herself in a position of dependence. France constantly needed its assistance in order to
avoid monetary collapse. It was from America that she
received the weapons for her soldiers. France's security
was dependent entirely on its protection. With regard to
the international undertakings in which its leaders at that
time were taking part, it was often with a view to dissolv-
ing France in them, as if self-renouncement were henceforth its sole possibility and even its only ambition, while
these undertakings in the guise of integration were automatically taking American authority as a postulate. This
was the case with regard to the project for a so-called
supranational Europe, in which France as such would have
disappeared, except to pay and to orate; a Europe governed in appearance by anonymous, technocratic and
stateless committees; in other words, a Europe without
political reality, without economic drive, without a capacity for defense, and therefore doomed, in the face of the
Soviet bloc, to being nothing more than a dependent of

that great Western power, which itself had a policy, an economy and a defense—the United States of America.[23]

De Gaulle opposes not the Alliance, but the concept of integration on which it is based. In his view, to assign tasks on the basis of a division of labor will erode France's identity:

It is intolerable for a great State to leave its destiny up to the decisions and action of another State, however friendly it may be. In addition, it happens that, in integration . . . the integrated country loses interest in its national defense, since it is not responsible for it. The whole structure of the Alliance then loses its resilience and its strength.[24]

Integration would lead to an abdication of responsibility and a sense of impotence. Ultimately, this would demoralize France's foreign policy. It would oblige France and Europe to accept the tutelage of the United States forever.

Thus De Gaulle, in 1959, withdrew the French fleet from NATO command. He argued that naval power by definition was designed for use in areas not protected by NATO commitments. According to De Gaulle, this was the reason that the major portion of the American and British fleets remained under national control. When the French army returned from Algiers, most of it was stationed in France and not "integrated" into NATO. This was done not only because of De Gaulle's objection to the concept of integration but also for a more mundane reason, which showed how brittle the seeming cohesiveness and power of France really was:

. . . it is absolutely necessary, morally and politically, for us to make our army a more integral part of the nation. Therefore, it is necessary for us to restation it, for the most part, on our soil; for us to give it once again a direct re-

[23] Press Conference on July 29, 1963, *Major Addresses*, pp. 233–234.

[24] Press Conference on April 11, 1961, *Major Addresses*, p. 124.

sponsibility in the external security of the country; in short, for our defense to become once again a national defense.[25]

In De Gaulle's judgment, twenty-five years of humiliating conflict and several military revolts against legitimate authority made it more important to integrate the French army into French society than into NATO.

Few of De Gaulle's policies have so embroiled him with America as his insistence on an autonomous nuclear striking force. He argued:

We are in the atomic age and we are a country that can be destroyed at any moment unless the aggressor is deterred from the undertaking by the certainty that he too will suffer frightful destruction. This justifies both alliance and independence. The Americans, our allies and our friends, have for a long time, alone, possessed a nuclear arsenal. So long as they alone had such an arsenal and so long as they showed their will to use it immediately if Europe were attacked—for at that time Europe alone could be attacked—the Americans acted in such a way that for France the question of an invasion hardly arose, since an attack was beyond all probability. . . . It is impossible to overestimate the extent of the service, most fortunately passive, that the Americans at that time, in that way, rendered to the freedom of the world.

Since then the Soviets have also acquired a nuclear arsenal, and that arsenal is powerful enough to endanger the very life of America. Naturally, I am not making an evaluation—if indeed it is possible to find a relation between the degree of one death and the degree of another—but the new and gigantic fact is there. From then on, the Americans found and are finding themselves confronted with the possibility of direct destruction.[26]

[25] Press Conference on May 15, 1962, *Major Addresses*, pp. 180–181.
[26] Press Conference on January 14, 1963, *Major Addresses*, pp. 216–217.

These views have caused American spokesmen to charge De Gaulle with fomenting distrust of the United States. He has been lectured on his ignorance of the technical requirements of nuclear strategy and ridiculed for excessive pretensions. Actually, his analysis of the situation does not differ radically from Secretary McNamara's. Both agree that the growing Soviet nuclear arsenal confronts the United States with an unprecedented challenge. Both insist that NATO strategy must be adapted to new realities. They disagree less in their analysis than in the conclusions to be drawn from it. Looking at NATO from the point of view of division of labor, the United States considers French resources better spent on conventional forces than on nuclear arms. From the perspective of vindicating France's identity, De Gaulle is not so concerned with the technical aspects of strategy as with the political problem of choice. The United States considers central control over nuclear weapons crucial for the contingency of general war; De Gaulle gives priority to France's impact on the conduct of day-to-day diplomacy. Secretary McNamara strives for strategic options; President de Gaulle seeks political ones.[27]

Differences between France and the United States over the future of Europe have been compounded by disagreements over the scope of Atlantic policy. These have gone through two contradictory phases. During his first three years in office (from 1958–1961), De Gaulle repeatedly urged the coordination of Western policies on a world-wide basis. In September 1958, he proposed a global Directorate composed of the United States, Great Britain and France. The United States rejected this with the argument that it could not designate one of its European partners to speak for the others. No attempt was made to explore De Gaulle's reaction to the possibility of a wider forum.

[27] For a fuller discussion of the strategic problems, see Chapters 4, 5 and 6.

De Gaulle returned to the theme of the need for co-ordination in his press conference of March 25, 1959.[28] In 1960, he made yet another plea for a common Western world-wide policy:

We feel that, at least among the world powers of the West, there must be something organized—where the Alliance is concerned—as to their political conduct and, should the occasion arise, their strategic conduct outside Europe, especially in the Middle East, and in Africa, where these three powers are constantly involved. Furthermore, if there is no agreement among the principal members of the Atlantic Alliance on matters other than Europe, how can the Alliance be indefinitely maintained in Europe? This must be remedied.[29]

This idea was pressed particularly urgently with respect to the Congo crisis in 1960.

When nothing came of these proposals, De Gaulle reverted to his usual, perhaps preferred, tactic of acting unilaterally and trying to force his partners' hand. After 1961, he stopped urging concerted Western action. Instead, he stressed that only a strong Europe would receive a respectful hearing from the United States or the U.S.S.R. Increasingly, De Gaulle seemed to expect that the development of Europe's economic strength and sense of identity would leave the United States no choice but to concede a coordination of policy.

This is not to say that De Gaulle's policy was primarily a reaction to being rebuffed by the United States. Rather, two changes in the international situation caused him to consider American support less crucial and made independent action appear rewarding. When he proposed the Directorate, a global showdown appeared possible. The Lebanese crisis had just occurred; Soviet intransigence was at its height. This impelled De Gaulle to try to insure American support in case war proved unavoidable. Since 1961

[28] Press Conference on March 25, 1959, *Major Addresses*, p. 49.
[29] Press Conference on September 5, 1960, *Major Addresses*, p. 96.

the Soviet military threat has seemed to recede, and the need for concerted action has diminished proportionately. Indeed, with the growth of American involvement in Asia and Latin America, the shoe is now somewhat on the other foot. It is the United States which presses its European allies to share its global responsibilities and the Europeans who are reluctant to assume world-wide commitments.

The reduction in the Soviet threat has brought to the surface sharply conflicting views of East-West relations. As in most other controversies, each side has accused the other of the same offense: of planning a settlement, if not at the expense of, at least to the exclusion of its ally. In the United States, De Gaulle's comment that Europe extends from the Atlantic to the Urals is often cited as proof of a thinly veiled desire to negotiate directly with Moscow. In France, United States bilateral dealings with the Soviet Union are taken as an indication that the United States is seeking a separate accommodation with the U.S.S.R.

At times both sides seem primarily concerned with scoring debating points. De Gaulle's statement that one day Europe would again extend from the Atlantic to the Urals did not imply a deal with the Soviet Union:

On our old continent, the organization of a western group, at the very least equivalent to that which exists in the east, may one day, without risk to the independence and the freedom of each nation and taking into account the probable evolution of political regimes, establish a European entente from the Atlantic to the Urals. Then Europe, no longer split in two by ambitions and ideologies that would become out-of-date, would again be the heart of civilization.[30]

The reorganization of Europe to which De Gaulle refers is to take place *after* Communist ideology no longer dominates in the Soviet Union, that is, when Russia is once more a national, and not an ideological, state pursuing

[30] Press Conference on May 31, 1960, *Major Addresses*, p. 78.

a policy dictated by its national interests. This is the precise eventuality postulated by four American postwar administrations as the prerequisite of a final settlement.

Indeed, French and American analyses of Soviet trends are not so different as the controversy sometimes suggests. Both are of the view that at some point the Soviet system will be transformed. Both believe that this transformation will mark the starting point for fruitful negotiations. They disagree not over the fact of evolution but its nature, not over the ultimate desirability of a diplomatic settlement but about who will be the spokesman for the West when it takes place. Above all, they differ about the nature of a stable international order and the role of individuals in relation to it.

The United States has a tendency to believe that peace and stability are "natural." Crises must, therefore, be caused by personal ill-will rather than by objective conditions. If tension persists, it is because Communist leaders continue to be unreasonable; it can be alleviated by establishing an atmosphere of trust and good personal relations or by a change of heart on the part of the Soviets. As a result, United States policy toward the Soviet Union has oscillated between two opposite approaches: During periods of tension, the United States tends to assume that Soviet policy is conducted by highly purposeful, ideologically inspired men operating according to careful, long-range plans. During periods of detente, American leaders have often acted as if a settlement could be achieved by good personal relations with their Communist counterparts. Either approach leads to an avoidance of concreteness. When the Soviets are aggressive, negotiations are believed to be useless, and, when they are conciliatory, there is a reluctance to disturb the favorable atmosphere. In either case, American policy statements envisage a world where all conflict has ended and nations live under "the rule of law."

De Gaulle's view is more historical. Peace to him is not a final settlement but a new, perhaps more stable, balance of forces. "Now, in the last analysis and as always, it is only in equilibrium that the world will find peace."[31] An equilibrium can never be permanent but must be adjusted in constant struggles. Tension, according to De Gaulle, is not caused so much by the personal attitudes of individual Communist leaders as by the dynamics of the system which they represent. To him, internal instability is the distinguishing feature of Communist leadership groups.

During my lifetime, Communist ideology has been personified by many people. . . . Each of these holders in his turn condemns, excommunicates, crushes and at times kills the others. In any event, he firmly fights against the personality cult of the others.[32]

Having erected an unnatural system, Soviet leaders are under constant pressure to divert attention by foreign adventures.[33]

. . . there is in this uproar of imprecations and demands organized by the Soviets something so arbitrary and so artificial that one is led to attribute it either to the premeditated unleashing of frantic ambitions, or to the desire of drawing attention away from great difficulties: this second hypothesis seems all the more plausible to me since, despite the coercions, isolation and acts of force in which the Communist system encloses the countries which are under its yoke, and despite certain collective successes which it has achieved by drawing upon the substance of its subjects, actually its gaps, its shortages, its internal failures, and above that its character of inhuman oppression, are felt more and more by the elites and the masses, whom it is more and more difficult to deceive and to subjugate.[34]

[31] Address on May 3, 1960, *Major Addresses*, p. 78.
[32] Press Conference on July 29, 1963, *Major Addresses*, p. 236.
[33] Press Conference on September 5, 1960, *Major Addresses*, p. 84.
[34] Press Conference on September 5, 1961, *Major Addresses*, p. 140.

Since in De Gaulle's view Soviet aggressiveness does not reflect a real grievance but domestic instability, it must be resisted and not accommodated by the West. To yield to Soviet blackmail would not alleviate internal Soviet stresses but only supply an incentive for further demands. Thus during the Berlin crisis De Gaulle spoke as follows:

. . . we do not allow ourselves to be moved by all the tumult, all the flow of invective, of formal notifications, of threats launched by certain countries against other lands and especially against ours. This is all the more true in that we realize the tactical element that enters into all this staging by those who, so to speak, make it their job to upset others.

. . . in their camps the struggle between political trends, the intrigues of clans, the rivalries of individuals periodically lead to implacable crises, whose sequels—or even whose premonitory symptoms—cannot help but unsettle them. Moreover, we know that in those countries there are conflicting national grievances in spite of the absolutism of their ideology. We realize therefore only too well that they readily indulge in virulent utterances and sensational outbursts in order to lead people astray—within their own country and outside—without, however, overstepping certain bounds.[35]

De Gaulle rejected the "exploratory" conversations on Berlin urged by the United States and Britain as a means of determining Soviet intentions. He refused to join the talks because:

. . . so long as the Soviet Union does not put a stop to its threats and its injunctions and bring about an actual easing of the international situation, we believe that we have spared our allies and ourselves the catastrophic retreat, dramatic rupture or tragi-comical engulfment, in which the conference would obviously have ended.[36]

[35] Press Conference on September 5, 1960, *Major Addresses,* pp. 84–85.
[36] Address on February 5, 1962, *Major Addresses,* p. 160.

And he did not participate in the Geneva disarmament conference, predicting that it would do nothing except present irreconcilable plans.[37]

Views differ, finally, about the significance of the Sino-Soviet split and about policy toward Communist China. The United States, convinced of the importance of intentions in the conduct of foreign policy, is tempted to back the Communist power which professes the more peaceful goals. De Gaulle, believing that an equilibrium is the only reliable basis for stability, is more concerned with establishing a counterweight to the stronger Communist partner. He is prepared, if necessary, to play off its weaker Communist opponent against it. The United States, with its global responsibilities, sees in Communist China an objective threat to its interests. De Gaulle, leading a country primarily concerned with European affairs, considers a Russia extending its power into the center of Europe as the principal danger. China, to him, is a distant country which could become useful in diverting Soviet energies. What is involved here is a certain divergence of American and European interests; De Gaulle's analysis is far from unique in Europe, even if his methods of implementing it are.

In short, peace according to De Gaulle is achieved not by a personal reconciliation but by the establishment of a more stable equilibrium. France and Europe must contribute in bringing about this balance not as the object of policy but as its author. De Gaulle is thus concerned not only with the fact of negotiations but also with France's role in them. He would object to *any* settlement that France did not help to formulate—regardless of his opinion of its substance. The major thrust of De Gaulle's policy is to make it impossible for the United States to deal with the Soviet Union over the heads of France and the rest of Europe.

De Gaulle's thought is remarkably consistent. Convinced

[37] Press Conference on May 15, 1962, *Major Addresses*, p. 181.

that only those capable of assuming responsibility can form meaningful associations, he can logically affirm his faith in the Atlantic Alliance while insisting on the identity of Europe and the uniqueness of France. To De Gaulle, the two notions are complementary—though this may seem disingenuous or even cynical to many Americans.

While De Gaulle's tactics have frequently been brutal, he has faced a very special challenge. Even in the best of circumstances, any leader of a country which has been ravaged by two world wars, and which barely avoided civil war in 1958, in 1960 and again in 1962, would have had to face the problem of restoring France's faith in itself. How well De Gaulle has succeeded is shown by the fact that three years after the end of the Algerian war France, far from being torn to pieces by internal schisms —as most observers expected—is the European country most active in international affairs.

Although De Gaulle has often exaggerated his psychological mission, he has posed an important question which the West has yet to answer. There is merit in his contention that a political unit must mean something to itself before it can have meaning to others. Before a state can contribute usefully to common decisions, it must be convinced that its opinions matter. The tendency of his opponents to refuse to take his challenge seriously and to treat De Gaulle as a relic to be outwaited has prevented a meaningful discussion from which a new common conception of Atlantic relations might have emerged. Difficult as it may be to deal with De Gaulle's France, we would do well to remember that it contributes to the general interests of the West far more than a France wracked by dissension or abdicating from the international stage.

But if his critics have shown little compassion for his special circumstances, De Gaulle has often thwarted his own aims by his abrupt tactics and his imperious style. Not comfortable with the give and take of negotiations, the French President has moved through a series of *faits accomplis* to force his allies to accept his objectives. A rationalist, he has acted as if his views were certain to prevail by virtue of their inherent validity and that the feelings of other statesmen were, therefore, irrelevant. A profound believer in historical necessity, he has acted as if the logic of events would always override the sensibilities of others.

No doubt, this is a heroic posture. But man is not governed by reason alone. History may appear inevitable in retrospect; but it is made by men who cannot always distinguish their emotion from their analysis. The paradox of De Gaulle's position is that he claims to speak for Europe, but he has not found it possible to create a following outside of France that considers him a European statesman. He has alienated many potential supporters by his excessive rationalism and unilateral tactics. Many individuals who share De Gaulle's aspiration that Europe play a more autonomous role in world affairs have been driven into opposition by his wounding insistence on intellectual submission to his maxims. His rigid defense of an extreme conception of sovereignty has antagonized even those who do not see the choice between a federal or confederated Europe as an issue of principle. Although France and the United States seem to agree on the principle of a strong and autonomous Europe, De Gaulle's methods suggest that he will cooperate only if others accept his unilateral pronouncements. His tactics create the impression that he desires autonomy not to enhance the unity of the West but to enable him to pursue policies contradictory, if not hostile, to those of the United States.

Ironically, De Gaulle has become a symbol on both sides of the Atlantic of principles contrary to his pronouncements and probably to his intentions. He has enabled many in Europe not previously noted for their devotion either to European unity or to Atlantic partnership to advocate some ideal model of either relationship in order to thwart whatever progress is possible now. By evoking so many memories of authoritarian rule, De Gaulle has polarized the discussion within Europe in a manner that

makes it next to impossible to come to grips with the substance of his thought. A strong Europe was bound to present a challenge to American leadership. But by couching
this challenge so woundingly, De Gaulle has spurred
American self-righteousness rather than the objective reexamination of Atlantic relationships which the situation
demands.

History will probably demonstrate that De Gaulle's conceptions—as distinct from his style—were greater than
those of most of his critics. But a statesman must work
with the material at hand. If the sweep of his conceptions
exceeds the capacity of his environment to absorb them,
he will fail regardless of the validity of his insights. If his
style makes him unassimilable, it becomes irrelevant
whether he is right or wrong. Great men build truly only
if they remember that their achievement must be maintained by the less gifted individuals who are likely to follow them. A structure which can be preserved only if
there is a great man in each generation is inherently fragile. This may be the nemesis of De Gaulle's success.

Though De Gaulle has performed an enormous feat in
lifting his country's sights almost by an act of will, there
exist objective limits which great and strong-willed statesmanship may extend but cannot change altogether. De
Gaulle's insistence that France and the United States are
equal is true in a moral sense, but if pushed too far it must
bring into the open a permanent disparity of strength. The
superiority of American resources is likely to prevail in
any confrontation regardless of the validity of the competing views. By generating so much personal ill-will
among American leaders, De Gaulle may rend the fabric
of illusion on which his policy depends. The irony of the
Franco-American rivalry is that De Gaulle has conceptions greater than his strength, while United States power
has been greater than its conceptions.

In the meantime, there is something of a Greek tragedy
about the dispute between the United States and France.
Each chief actor, following the laws of his nature, is bring-

ing about consequences quite different from those intended. Either the "American" or the "French" concept of Atlantic relationship might have succeeded. Competing as they do—with no comprehension by one side of the real intentions of the other—they may bring on what each side professes to fear most: a divided, suspicious Europe absorbed once again in working out its ancient rivalries. Tragedy, to many Americans at least, is to find oneself thwarted in what is ardently desired. But there is another and perhaps more poignant tragedy, that of fulfilling one's desires and then finding them empty.

Chapter Three

THE BERLIN CRISIS AND
THE NASSAU AGREEMENT:
THE FEDERAL REPUBLIC AND
GREAT BRITAIN UNTIL
JANUARY 1963

THE PROBLEM OF GERMANY: EVENTS LEADING TO THE FRANCO-GERMAN TREATY OF COLLABORATION

Germany has held the key to the stability of Europe for at least three centuries. In the twentieth century the peace of Europe has been violated twice by a powerful and unified Germany. But prior to 1871, when Germany was composed of a group of competing states, it was the arena of conflict for other European powers which sought to perpetuate its divisions, thwart its national aspirations and prevent one another from gaining a preponderant influence.

Considering this history it was inevitable that Germany, when it was finally unified in 1871, should identify security with sufficient strength to defend itself against all of its neighbors simultaneously. But this effort, however understandable, proved fatal to the stability of Europe. Germany's strength, coupled with its central location, produced a vicious circle. A country powerful enough to defend itself against all its neighbors simultaneously would also be strong enough to defeat each of them singly. Moreover, the effort to develop such strength required a mobilization of resources and an exaltation of national feelings certain to disquiet the other European countries. Bismarck, who unified Germany, spoke of "the nightmare of hostile coalitions." It was Germany's tragedy that the effort to prevent these coalitions made them inevitable. Germany has been either too weak or too powerful for the peace of Europe.

Ideally, Germany should be strong enough to defend itself but not to attack; it should be united so that its frustrations do not erupt into conflict and its divisions do not encourage the rivalries of other countries, but not so nationalistic that it disquiets its neighbors. To bring about such a Germany has been a major goal of Western policy since the end of World War II.

The effort to define a new role for Germany faces major psychological problems. Every German over fifty years of age has lived through three revolutions. He has known four different regimes, each claiming to be morally antithetical to its predecessor. He has seen Germany lose two world wars and has experienced two catastrophic inflations. Every German over thirty-five has witnessed the trauma of the Nazi period, of World War II and of the postwar collapse. The Nazi experience has been so completely suppressed or sublimated into a vague feeling of generalized guilt that it is no longer a problem as such. But the rootlessness produced by blotting out twelve years of history is relevant. Germany has suffered too many breaks in historical continuity and too many shocks. Great national prosperity has developed at the same time that national, political and territorial integrity has been lost. The incongruity of this situation contributes to the insecurity of German leadership groups, the stridency and legalism of whose disputes often hide a lack of inner assurance.

Chancellor Adenauer's great achievement—just as De Gaulle's—was that he understood the psychological needs of his country. He was aided by wise and far-sighted American statesmen who helped reintroduce Germany into the community of nations. In order to prevent the latent nihilism in Germany from again menacing the peace, Adenauer sought to give the Federal Republic a stake in something larger than itself. The so-called rigidity decried by many of his critics was in fact the reverse side of his attempt to teach his people habits of reliability in international affairs. He realized that Germany was too exposed geographically and too vulnerable psychologically and politically to be able to sustain a very active policy. He understood that a divided and rootless country, viewed with suspicion and fear, would be excessively tempted by either nationalism or neutralism, or both, if forced to undertake an autonomous foreign policy. The fabric of German political life might not withstand the pressures inherent in such a course.

Adenauer, therefore, sought to submerge narrowly German interests in a wider community. First he developed intimate ties with the United States which caused the opposition parties to call him the Chancellor of the Allies. Later, when United States policy on Berlin seemed to threaten vital German interests, he renewed his always strong tendency for close association with France. This culminated in the Franco-German Treaty of Collaboration of January 1963. In both cases, his major concern was to assure for the Federal Republic the moral and physical backing of a senior partner. In the case of the treaty with France, diplomatic advantage was reinforced by psychological need. For the first time in its history as a nation, Germany had a friendly country as a neighbor to the West. Perhaps Chancellor Adenauer's most notable achievement was to bring about the optical illusion that conditions in the Federal Republic were as firm and stable as his own policy.

This is not the case, however. For the first twenty years after the collapse of the Third Reich, German energies were absorbed in reconstruction, and German politics were dominated by a man whose formative experience was in the last century. But Germany's uncertain sense of identity could take surprising forms. This is all the more true because since 1961 the German situation has become more fluid under the impact of four events: (1) the Berlin Crisis and Anglo-American negotiating tactics until the end of 1962; (2) the Berlin Wall; (3) De Gaulle's European policy and the United States reaction to it; and (4) United States pressures for diplomatic flexibility.

The Berlin crisis was crucial because it emphasized a serious potential for tension within the Alliance: the difference between the German quest for national unity and the equally understandable desire of the rest of the Allies for stability. Of course, no alliance can perfectly reconcile the objectives of all of its members. But the minimum condition for effectiveness is that the requirements of the alliance should not clash with the deepest aspirations of one or more of the partners.

The Berlin issue has proved sensitive not so much because the city is physically vulnerable, but because all of Germany is psychologically vulnerable. Not all of Germany's allies accept the division of Germany, and some might prefer a unified Germany; but none makes reunification a major goal. Thus during the Berlin crises of 1959–1960 and 1961–1962, many in the West argued that the logical solution was to negotiate new procedures for access to Berlin in return for accepting the "fact" of a divided Germany. To many influential Americans and Britishers, the continuation of a status quo which had persisted for a decade and a half appeared a small price to pay for a promise of stability.

However, acceptance by the West of the division of Germany as permanent would upset the domestic equilibrium of the Federal Republic; this is one of the reasons that the Soviets are so eager to secure Western recognition of

the status quo in Germany. The division of Germany may
be unavoidable; but the cohesion of the Atlantic Alliance
requires that there is no ambiguity about the reason for
it. If the West tacitly or explicitly abandoned the principle
of German national unity—by collaborating with the Soviets to keep Germany divided—Germans would consider it
a sacrifice of their basic interests. No German political
leader can accept as permanent the subjugation of 17 million of his compatriots—all German political parties are
agreed on this point. His minimum goal must be to ameliorate conditions in East Germany—a goal that he will be
under increasing pressure to pursue independently if his
allies prove indifferent to it.

This is why the building of the Wall in Berlin and the
hesitant Western response to it gave such a shock to German political life. Many in the West considered the Wall
primarily as another unilateral abrogation of a treaty obligation by the Soviets and as an act of inhumanity to the
people of Berlin. In Germany, the Wall shattered the previous hopes for unification. For better or worse, the policy
of the Federal Republic had been based on the premise
that there was no inconsistency between Germany's national aspirations and its Western orientation. In fact, the
Western Alliance had been sold to the German public
with the argument that it represented the best method to
achieve these aspirations.

The partition of Berlin marked the end of the belief
that German unification would more or less automatically
follow the strengthening of the Atlantic Alliance. Since
then, the Federal Republic has groped for a new approach
to the question of German unity and to the alleviation
of conditions in East Germany. Some have begun to argue
that these objectives must be sought by unilateral initiatives if necessary. Others advocate a policy of relaxation.
Still others favor maximum pressure. The challenge to
Western policy is to prevent the Alliance from seeming an
obstacle to legitimate German aspirations, while not let-

ting German national aspirations transcend all other imperatives.

To strike this balance would be difficult even in a cohesive alliance. It has proved impossible in the face of a Franco-American rivalry. President Kennedy had been in office less than six months when Khrushchev's Berlin ultimatum confronted his administration with a direct challenge. The Kennedy Administration thereupon coupled a drastic build-up of American military strength with a diplomacy based on the unexceptionable proposition that a showdown could not be faced until all honorable means of compromise had been exhausted. It was widely assumed that the primary Soviet goal was to stabilize conditions in Central Europe. The United States was, therefore, inclined to seek some way to deal with the immediate irritant—the problem of Berlin—by making concessions that might enhance the status of the East German authorities without impairing the physical means of access to Berlin. American policymakers assumed that progress on the national question would be achieved by increasing technical contacts between East and West Germany. In these contacts, it was supposed, the superior moral strength of West Germany could not fail to make itself felt.

All these elements were contained in the United States plan which the Germans leaked to the press in April 1962 in order to torpedo it. It provided for an International Access Authority in which East Germany would enjoy the same status as the Federal Republic; it included proposals for a number of East-West German commissions to deal with technical problems, a nonaggression treaty between NATO and the Warsaw Pact, and an agreement to prevent the spread of nuclear weapons to other countries.

These initiatives produced conflicting emotions among the leaders of the Federal Republic. Conscious of the danger of being accused of bellicosity, they accepted the need for negotiations. But Chancellor Adenauer and his associates were extremely uneasy about the way the issue had been posed. They held that Soviet "salami tactics" had already curtailed West Berlin's margin of safety so sharply that any further concessions were likely to undermine its viability. They were torn between the desire for progress on the German question and the fear that any negotiation would result in further undermining the freedom of Berlin. They remembered that at the Foreign Ministers' Conference in Geneva in 1959 the Western powers first coupled a proposal on German unification with some concessions on Berlin. When the Soviets refused even to discuss unification, the West refrained from pushing the German plan, but still allowed possible modifications of Berlin's status to remain on the agenda.

The German government, having based its entire postwar policy on close ties with the West and especially with the United States, chose not to make public the full extent of its disquiet. Similarly, the United States preferred to stress German agreement to specific formulas in order to maintain the appearance of Allied unity. However, nominal German agreement frequently depended on Chancellor Adenauer's knowledge that President de Gaulle would exercise his veto in Allied councils.

One result was that much of the polemic between Washington and Bonn was conducted by means of inspired leaks to the press. During the summer and fall of 1961, many American newspapers pointed out that Germany's bills for World War II would be coming due. The United States was said to be delaying proposals until after the German elections scheduled for that fall so that a new government would be able to bear the brunt of the unpleasant decisions which were required. There were demands for "initiatives" and "imagination" from the Germans. According to a prevalent theory, it was safe to press the Germans for concessions because, as the saying went, "Where are the Germans going to go?"

On the German side, the suspicion was frequently voiced that sooner or later the United States would confront Germany with a *fait accompli*. Planted stories expressed doubt about the validity of the United States nuclear guarantee. The frequent demand that the Germans undertake "initiatives," it was said, really was a euphemism for an American desire that they should offer unpalatable concessions which we were reluctant to make ourselves.

A more important result of this atmosphere of distrust between Bonn and Washington was the emergence of France as guardian of the Federal Republic's interests—which answered the rhetorical question of where Germany might go. This, in turn, laid the basis for the close Franco-German cooperation which existed during the remainder of Chancellor Adenauer's term in office and which gave France the psychological support it needed for excluding Britain from the Common Market.

France's role has not been without its own ambivalence. French leaders are not likely to have transcended their historical reflexes so thoroughly as to have become believers in a powerful and self-confident Germany for its own sake. But President de Gaulle has understood that the most dangerous kind of Germany is one that feels forsaken by its allies and is thrown back on a purely national policy. This is why from the beginning of his tenure De Gaulle has sought to demonstrate that the Federal Republic would not stand alone. When rejecting—sometimes brutally—the American efforts to devise negotiating formulas, De Gaulle came to express the true convictions of the German government better than it dared to do itself.

The conflicting policies of the United States, Great Britain, France and the Federal Republic created a diplomacy that combined the disadvantage of Allied disunity with the inability to gain any real benefit from negotiations with the Soviets. France refused to negotiate. The Federal Republic approved diplomatic contacts with the Soviets only with great misgivings. The "exploratory talks" with Foreign Minister Gromyko were first conducted by Secretary Rusk and later by Ambassador Thompson. Thus, the Federal Republic, on an issue affecting it most immediately, stood on the sidelines, in a position to criticize the unfavorable features of specific proposals without having to weigh them against alternative courses. By assuming the role of chief negotiator, the United States played into the hands of President de Gaulle and disquieted the Germans, all without being able to bring about a settlement. Since we could not commit the West as a whole, the Soviets were in a position to treat our offers as fishing expeditions or to engage in fishing expeditions of their own. If they considered Allied discord a feint, this gave them an incentive to be rigid. If they took it seriously, they could, in effect, bank every concession and use it as the starting point for the next round of talks.

The longer negotiations were conducted in this manner, the more relations between Bonn and Washington suffered. The mere fact of bilateral negotiations raised the specter of a United States-Soviet accommodation at the expense of our Allies. Our tactics thus encouraged the Franco-German entente. The French inclination to create a new grouping in Europe would probably have been pursued in any case; but it was given impetus and opportunity by German uneasiness about Anglo-American negotiating tactics.

This was the situation when Chancellor Adenauer finally put an end to the "exploratory talks" by publicly expressing his dissatisfaction with them. Throughout 1962, American-German relations remained wary, while the Federal Republic moved ever closer to an intimate association with France.

Thus, by the end of 1962, while NATO was still going through protestations of unity, serious fissures had appeared. France had formulated an explicit challenge to American pre-eminence within NATO. The Federal Republic was torn between disquiet over American policy and the knowledge that its military security depended on American support. Great Britain's application for membership in the Common Market was stalled. Matters were brought to a head by De Gaulle's press conference of January 14, 1963, excluding Britain from the Common Market. This was followed within two weeks by the Franco-German Treaty of Collaboration.

The first United States reaction was stunned outrage at what was seen as an embryo European organization based on De Gaulle's conceptions. This was followed by a deliberate policy of wooing the Federal Republic away from its French ties. The focus of America's European policy shifted more and more toward Germany. In the military, diplomatic and economic fields strenous efforts were made to forge new United States-German links. The practical consequence—whatever the intention—was to reduce Germany's interest in the treaty with France— a process which was accelerated by the retirement of Chancellor Adenauer and the installation of a new government. Whereas the previous policy ran the risk of a German estrangement from the Alliance, the succeeding policy, by giving the impression of a special United States-German relationship, was in danger of eventually producing an estrangement of the other Allies. Finally, another change of course restored more balance to our European policy. By then, however, many German leaders who had staked their careers on following our lead found themselves in an extremely exposed position. Before dealing with these problems, it is important to examine the role of Great Britain, the ally which has prided itself on its special relationship with the United States during the entire postwar period.

GREAT BRITAIN AND EUROPE: THE NASSAU AGREEMENT

Great Britain's relations to the Continent in the postwar period have been extraordinarily ambivalent. In the years immediately following the war, the countries of the Continent were on the verge of chaos. The quest for a modicum of stability overrode all other considerations.

Great Britain alone seemed to possess a structure capable of sustaining a long-range, orderly policy. During this period, Britain could have had the leadership of Europe for the asking. It would have seemed inconceivable that Europe might exclude Britain from its community—assuming that it would ever be able to form one.

Yet it was precisely the memory of its recent isolation that prevented Britain from seizing its opportunity. Throughout Britain's history, the threats to its security had come from the Continent, which in Britain significantly is called Europe. Britain's historic policy had been to prevent the emergence of a powerful and united Continent. To promote the unity of Europe, to submerge Britain in such a structure and to substitute European for American and Commonwealth connections, all this has represented a wrench with tradition which few in Britain have been prepared to make.

The memory of the war reinforced this hesitation. The countries of the Continent had surrendered and forced Britain to fight alone. In the late forties, these countries were still wracked by internal dissension. Although Britain was geographically close to Europe, its emotional ties were to its recent ally across the sea and to the Commonwealth. Long before anyone on the Continent could even imagine excluding Britain from whatever structure might be formed, Britain had made a tentative choice against the Continent.

The more the memory of the war receded, the more apparent it became that total defeat may be more conducive to making a new start than partial victory. For Great Britain, the tremendous exertions of the war did not lead to a well-deserved respite. On the contrary, Britain was obliged to undertake another major effort to adjust to a loss of international influence—a task which was made even more difficult by the memory of the recent heroic effort. While defeat enabled the Continent to free itself from the shackles of traditional nostalgia, Britain's policy, courageous and steadfast during two difficult decades, now began to turn stagnant. Its exertions had consumed so much energy that Britain never seemed able to decide which option to pursue: close relations with the United States, a new concept of Commonwealth or an unreserved entry into Europe. By trying to combine all three, Britain ran the risk of losing each. The roots of Britain's exclusion from the Continent go deeper than one individual's arbitrary decision.

This ambivalence has been described by some as Britain's search for identity. But the real problem is not that Britain has lacked an identity. Rather it is that its sense of identity has been incompatible with an unreserved entry into Europe. Britain's coolness toward Europe has been a consistent feature of the postwar period. It refused to join the Schuman Plan. It was not part of the abortive European Defense Community. Britain opposed the Common Market and applied for membership only after it was well-established and thriving. Britain has rejected the possibility of eventually transforming the proposed NATO multilateral force into a European force—indeed, one of its motives for even considering this scheme is to obtain a veto over such a development.[1]

Throughout, Britain's views on the organization of Europe have been quite different from those of the European integrationists who so passionately championed her cause. They have, in fact, not been easy to distinguish from those of President de Gaulle except that they have been stated in a more accommodating fashion. Britain has been no more prepared than De Gaulle to join an "integrated," "supranational" Europe. Thus, in proposing that Britain enter the Common Market, Prime Minister Macmillan told the House of Commons:

A number of years have passed since the movement began which culminated in the Treaty of Rome and I am bound to say that I do not see any signs of the members of the Community losing their national identity because

[1] See Chapter 5.

they have delegated a measure of their sovereignty. This problem of sovereignty, to which we must, of course, attach the highest importance is, in the end, perhaps a matter of degree. I fully accept that there are some forces in Europe which would like a genuine federalist system. . . . They would like Europe to turn itself into a sort of United States, but I believe this to be a completely false analogy.

. . . The alternative concept, the only practical concept, would be a confederation, a commonwealth if hon. Members would like to call it that—what I think General de Gaulle has called *Europe des patries*—which would retain the great traditions and the pride of individual nations while working together in clearly defined spheres for their common interest. This seems to me a concept more in tune with the national traditions of European countries and, in particular, of our own.[2]

The same thought was expressed by Reginald Maudling, then President of the Board of Trade:

. . . we have seen in the last year or two the development of the European *patrie* of General de Gaulle and it is clear, I should have thought, that the Governments of the Six are not supporters of the conception of a political federation. Therefore, it is fair to say that neither by the terms of the Treaty itself nor by the expressed views of the governments concerned in the Community would our membership commit ourselves in any way to ultimate political federation.[3]

To be sure, Britain's attitude toward European integration was less theoretical than De Gaulle's and therefore easier for American policymakers to accept. It advanced no general maxims about the relationship between national identity and cooperative efforts. It insisted simply that supranationalism violated not universal rules but the lessons of British history.

[2] *Hansard,* Fifth Series, Vol. 645, Commons (July 24–August 4, 1961), Cols. 1490–1491.
[3] *Ibid.,* Col. 1958.

Resistance to supranationalism has had an emotional basis as well. Britain had always considered itself primarily a world power and not a European power. Its sense of identity was bound up with relations across the sea, not across the Channel. Its emotional ties were less with Europe than with the "special relationship" with the United States.

This relationship is difficult to define, and there is no doubt that President de Gaulle sees it as more formal than it really is. Unquestionably the enormous prestige gained by Britain during the war has played a major role. Unique ties of language and culture encourage many informal connections. Anglo-American relations would therefore be "special" whatever the formal arrangements.

British diplomacy has skillfully exploited these assets. De Gaulle's tactics consist of submitting a proposal preemptorily and with a minimum of explanation. If the proposal is rejected, he then proceeds to implement it unilaterally in order to create a *fait accompli* to which his allies must adjust. British tactics have been more subtle. Britain never contests an abstract or theoretical point. It almost never disagrees openly with fundamental American policies. Instead, British policy usually concedes us the liturgy while seeking to shape its implementation through intensive formal and informal consultation. De Gaulle has often been deliberately difficult to insure that he cannot be overlooked, while Britain has been conciliatory to make it seem natural for the United States to solicit its views before major action is taken. Whatever the "reality" of the "special relationship," Britain has tried hard to give the impression to the outside world that American policy is strongly influenced, if not guided, by London.

In the sixties, this policy became less effective for a number of reasons. For one thing, the "special relationship" has never had the same psychological significance for the United States that it did for Britain. The memory of Britain's wartime effort, despite the very great prestige gained by it, has diminished with time. As the postwar period progressed, many influential Americans have come to believe that Britain has been claiming influence out of proportion to its power. Consequently, they have pressed Britain to substitute close association with Europe for the special ties across the Atlantic. This school of thought has objected to giving Britain a preferential voice or even the appearance of it. They believe that Britain should be treated as simply one other European country that should seek its fulfillment in Europe.

The two events that underlined the decline of Britain's influence in Washington most vividly were the Suez crisis and the cancellation of the Skybolt missile. The former demonstrated the end of Britain's capacity for major independent action; the latter showed the hollowness of Britain's aspiration to military autonomy. In both instances, the wounds were to some extent self-inflicted— more in the case of Suez than in the case of Skybolt. In both instances, brutal and unfeeling American actions aggravated an already difficult situation. After Suez much of the previous assurance disappeared from British diplomacy.[4] Britain increasingly tended to substitute maneuver for commitment and tried to add to its influence while reducing its responsibilities—a combination impossible to sustain in the long run.

But the "special relationship" lasted long enough to bring about a number of illusions in Allied relationships. Where Britain tended to exaggerate its special influence in Washington, the United States may have overestimated the extent of Britain's pliability. It became an axiom of United States policy that Britain's entry into a suprana-

[4] It is interesting to compare the reactions of Britain and France to Suez. Britain, having based its entire policy on close association with the United States, suffered a severe psychological blow. France, having fewer illusions about its determining role in Washington, decided to accelerate its autonomy. The French nuclear program was much more the result of Suez than of the British example.

tional Europe would be a guarantee of Atlantic partnership. This is why Washington championed Britain's entry into the Common Market so ardently and why it was so outraged when this policy was thwarted.

It is possible, however, that the American view was overoptimistic. To be sure, Britain's political maturity would have weighed heavily in Europe's councils. With Britain playing a leading role, the policy of a united Europe would have been more subtle, more skillful and, at least in form, less demanding. Nevertheless, the Conservative government's arguments on behalf of Britain's entry into Europe always emphasized that only as part of a united Europe would Britain carry weight with the United States, that basically the United States respected only strength. One ironic result of Britain's entry into Europe might well have been that Europe would henceforth have conducted De Gaulle's policies with British methods.

By 1962 the chief remaining symbol of the special Anglo-American relationship was in the nuclear field. An amendment to the United States Atomic Energy Act in 1954 permitted United States assistance to the British nuclear program. This corrected an inequity in the original law which, despite close wartime collaboration in research between Britain and the United States, prohibited the sharing of nuclear information with foreign countries. American technology was also made available for the development of delivery vehicles for the British retaliatory force. No such assistance has been extended to any other ally.

The "independent" British deterrent has been composed of about 175 V-bombers which are threatened with obsolescence. Accordingly, in 1957, Britain began to develop a missile called the Blue Streak—similar to first-generation American liquid-fuel missiles such as Jupiter or Thor. Because this development was extremely expensive—as is true of all first-generation weapons—it was abandoned in February 1960 in favor of an air-to-surface weapon then under development in the United States, the ill-fated Skybolt.

Throughout the spring and summer of 1960, the Conservative government was under constant attack by Labor on two grounds: (1) By relying on a weapon to be developed by a foreign country, Britain admitted that an "independent" British deterrent was impossible and (2) if there really was a need for an independent deterrent, it was dangerous to rely on Skybolt, since the weapons did not yet exist and since, as George Brown, then Labor's spokesman on defense matters, said, "the Americans have not bought it." The Conservative government countered by referring to an "agreement" by the United States to supply Skybolt. This was never contradicted by either the Eisenhower or the Kennedy Administration.

The debate became more intense after the Kennedy Administration took office. President Kennedy and Secretary McNamara publicly deprecated the utility of independent nuclear forces. They were supported by the British Opposition. In 1962, Harold Wilson, then foreign affairs spokesman for the Labor Party, insisted after a visit to Washington that the United States did not consider the British retaliatory force strategically significant and that the British defense effort would make a greater contribution if channeled in other directions. This was denied by the Conservative government. Labor then challenged the Conservative government to produce a single official American statement affirming that the United States valued the British deterrent. This the Conservative government was unable to do.

Thus, when the Skybolt program was canceled in December 1962, conditions were not conducive to calm deliberation. The uproar the cancellation produced had little to do with the technical merits of Skybolt or with the strategic posture of Great Britain. No one was concerned over a possible deterrent gap in the interval between the time the V-bombers became obsolete and a new weapons system could be developed to replace Skybolt.

What was at stake was a fiction on which Britain's postwar policy had been based and for which successive British governments expended 10 billion dollars. British independence in the field of strategy—whatever its "real" significance—was literally a matter of life or death for the Conservative government. And governments are notoriously slow to appreciate the technical merits of arguments that threaten their existence. As a result, a conference between President Kennedy and Prime Minister Macmillan, which had been scheduled originally to review the world situation after the Cuban missile crisis, was transformed into a redefinition of nuclear relationships. The Nassau Agreement was the result.

The Nassau Agreement is a document of extraordinary ambiguity, reflecting an attempt to reconcile the American quest for the integration of all the nuclear forces of the Alliance with the British desire to maintain a measure of independence. The United States agreed to supply Polaris missiles to Great Britain. Britain was to construct the submarines and to provide the warheads. The British Polaris submarines, armed with American missiles and British warheads, were then to be subscribed to a NATO "multilateral" force that the United States and Great Britain pledged themselves to establish. It was to include the British Bomber Command, some United States Polaris forces and other tactical forces in Europe. Another paragraph stated that the purpose of the two governments was "the development of a NATO multilateral force in the closest consultation with other NATO allies." Great Britain committed itself to use its nuclear forces "for the purpose of the international defense of the Western Alliance" except "where the supreme national interest was at stake." The same qualification appeared in the provision that both governments agreed that Western defense "is indivisible and . . . in *all ordinary circumstances of crisis or danger* [emphasis added] it is this very unity which is the best protection of the West." Finally Great Britain and the United States agreed that NATO in addition to having a nuclear "shield" should have a non-nuclear "sword," thus reversing the traditional NATO strategic concept.[5]

This agreement was transmitted to President de Gaulle after it was published. In an accompanying memorandum, the United States offered to sell Polaris missiles to France on the same terms as to Great Britain.

The Nassau Agreement attempted a *tour de force*. It tried to reconcile integration with independence, the American belief in the need for an indivisible nuclear strategy with the British desire for autonomy.

But the price was high, and in practice the various clauses of the Nassau Agreement tended to cancel each other out. For example, what was the significance of subscribing the British retaliatory force to NATO while at the same time reserving the right of independent action when the supreme national interest was at stake? As President Kennedy pointed out shortly after the Nassau Agreement was signed, the supreme national interest is automatically involved when a country considers the use of nuclear weapons. Similarly, what was the meaning of the phrase that a unified strategy was the best protection in "ordinary" circumstances? To what "extraordinary" contingencies did the escape clause refer? Moreover, it was not clear whether the multilateral force described in paragraph six—to be composed of national contributions—was the same as that in paragraph seven. In other words, did the commitment imply only that national contingents be assigned to NATO or did it involve also an undertaking to establish a mixed-manned fleet (the MLF)?[6] Britain was to urge the first interpretation; the United States defended the latter one. Finally, what was the meaning of the reversal of the traditional notions of "shield" and

[5] Text, Joint Communique and Attached Statement on nuclear defense systems issued on December 21, 1962, by President Kennedy and Prime Minister Macmillan, *DOSB*, Vol. XLVIII, No. 1229 (January 14, 1963), pp. 44–45. See also Chapter 4.

[6] See Chapter 5.

"sword" in NATO strategy? Did it imply that the United States and Great Britain were proposing to resist a conventional attack in Europe primarily with conventional means?

Thus even an individual less inclined to exploit Allied discord than President de Gaulle would have been likely to view the Nassau Agreement with suspicion. Indeed, reaction to the Nassau Agreement all over Europe ranged from cool to hostile. In Germany, the grouping of NATO's nuclear forces into a special nuclear command revived fears of a possible nuclear disengagement. The Labor Party interpreted the Nassau Agreement as proving the validity of their previous contention that British nuclear independence was a sham. The Agreement did not satisfy those in the United States who had been pressing for an integrated strategy. And it was, of course, rejected out of hand by President de Gaulle.

The Nassau Agreement could not have been timed more disastrously for Britain's application for membership in the Common Market. If Britain overestimated its special ties with the United States, De Gaulle took them at face value. He has never forgotten Churchill's statement that if Britain were forced to choose between Europe and the open sea, it would unhesitatingly choose the latter.[7] The difference between the tenacity with which Britain had argued about the economic conditions of its entry into Europe and the willingness to settle its nuclear future in a three-day conference with the United States seemed to reflect Britain's priorities. Britain's special relation with the United States in the nuclear field could have two meanings: It was either a challenge to De Gaulle's contention that a united Europe required its own defense; or else it seemed designed to assure Britain a pre-eminent place in a united Europe. Neither contingency was attractive to De Gaulle.

[7] Charles de Gaulle, *The War Memoirs of Charles de Gaulle, Unity, 1942–1944,* translated by Richard Howard (New York: Simon and Schuster, 1959), p. 253.

Moreover, if the integration envisaged by the Nassau Agreement did not go far enough for some Americans, it was much too sweeping for President de Gaulle. He was likely to object to the integration of nuclear forces whatever its actual significance. He said that the proposed assignment of nuclear forces to NATO involved:

. . . a web of liaisons, transmissions and interferences within itself . . . such that, if an integral part were suddenly snatched from it, there would be a strong risk of paralyzing it just at the moment, perhaps, when it should act.[8]

And he asked how in practice integration could be reconciled with independent disposition, putting his finger on the key evasion of the Nassau Agreement. At the same time, he agreed that cooperation between the national nuclear forces within NATO was both possible and desirable. It is symptomatic that, while arguing the relative merits of integration and coordination, neither side has yet defined what common action might be possible under one label that is not possible under the other.

The way the Nassau Agreement was negotiated created as many problems as its content and timing. Given De Gaulle's wartime experiences and his view of France's role in the world, it was against all probability that he would accept a proposal negotiated privately by the "Anglo-Saxons" and revealed to Paris only after it had been released to the press. It should have come as no surprise that, at the press conference where he rejected French participation in the Nassau Agreement, De Gaulle commented acidly: "Of course, I am only speaking of this proposal and agreement because they have been published and because their content is known."[9]

Moreover, the actual terms of the Agreement seemed to De Gaulle to perpetuate the discriminatory treatment

[8] Press Conference on January 14, 1963, *Major Addresses*, p. 219.
[9] *Ibid.*, p. 218.

that he had opposed throughout his public career. France possessed neither submarines nor warheads for the Polaris missiles. Thus, the Nassau Agreement could bring benefits to France only after many years. Britain's experience with the Skybolt program reduced the already small incentive of France to make itself dependent on the promise of future delivery of United States missiles—all the more so as France was not offered the information about the construction of nuclear warheads which was essential if the missiles were to be useful.

There have been endless debates whether the Nassau Agreement precipitated De Gaulle's decision to veto British membership in the Common Market, whether it was a pretext or—as is most likely—whether it was simply a contributory cause. It is not necessary to decide this question to realize that the Nassau Agreement exacerbated an already difficult situation and placed the issue of British entry into the Common Market in the most adverse light imaginable. Britain's application was bound to raise the question whether it was consistent with the aspirations of a united Europe for one of its members to have an exclusive relationship with the United States on so vital a subject as nuclear strategy or whether it should share its nuclear knowledge with its new partners.

The Nassau Agreement brought this issue to a head prematurely. Britain had received an abrupt rebuff on the Skybolt issue. Yet it never seems seriously to have considered that it might use this opportunity for closer cooperation with its European partners in the military field. Instead, it concluded an agreement with the United States without even consulting France, the other European nuclear power, and it developed a nuclear plan for NATO without the participation of its prospective partners in the Common Market. It agreed to reverse the traditional significance of "sword" and "shield" in NATO doctrine without consulting any other NATO ally. Perhaps President de Gaulle had decided on a veto whatever happened.

But if he still hesitated, the Nassau Agreement was likely to tip the scales.

In retrospect, the failure of Britain to consult with France and its other European allies before committing itself to the Nassau Agreement seems a crucial missed opportunity. It will never be known what the reaction would have been if Britain had made such an overture before the Bahamas meeting. Even had it failed, it would have placed the subsequent debate in a far better context.

As it was, De Gaulle, in his press conference of January 14, 1963, abruptly and brutally vetoed British membership in the Common Market and rejected the Nassau offer. The date marks an important watershed in Atlantic relations. De Gaulle's action exploded the premises on which much of previous thinking had been based. The belief in an automatic progression from economic to political integration suddenly stood in need of reexamination. The concept of an Atlantic partnership between the United States and a united Europe, including Great Britain, was seriously challenged. It was now clear that conflicting approaches to Atlantic relationships were confronting each other.

The debate was confused by the way the lines were drawn, which made it dangerous to take either criticism or support of United States positions at face value. France's claim that it spoke for Europe was belied by the fact that on economic issues Germany and the Netherlands tended to side with Great Britain and in the field of strategy the Federal Republic leaned toward the United States. Many in Europe were disquieted by De Gaulle's tactics even when they basically agreed with his policies —as in the case of the recognition of Communist China and his proposal for the neutralization of Southeast Asia.

At the same time, opposition to De Gaulle does not guarantee support of United States policies. British policy often differs from that of De Gaulle only in the greater subtlety of British methods. Much domestic French criticism is due to the frustration of the divided Opposition that sees its policies carried out by the incumbent. All over Europe, left-wing groups violently oppose De Gaulle's imperious style, seeing in him a direct descendant of the dictators of the thirties. But this does not mean that they object to Third Force policies as such or that their long-term alternative is close association with the United States. The Federal Republic maneuvers uneasily between relying on the military protection of the United States and the diplomatic cover of France.

The press conference of January 14, 1963, ushered in a period of frantic diplomatic activity in which the United States strove hard to vindicate its previous conception and France aloofly pursued her own course. What started out as a dispute about the internal structure of Europe and its role runs the risk of fragmenting Europe or of shifting the balance within Europe in unexpected directions. The result is a stalemate which is seen most obviously in the field of strategy.

PART THREE

The Strategic Issues

Chapter Four

THE NATURE OF THE STRATEGIC DEBATE

AMERICAN STRATEGIC DOCTRINE AND NATO POLICY

When the Atlantic Alliance was formed in 1949, Soviet aggression was believed to be imminent. As a result, there was a natural preoccupation with military security. Allied cohesion grew greatest with respect to strategic matters. An integrated headquarters staffed by officers of various nationalities was set up near Paris (SHAPE). A joint defense plan was developed. Some agreement about the nature of the common defense has always been central to the cohesiveness of NATO.

In recent years, such agreement has been difficult to achieve, and for good reasons.[1] Weapons are novel and untested—and everything depends on them. Offensive power has far outstripped defensive power. Every ally —no matter how powerful—faces a level of destruction which in the past would have been considered catastrophic. Finally, modern technology makes available more choices than the Alliance can afford to implement. High risk combines with multiple choice to produce controversy.

[1] See also Chapter 1.

Whether the Allies choose land- or sea-based missiles, whether they emphasize nuclear or conventional weapons depends less on technology than on strategic doctrine. Strategic doctrine, as here used, does not connote something abstract or dogmatic. In the absence of any relevant experience, its role is to define the likely dangers and how to deal with them, to project feasible goals and outline plans for attaining them. It must furnish a mode of action for the circumstances it defines as "ordinary." Its adequacy will be demonstrated by whether these events do in fact occur and whether the forces and procedures developed in anticipating them are adequate to deal with the real challenges.

In the interwar period French strategic doctrine exalted the value of the strategic defensive and built its plans around the Maginot Line. However, the likely German attempts to overthrow the Treaty of Versailles could be prevented only by French offensive action. The Maginot Line could prove useful, in other words, only after the Versailles settlement was already overturned. Thus French strategic doctrine contributed to the paralysis of French foreign policy. When German armies reoccupied the Rhineland and attacked France's allies in Eastern Europe, French power remained passive and French diplomacy stood impotent. Even when the long-awaited attack in the West finally came, it took place in an area which had not been fortified.

If a mistaken strategic doctrine absorbs energy in reconciling what happens with what is expected, an excessively complicated or esoteric doctrine can break down under the stress of decision-making. The Schlieffen Plan, Germany's military design for World War I, provided for every contingency except the psychological strain on the commander. It failed largely because the German leaders lost their nerve. In the face of Russian advances into East Germany—which were foreseen by the Schlieffen Plan—the Germans rushed reinforcements from the West and thus weakened their offensive thrust at the crucial moment. It adds to the irony of the situation that these reinforcements were in transit when the decisive battles in both the East *and* the West were being fought.

But if there is no doctrine at all and a society operates pragmatically, solving problems "on their merits" as the saying goes, every event becomes a special case. More energy is spent on deciding where one is than where one is going. Each event is compartmentalized and dealt with under pressure by experts in the special difficulties it involves without an adequate consideration of its relation to other occurrences. American policy has been shaped by this approach.

The problem of agreeing on strategic doctrine is complex within each government. The difficulty has been magnified within the Alliance because disputes about strategy become symbols for larger disagreements on policy. To be sure, differences of opinion about strategy have been real enough. But their urgency is due to the fact that something deeper than the analysis of weapons systems is involved. Disputes have become exacerbated because the United States and its European critics have rarely been talking about the same thing.

The United States has stressed the technical adequacy of its strategic views and the analytic accuracy of its strategic assessments. Our European critics have emphasized the political and psychological framework within which these decisions will have to be implemented. The United States has reiterated its formal commitment to the defense of Europe—as if a legal clause could settle the problems of credibility in the nuclear age once and for all. Our European Allies are wary of even the most solemn undertakings. Too many of them have seen alliances disintegrate not to be concerned over the impact of the unprecedented stress of nuclear war on obligations incurred many years before under completely different circumstances.

The sense of insecurity of most of our European Allies has been magnified by the one-sided relationship that has grown up in the military field within the Alliance. In no other area has the dependence of Europe on the United States been so great or so prolonged. In every other field American policy has deliberately sought to reduce Europe's dependence on the United States; in the military sphere the thrust of United States policy has been to make our tutelage more bearable.

When the United States gave economic assistance to Europe after World War II, it tried to induce its European Allies to assume responsibility for developing a joint program and a system for dividing up the total available aid. Though United States representatives played an active and important advisory role, the basic scheme was European. This cooperative effort spawned the Schuman Plan and later the Common Market. It encouraged the emergence of a responsible group of European leaders, dedicated to Atlantic partnership and experienced in working with the United States. The Atlantic Alliance owes a great deal to the habits of cooperation and mutual respect developed during the Marshall Plan.

In the military field, by contrast, the United States never encouraged the emergence of a specifically European point of view. It made no effort to stimulate European institutions comparable to those it fostered in the economic sphere. The Western European Union (WEU), which originally had been expected to play that role, has remained dormant. Thus NATO strategy has always been based on more or less unilateral American conceptions. The consultative role of our European Allies has been confined in effect to the technical implementation of American views. No specifically European concept of defense—and no real European sense of responsibility—has developed.

This state of affairs had many causes. At the beginning of NATO, our Allies, remembering our tradition of isolationism, actively encouraged a predominant United States military role. A hegemonial position for the United States seemed the best guarantee of our commitment to the defense of Europe. Later on, many Allies used our dominant position as an excuse to avoid difficult domestic choices. They encouraged us to assume the burden of defense expenditures and the stress of difficult strategic decisions. We acquiesced because we were psychologically more deeply engaged in the military than in the economic field. Most importantly, the United States possessed a monopoly of nuclear weapons on which the security of the West was believed to depend.

However valid the reasons, the imbalance in responsibility between us and our European partners could not be healthy in the long run. It was unprecedented that the defense of an area so rich and potentially so powerful as Europe should be left to a country 3,000 miles away and with a recent history of isolationism. The result has been that many of our Allies have seen their role primarily as that of lobbyists trying to sway decisions not their own. They have either abdicated from the strategic field altogether or emphasized a military posture which makes no provision for the possibility that deterrence might fail.

This attitude contributes to Allied discord. Charged with the major responsibility for the common defense, the United States has been obliged to adapt its strategy to a rapidly changing technology. Many of our Allies, on the other hand, cling to the status quo as the best guarantee of our reliability. Unilateral change of our strategic views has a symbolic quality for them. If we are able to alter our views about strategy, might not the same be true of other commitments? If our Allies were primarily concerned with the technical aspects of strategy, they should be worried if we follow an existing doctrine after circumstances change. It is a measure of Europe's abdication from serious concern with defense that the opposite has been the case.

The United States, in turn, has fallen into the habit of dealing with its European Allies, except Great Britain, almost psychotherapeutically. It has tended to confuse periodic briefings and reassurance with consultation and it has sought to muffle expressions of concern rather than deal with the underlying causes. This is the psychological background of the strategic debate that has been taking place since the beginning of NATO and with particular intensity since the change in United States strategic concepts in 1961.

In order to understand the reaction of our Allies to this change, it is necessary to examine briefly the doctrine that was replaced. When the Korean War first raised the specter of a Soviet attack on Europe, NATO developed the Lisbon goals, which envisaged a largely conventional defense of Europe. These provided for some thirty-five to forty regular and some fifty-five to sixty reserve divisions. It soon became apparent, however, that no European ally was prepared to make the sacrifices necessary to raise these forces.

The advent of the Eisenhower Administration in 1953 led to a new defense policy—called the New Look—which placed much greater emphasis on nuclear forces. In 1957 the United States submitted to NATO what came to be known as the Radford Plan—initially to the dismay of the Europeans. This plan started from the premise that NATO was permanently inferior in conventional strength to the hordes of easily-mobilized Soviet manpower. To base NATO's strategy on resisting a Soviet attack with conventional weapons was to emphasize Communist superiority. Therefore, the defense of NATO should depend on nuclear weapons. Any attack on Europe would involve general nuclear war. The purpose of the military establishment on the Continent was primarily to delay a Soviet advance long enough for the effects of nuclear war to make themselves felt. The ground forces were to be a "trip wire" or a "plate glass window."

As a result, large numbers of tactical nuclear weapons were shipped into Europe under the so-called double-veto system. This required the consent of both the United States and the host country before nuclear weapons could be used. Moreover, the definition of "tactical" was such that the Supreme Allied Commander, Europe (SACEUR) was to be able to destroy all Soviet weapons aimed at Europe. The nuclear arsenal in Europe thus included some weapons of a range and destructiveness indistinguishable from those in the arsenal of the Strategic Air Command (SAC). They could be called "tactical" only in the sense that they were stationed in Europe and not in the United States and that they were controlled by SACEUR rather than the commanding general of SAC.

According to this strategic concept, conventional weapons played a minor role. Their function was to deal with minor incursions; they were to act as a screen to determine that a full-scale Soviet attack was taking place. Though there was some talk of a "pause" before nuclear weapons might be used, the logistic system of NATO left little doubt about the real emphasis of NATO strategy. None of NATO's conventional forces had supplies for more than two weeks, and several national contingents were considerably worse off. In case of large-scale Soviet attack, nuclear weapons would have to be used practically from the outset. "The pause," General Norstad was reported to have observed, "will probably take place *before* the outbreak of hostilities." NATO doctrine described conventional weapons as the "shield" and nuclear weapons as the "sword" of the Alliance.

Almost concurrently with the disclosure of the Radford Plan in 1957, the United States came to believe that it was inferior to the Soviet Union in long-range missiles. In order to close this "missile gap," the United States pressed its NATO allies to permit the installation of intermediate-range ballistic missiles on their territory. These were thought to be essential to the over-all strategic posture of the West. The concern of some of our Allies regarding the vulnerability of these missiles was rejected. It was argued that the Soviets would not be able to launch a blow against our European bases without an unacceptable risk of an all-out United States counterblow and that a coordinated Soviet attack against the United States overseas and domestic bases would prove technically difficult. In pursuit of these policies, intermediate-range missiles (IRBM's) were stationed in Italy, Turkey and Great Britain.[2]

The stationing of these missiles in Europe tended to establish an inextricable link between the defense of Europe and that of the United States. As long as the United States believed that its European bases were essential to redress the strategic balance, an attack on Europe would threaten the survival of the United States immediately rather than indirectly. Deployment rather than a decision taken at the moment of attack would determine the American response.

With the advent of a new United States administration in 1961, these policies were drastically and suddenly changed. Starting early in 1961, the Kennedy Administration developed a four-pronged strategic theory which has remained essentially unchanged under President Johnson.

1. *Flexible Response:* When it took office, the Kennedy Administration found itself confronted with a strategy for general war which emphasized a single all-out response. If general nuclear war proved inevitable, the goal was to be to destroy the opposing society virtually with one blow.

The Kennedy Administration sought to replace this strategy with a doctrine which offered more alternatives. It attempted to develop the maximum number of options even for the contingency of general nuclear war—a strategy summed up in the phrase "flexible response." In 1962, this strategy was described by Secretary of Defense McNamara as follows:

. . . our forces can be used in several different ways. We may have to retaliate with a single massive attack. Or, we may be able to use our retaliatory forces to limit damage done to ourselves, and our allies, by knocking out the enemy's bases before he has had time to launch his second

[2] The IRBM's in Italy and Turkey were under SACEUR; those in Great Britain were not part of NATO.

salvos. We may seek to terminate a war on favorable terms by using our forces as a bargaining weapon—by threatening further attack.

In any case, our large reserve of protected firepower would give an enemy an incentive to avoid our cities and to stop a war. Our new policy gives us the flexibility to choose among several operational plans, but does not require that we make any advance commitment with respect to doctrine or targets. We shall be committed only to a system that gives us the ability to use our forces in a controlled and deliberate way, so as best to pursue the interests of the United States, our Allies, and the rest of the Free World.[3]

Official explanations about how this capability for flexible response would be used have not always been consistent. Criticizing the nuclear forces of Britain and France, Secretary McNamara argued that the United States proposed to rely on a counterforce strategy and confine its initial attacks to military targets:

The U.S. has come to the conclusion that to the extent feasible, basic military strategy in a possible general nuclear war should be approached in much the same way that more conventional military operations have been regarded in the past. That is to say, principal military objectives . . . should be the destruction of the enemy's military forces, not of his civilian population.[4]

Throughout 1962 Secretary McNamara insisted that the United States had the capability to destroy the entire Soviet military target system even *after* absorbing a first blow. The corollary was, of course, that the United States

[3] Robert S. McNamara, address before the Fellows of the American Bar Foundation Dinner, Chicago, Illinois, February 17, 1962, Department of Defense, Office of Public Affairs, News Release No. 239-262 (February 17, 1962), pp. 6–7.

[4] McNamara, address at the Commencement Exercises, University of Michigan, Ann Arbor, Michigan, June 16, 1962, Department of Defense, Office of Public Affairs, News Release No. 980-62, June 16, 1962, p. 9. See also statement on RS-70, *New York Times,* March 16, 1962.

would be able to overwhelm Soviet strategic forces by striking first, for instance, in response to an attack on Europe. But if this assessment was correct, the purpose of building up conventional forces in Europe was far from obvious. If Soviet strategic forces were indeed so much more vulnerable than ours, a Soviet conventional attack on Europe would be too risky to be at all probable. NATO strategy could continue to rely primarily on United States strategic nuclear power.

More recently Secretary McNamara has been less sanguine about the prospects for a counterforce strategy. He has argued that the growing size of the opposing strategic forces requires us to define more modest objectives than the original counterforce doctrine had seemed to imply. He now maintains that no matter how large our strategic forces, they will not be able to prevent vast damage. The strategy of flexible response is not designed to achieve victory in the traditional sense; its function is to limit damage by destroying the largest possible number of weapons which an aggressor might hold in reserve after he has launched an initial blow:

. . . a "damage-limiting" strategy appears to be the most practical and effective course for us to follow. . . . While there are still some differences of judgment on just how large such a [U.S. strategic] force should be, there is general agreement that it should be large enough to ensure the destruction, singly or in combination, of the Soviet Union, Communist China, and the Communist satellites as national societies, under the worst possible circumstances of war outbreak that can reasonably be postulated, and, in addition, to destroy their warmaking capability so as to limit, to the extent practicable, damage to this country and to our Allies.[5]

2. *Hostility to National Nuclear Forces:* Flexible response, however its objectives are defined, presupposes

[5] McNamara, *Hearings, Department of Defense, Appropriations for 1965*, House Appropriations Subcommittee (88th Cong., 2nd sess., 1964, Part 4), pp. 27–28.

a centralized system of command and control and highly invulnerable strategic forces. The possibility of conducting nuclear war discriminately depends on an over-all plan controlled by individuals familiar with the strategic context. United States doctrine has considered the existence of strategic nuclear forces not under United States control inconsistent with these requirements. Said Secretary McNamara:

We are convinced that a general nuclear war target system is indivisible, and if, despite all our efforts, nuclear war should occur, our best hope lies in conducting a centrally controlled campaign against all of the enemy's vital nuclear capabilities, while retaining reserve forces, all centrally controlled.[6]

President Kennedy described the French nuclear program as "inimical" to NATO. Secretary McNamara called European nuclear forces "dangerous," "expensive," "prone to obsolescence" and "lacking in credibility." Under Secretary Ball has criticized these nuclear forces because "the road toward nuclear proliferation has no logical ending."[7]

At first, these criticisms were directed against the French nuclear program alone. However, they could be applied with equal logic to the British strategic force, although it has been in existence with American support for over a decade. Robert Bowie, one of the most eloquent defenders of official nuclear policy, has made this explicit.[8]

In short, the requirement of central control is interpreted by the Pentagon to mean the integration of stra-

[6] McNamara, address at the Commencement Exercises, University of Michigan, June 16, 1962, *op. cit.*, p. 11.

[7] George Ball, "NATO and World Responsibility," *The Atlantic Community Quarterly*, Vol. 2, No. 2 (Summer 1964), p. 211.

[8] Robert Bowie, "Tensions Within the Alliance," *Foreign Affairs*, Vol. 43, No. 1 (October 1963), p. 66.

————, "Strategy and the Atlantic Alliance," *International Organization*, Special issue on the Atlantic Community, Vol. 17, No. 3 (Summer 1963), pp. 722–726.

tegic nuclear forces in a way that forecloses the technical
possibility of independent use. If any of our Allies are to
have nuclear forces of their own—and the clear United
States preference is that they do not—these must be an
adjunct to United States strategic forces and, for all practical purposes, subject to American control.

3. *Tactical Nuclear Weapons:* United States strategic doctrine has shown considerable ambivalence about tactical
nuclear weapons which were previously considered the
key element of the military establishment on the Continent. On the one hand, the number of tactical nuclear
weapons on the Continent has been considerably increased, according to official Pentagon estimates, by some
60 per cent. On the other hand, tactical nuclear weapons
do not really fit the Administration's strategic concept.

Tactical nuclear weapons in the hands of front-line
units are extremely difficult to subject to the central command and control envisaged by the new doctrine. The
Administration has repeatedly stressed the danger of
escalation. As the then Deputy Secretary of Defense Gilpatric put it, "I, for one, have never believed in a so-called
limited nuclear war. I just don't know how you build a
limit into it once you start using any kind of a nuclear
bang."[9] And in the spring of 1961, Secretary McNamara
said that, in his concept, limited war in effect excluded
the use of *any* nuclear weapons. "I think by 'limited' war
we simply mean war that is carried on for the most part
with non-nuclear weapons. . . ."[10] Deputy Assistant
Secretary of Defense Alain C. Enthoven said on February
10, 1963:

There has been, in recent years, the development of small
nuclear weapons having yields equivalent to a few thousand tons of TNT or less. The day will come, if it has not

[9] *New York Times,* June 7, 1961.
[10] McNamara, *Department of Defense, Appropriations for 1962,
Hearings,* Committee on Appropriations, House Subcommittee
(87th Cong., 1st sess., 1961, Part 3), p. 136.

already, when there will be nuclear weapons of smaller yield than the largest high explosive weapons. When that day comes, will there no longer be a distinction between nuclear and conventional weapons? Some have argued to that effect. But they are mistaken. There is and will remain an important distinction, a "firebreak" if you like, between nuclear and non-nuclear war, a recognizable qualitative distinction that both combatants can recognize and agree upon, if they want to agree upon one. And in the nuclear age they will have a very powerful incentive to agree upon this distinction and limitation, because if they do not there does not appear to be another easily recognizable limitation on weapons—no other obvious "firebreak"—all the way up the destructive spectrum to large-scale thermonuclear war.[11]

If any use of nuclear weapons is likely to lead to an uncontrolled general nuclear exchange, it follows that many of the Administration's strictures against independent nuclear forces apply also to the tactical nuclear weapons on the Continent. Administration statements have made clear that the tactical nuclear weapons in Europe were too vulnerable to serve as reliable second-strike weapons and thus were not needed to deter or to fight a general nuclear war:

Last year I told this Committee "there is no question but that, today, our Strategic Retaliatory Forces are fully capable of destroying the Soviet target system, even after absorbing an initial surprise attack." This statement is still true. . . .

Allowing for losses from an initial enemy attack and attrition en-route to target, we calculate that our forces today could still destroy the Soviet Union without any help from the deployed tactical air units or carrier task forces or THOR or JUPITER IRBM'S.[12]

---

[11] Alain C. Enthoven, U.S. Senate, Committee on Armed Services, *Military Procurement Authorization: Fiscal Year 1964; Hearings on H.R. 2440* (88th Cong., 1st sess., 1963), p. 168.

[12] McNamara, statement before the House Armed Services Committee, *The Fiscal Years 1964–68, Defense Program and 1964 Defense Budget* (January 30, 1963), p. 29.

If official doctrine is ambivalent about tactical nuclear weapons, it is hostile to the overseas deployment of strategic delivery systems. Accordingly, the intermediate-range ballistic missiles were withdrawn from Britain, Italy and Turkey in 1963. This was justified by the argument that new weapons such as the Polaris missiles are more effective and that land-based missiles are too vulnerable.

4. *Conventional Defense:* If European national nuclear forces are irrelevant or worse and tactical nuclear weapons are overvalued, it follows that American strategic doctrine considers Europe's optimum contribution to be in the field of conventional defense. This argument has been pressed insistently. "The decision to employ tactical nuclear weapons," testified Secretary McNamara before the House Armed Services Committee in January 1963, "should not be forced upon us simply because we have no other way to cope with a particular situation."[13]

The corollary is that the most desirable objective is to resist a Soviet conventional attack with purely conventional means. Secretary McNamara added that existing NATO conventional capabilities were adequate to deal with any "major incursion." Nevertheless, he urged that they be strengthened to give us "capabilities for dealing with even larger Soviet attacks"—in other words, a massive, sustained Soviet offensive. This view was made explicit by Alain C. Enthoven a little later that year:

. . . we will have no sensible alternative to building up our conventional forces to the point at which they can safely resist all forms of non-nuclear aggression. Our forces will be adequate if we can never be forced because of weakness to be the first to have to resort to nuclear weapons.[14]

This feature of the new United States strategic doctrine was vividly symbolized in the Nassau Agreement which

[13] McNamara, statement . . . , p. 18.
[14] Enthoven, address to the Loyola University Forum for National Affairs, Los Angeles, February 10, 1963. Cited in *Survival*, Vol. V, No. 3 (May–June 1963), p. 98.

reversed the traditional NATO concepts of "shield" and "sword." In the new formulation, decided bilaterally by Great Britain and the United States, nuclear weapons were described as the "shield" and the conventional weapons as the "sword" of the Alliance—implying a preference for a largely conventional defense of Europe.

The new strategic doctrine made a sharp debate almost inevitable. The drastic change of views within the space of less than five years cast into question either our steadiness or our judgment. Those Allied leaders who had staked their prestige on supporting the American doctrine of the fifties found themselves in the embarrassing position of seeing some of their opposition's arguments vindicated by a change of heart in Washington. This explains much of the bitterness of the dialogue.

Moreover, many of the changes decoupled deployment for general war from the defense of Europe. With American strategic forces located in the United States or at sea, the former military necessity to respond to an attack on Europe with nuclear retaliation was reduced. Together with the emphasis on conventional defense, this raised issues of nuclear control which had been muted when American nuclear retaliation had been believed to be automatic. The debate took on added urgency because the advent of a new, highly analytical administration in the United States coincided with the deliberate policy of President de Gaulle to assert a more independent role.

THE NATURE OF THE DEBATE: NUCLEAR OR CONVENTIONAL DEFENSE?

The strategic debate in the Alliance was at first given a slightly unreal quality by the desire of Washington to maintain an appearance of continuity. When the Kennedy Administration sought early in 1961 to convince NATO to strengthen its conventional forces, our Allies inquired whether the United States was reducing its reliance on nuclear weapons. We replied that the proposed build-up did not involve any lessened confidence in what had come to be called "The Deterrent." On the contrary, United States strategic forces were being expanded and made more invulnerable. The non-nuclear build-up, far from diminishing the credibility of our nuclear power, would actually enhance it.[15] According to official American statements, the NATO policy being promulgated was not new. We were simply asking our Allies to live up to their previous commitments. The goal was flexibility of response.

This curious dialogue, in which a change of emphasis in United States policy was defended in terms of traditional doctrines of NATO, produced new misgivings. Our Allies asked why, if the reliance on nuclear deterrence remained unimpaired, conventional forces had to be strengthened? Did not American efforts to build up conventional strength involve a risk? Since even thirty divisions would probably not be enough to stop a full-scale Soviet attack, a build-up might raise doubts about the American nuclear commitment and thus might make aggression more likely. The result was a paradoxical argument about whether an increase in NATO's strength would weaken its over-all defensive posture. The emphasis on conventional weapons had the strange consequence of exacerbating the issue of nuclear control.

This was no accident. As long as NATO strategy was nuclear and the United States had no obvious alternative to nuclear retaliation, our Allies were ready to acquiesce in the hegemonial position of the United States. They reasoned that this was the price which had to be paid for an automatic American nuclear response. However, one of the essential characteristics of the doctrine of flexible response is that American nuclear reaction will occur—if at all—deliberately and in stages. The very qualities that have made the new doctrine desirable for Americans raise questions for Europeans of how the American commitment

[15] McNamara, speech to the Fellows of the American Bar Foundation, Chicago, Illinois, February 17, 1962, *op. cit.*, p. 8.

will be interpreted under the stress of nuclear war. This, in turn, has brought to a head a long-standing difference in perspective between the American and the European approach to NATO.

Ever since the beginning of NATO, the military establishment on the Continent has been seen in symbolic terms by the Europeans and in military terms by the United States. When the Korean War seemed to indicate that Soviet aggression might be imminent, serious efforts were made to turn NATO into a more effective military instrument. However, given the enormous disparity in military and economic strength between the United States and Europe, the primary concern of the European countries was to commit the United States to their defense. They considered NATO above all a means to obtain American protection, by which they meant American nuclear protection.

At the same time, Europeans have had too much experience with the tenuousness of formal commitments not to strive for more tangible guarantees. This led to pressures for the stationing of American troops in Europe. European reasoning was similar to that ascribed to a French marshal in 1912 when he was asked how many British troops he wanted for the eventuality of a European war. He is reported to have replied: "We need only one, who we will make sure is killed on the first day of the war." In the nuclear age, the price of a guarantee has risen to close to five divisions.

With so many American troops permanently stationed in Europe, it was only sensible to try to give them some meaningful military mission. Even in the heyday of the doctrine of massive retaliation in the fifties, NATO forces were larger than the prevailing strategic concept seemed to demand. Indeed the number was somewhat inconsistent with it. Despite the United States commitment to a retaliatory strategy, we constantly pressed for a European contribution of ground forces. The Europeans, though they agreed to a succession of NATO force goals, never really believed in the doctrines used to rationalize them. Rather they considered their military contribution a fee to be paid for the United States nuclear protection. Our Allies agreed to our requests. But they tried to make certain that their actual contributions would be only large enough to induce us to keep a substantial military establishment in Europe, yet not so high as to provide a real alternative to nuclear retaliation. They were opposed to giving the conventional forces a central military mission; but they also resisted any hint of American withdrawal.

This ambivalence was brought into the open by the shift in United States strategic doctrine in 1961. The American attempt to strengthen conventional forces brought to the fore the issue of nuclear control, which for many Europeans had always been the crux of the matter. For the first time, United States strategic views were publicly challenged, at first hesitantly, then ever more explicitly. Europe had by now gained sufficient self-confidence so that the mere enunciation of an American policy no longer guaranteed its acceptance. The pre-emptory way in which the United States proceeded added ruffled feelings to substantive disagreements. And France compounded these problems by giving European doubts their most extreme formulation.

But while European concerns were understandable and inherent in the relationship which had grown up between Europe and the United States in the strategic field, by 1961 a changing technology had made a reassessment of NATO doctrine essential. Traditional NATO strategy assumed United States strategic preponderance. This superiority enabled us not only to prevent an attack on the United States but also to protect our Allies by what amounted to a unilateral American guarantee. The Soviet Union did possess superior conventional strength. But it could not use it for fear of triggering the Strategic Air Command. It could not attack the United States at the same time as Europe—even after it became technically able to do so—because, while this would have increased

American losses, a Soviet defeat would nevertheless have been inevitable. Until the middle sixties, the security of NATO thus depended essentially on the ability of the United States to destroy the Soviet retaliatory power—technically speaking, on the American capacity to conduct a counterforce disarming strategy.

Any prudent planning for NATO in the sixties had to start from the assumption that the utility of a counterforce strategy—in the sense of an ability to disarm the opponent —for the defense of Europe is bound to decline. Indeed, Secretary McNamara's statements in 1962 about the efficacy of a disarming strategy, while technically correct at the time they were made, were misleading if applied to foreseeable conditions. In the years ahead, the strategic and political significance of our numerical superiority in strategic weapons is certain to diminish.

For one thing, the more sophisticated missile systems which are now, or soon will be, in operation are dispersed, thus preventing one attacking missile from destroying more than one on the ground. Also, many missiles are protected in hardened underground sites, which means that more than one attacking missile is necessary to destroy a defending one. Other missiles will be mobile or based at sea, creating the need for coordinating many different forms of attack. These factors will greatly magnify the force required for a successful counterforce "disarming" strike.

The constantly mounting complexity of staging a missile attack is bound to reduce the political utility of a counterforce "disarming" strategy—perhaps even faster than is warranted by purely military considerations. In the face of risks that are certain to grow dramatically, it will become more and more difficult to convince political leaders to rely on a strategy based on fragmentary intelligence and to use large numbers of weapons for which there is no wartime operational experience. Even if the proportion of the opposing strategic force which we can destroy remains constant throughout the sixties—an unwarrantedly optimistic assumption—the absolute number left will rise. Thus the Soviet capability to devastate NATO countries in a counterblow will inevitably increase.

These factors are certain to reduce any President's readiness to initiate general war. Even our best efforts will not prevent the credibility of a counterforce "disarming" strategy from declining in the years ahead. It will grow ever more difficult to convince the Soviets that such a capability exists·or that we are prepared to run the risks it involves. This problem has been accurately described by Secretary McNamara as follows:

Fully hard ICBM sites can be destroyed but only at great cost in terms of the numbers of offensive weapons required to dig them out. Furthermore, in a second-strike situation we would be attacking, for the most part, empty sites from which the missiles had already been fired.

The value of trying to provide a capability to destroy a very high proportion of Soviet hard ICBM sites becomes even more questionable in view of the expected increase in the Soviet missile-launching submarine force. . . .[16]

Indeed, in his annual defense review before Congress in February 1965, Secretary McNamara explicitly abandoned the notion of counterforce strategy less than three years after seeking to base NATO policy on it. He stated that the new damage-limiting strategy might reduce American fatalities in a general war from 149 million to 122 million, provided there was warning of an hour or more.[17]

But if Secretary McNamara has been correct in insisting that an adaptation of NATO strategy was necessary, he has been less sensitive to the political and psychological implications of his insight. Although he coupled his most recent estimate of casualties with the customary assurance

[16] McNamara, *Military Procurement Authorizations: Fiscal Year 1964;* Senate Armed Services Committee (88th Cong., 1st sess., 1963), p. 41.
[17] *New York Times,* February 19, 1965.

of an unimpaired United States nuclear guarantee, the situation of NATO must inevitably be transformed when on the most favorable assumption a general nuclear war would kill over half of the United States population. The increasing vulnerability of civilian populations coupled with the growing invulnerability of retaliatory forces has produced a gap between the technical requirements of the new strategy and the political realities of an alliance of sovereign states. United States strategic doctrine seeks to make any American nuclear response depend on decisions taken in the light of circumstances when aggression is actually taking place. The very quality of deliberation which makes this strategy militarily desirable for the United States creates a sense of impotence or pressures for autonomy among our Allies. The central command and control system, which is the key feature of the new doctrine, is American. The United States will determine—to the extent that the enemy cooperates—how and with what weapons the war is to be fought and on what terms it will be concluded. The nature and timeliness of an eventual American response have thus become a central Allied concern which the Pentagon's 1965 casualty estimates will surely magnify.

These insecurities have been reinforced by simultaneous American pressures for the build-up of conventional forces. Secretary McNamara has argued that a build-up of conventional forces by the Europeans—indeed, a specialization by the Europeans in conventional weapons—would enhance the credibility of the nuclear arsenal:

If we have shown ourselves able and ready to engage in large-scale non-nuclear warfare in response to a Communist provocation, the Soviets can hardly misconstrue two things: first, that we regard this provocation as a challenge to our vital interests; and second, that we will use nuclear weapons to prevail, if this becomes necessary.[18]

[18] McNamara, address before the Fellows of the American Bar Foundation, Chicago, Illinois, February 17, 1962, *op. cit.*, p. 9.

This estimate has left many Europeans unconvinced. This is not because the Europeans fail to understand the notion of flexible response—though they do have trouble with some of its subtler applications. Rather it is that they reject its applicability for themselves. When the issue is Asia or Latin America, Europeans usually conceive even more "options" than the United States. With respect to the defense of Europe, their attitude is more rigid. Europeans are likely to agree with the following assessment of Soviet intentions by Secretary of the Navy Paul Nitze (then Assistant Secretary of Defense for International Security Affairs):

Communists demonstrate both a proclivity for bold political actions against a background of impressive military force and also careful calculation of risks and a staunch desire to keep events under their own control. Because they can be expected sensibly to avoid high risks of nuclear war or events leading to it, *their military actions against the West at any one moment are likely to be controlled in size and aimed at limited objectives* [emphasis added].[19]

But most Europeans would not consider that an attack on Central Europe could involve limited objectives. If Secretary Nitze is correct in his view that the Soviets recoil before a high risk of nuclear war, then a limited attack in Europe is likely only if the American nuclear guarantee has lost some of its credibility. For some Europeans, the remedy for this state of affairs is to build up nuclear forces of their own rather than additional conventional divisions too insignificant to affect the conventional balance but significant enough to underline American reluctance to face the risks of nuclear war.

This is well illustrated by European reactions to the arguments which we have used to justify the strengthen-

[19] Paul H. Nitze, address before the Cleveland Council on World Affairs, Cleveland, Ohio, March 2, 1963. Cited in William W. Kaufmann, *The McNamara Strategy* (New York: Harper & Row, 1964), pp. 130–131.

ing of NATO's conventional forces. The purpose of the conventional forces has been said to be to provide a "pause" in military operations in order to permit the Soviets to "appreciate the wider risks involved." The ground forces, in other words, are supposed to define a "threshold" below which nuclear weapons would not have to be used.

These arguments did not increase the European willingness to undertake a conventional build-up; instead they raised the issue of nuclear control in acute form. To begin with, it is far from certain that the Soviets will, in fact, confront increased risks of nuclear war after a given period of conventional conflict. Presumably the Soviets would have discounted in advance the threat of nuclear retaliation before launching a major attack on Central Europe. But if such an attack does take place, why should NATO's bargaining position be better at the end of a period of thirty days (the usual target date for the build-up)— when NATO's conventional forces would have presumably been decimated—than at the beginning? What if at that point the Soviets offered to negotiate after having gained possession of their prize? If nuclear war is too risky for the West at the start of the conflict, why should it not be even more risky when the local issue has in effect already been decided and when the devastation caused by a nuclear exchange may make the local situation seem irrelevant? If, on the other hand, it is argued that the Soviets would never dare to defeat NATO's ground forces lest this trigger a nuclear exchange, what is gained by increasing the number of NATO divisions beyond a level which forces the Soviets into a major commitment?

The same difficulty applies to the concept of a "threshold." This was defined by the then Deputy Secretary of Defense, Roswell Gilpatric, as follows: "The current doctrine is that if NATO forces were about to be overwhelmed by non-nuclear attacks from the bloc countries, NATO would make use of nuclear arms."[20] This raises two ques-

[20] *New York Times,* June 7, 1961.

tions: (1) Who determines whether the NATO conventional forces are being overwhelmed? (2) Assuming this determination is made, how are nuclear weapons then to be used?

With respect to the first of these issues, a question of definition arises: are the NATO forces "overwhelmed" when they are simply pushed back but still largely intact? What if the Soviets mass clearly overwhelming power in Eastern Europe, but have not yet launched an attack? If nuclear weapons are useful to prevent this contingency, why not to prevent others? Or it could be that in an otherwise successful defense, individual units of, say, division size would suffer setbacks. In view of the dispersal of nuclear weapons in Europe to divisional levels and below, it is likely that the location of nuclear stockpiles and delivery vehicles would decide the question of using nuclear weapons. In short, the deployment of nuclear weapons in Europe has been inconsistent with the announced United States strategic preference. This has raised the question about which is a better key to United States intentions: the pronouncements of our highest defense officials or the disposition of our forces.

Assuming, however, that it is possible to determine that NATO's conventional forces are being overwhelmed, this only shifts the concern to the issue of how nuclear weapons are to be used and who makes the decision to use them. If nuclear weapons are to be used only when NATO forces are at the point of being defeated, what is the sense in the nuclear establishment in Europe? If we assume that both sides have tactical nuclear weapons in adequate numbers and sizes, it is far from clear that the employment of these weapons would favor the defense at that stage of a battle. *After* a breakthrough has been achieved, battlefield employment of nuclear weapons may well favor the offense, whose units can by then be dispersed while the defense has to move into predictable areas. In short, if nuclear weapons are ever to be used tactically, it is likely that the optimum, perhaps the only appropriate, moment is early in military operations, or at least while the ground forces are reasonably intact and Soviet reserve forces have not yet appeared on the battlefield. If nuclear weapons are not to be used tactically, what is the sense of increasing their number in Europe?

These questions become all the more acute because the choice between nuclear and conventional war is no longer entirely up to the West. Whatever its preference, NATO will have to prepare for the introduction of nuclear weapons by the opponent. *Any* war will be nuclear, whether or not nuclear weapons are used, in the sense that deployment—even of conventional forces—will have to take place in a nuclear environment.

This in turn casts doubt about the feasibility of a large-scale conventional war in Central Europe. Preparations for such a war would have to assume that the Soviet Union discounts not only our strategic nuclear capability but also NATO's growing tactical nuclear establishment; for the United States has repeatedly announced that it would not accept a conventional defeat in Europe without using nuclear weapons. Even if the Soviets do not believe that we would risk the destruction of American cities by attacking the Soviet homeland, they can hardly expect that we would let the large stockpile of tactical nuclear weapons in Europe simply fall into their hands. Moreover these weapons are extremely vulnerable. Is it really sensible to assume that the Soviets would launch a large-scale conventional attack in Central Europe—which they would, of course, expect to win—without seeking to neutralize the nuclear weapons on the Continent?[21]

The issue of conventional defense has been muted since early in 1964 because the United States has apparently had second thoughts about its previous course. But it lasted long enough to make the issue of nuclear

[21] For a splendid analysis of this problem of the conventional defense of Europe see Bernard Brodie, "What Price Conventional Capabilities in Europe," *The Reporter*, Vol. 28, No. 11 (May 23, 1963), pp. 25–33.

control one of the central unresolved problems of the Alliance. As long as the United States insists on central control over the nuclear weapons of the Alliance, as well as total freedom of action with respect to them, the European incentive in the development of strategy is likely to be exactly the opposite of ours. Rather than permit a "pause" for "appreciating the wider risks involved," Europeans prefer to make our response as automatic as possible.

This has little to do with whether the United States could "afford" to lose Europe. It is rooted in the nature of sovereignty and is made more acute by the destructiveness of nuclear weapons. Robert Bowie has criticized British nuclear policy before the Assembly of the Western European Union as follows: "Britain . . . has retained a national command structure and the right to withdraw them at its option. This means that they *certainly* [emphasis added] could not be counted upon by any of the others to be available in case of need."[22] If this concern is valid when applied to British nuclear forces, which are, after all, assigned to NATO, it must be even stronger regarding United States strategic forces which remain under exclusive American control.

The debate about the level of conventional forces has hurt the Alliance in two other respects. It is dangerous to insist that a given form of defense is essential when allies are unable or unwilling to support it. Failure to reach the announced goals can then foster either a sense of impotence or a policy of neutrality. Moreover, as leader of the Alliance, the United States has a responsibility to consider whether its preferred schemes can be maintained over an extended period. If not, their benefits must be weighed against the loss of confidence engendered by frequent shifts of position. It is already apparent that in both Washington and London there is growing support for the view that conventional forces in Europe can be

[22] *Proceedings*, Assembly of Western European Union, Ninth Ordinary Session, Second Part, IV, December 1963, p. 125.

reduced. Such a step would have had unfortunate political consequences at any time; occurring two years after insistent American pressures that these forces be built up, the negative impact will be greatly increased.

If the United States has lacked consistency and, occasionally, psychological insight, some of our European critics have not helped matters by their insistence that existing NATO doctrine is sacrosanct and by the deliberate tendency—especially on the part of France—to put the worst possible construction on our actions. United States proposals for strengthening conventional forces have been treated with the same panic as later hints that some American troops might be withdrawn. Most Europeans do not want to give conventional forces a larger role because they fear that it will diminish the effectiveness of the nuclear deterrent. But they also have resisted a reduction of United States forces because they believe these represent the surest guarantee of American nuclear protection. It is just as difficult for Europeans to face the fact that these attitudes are inconsistent as it has been for Americans to admit that increased emphasis on local defense is incompatible with United States hegemony in nuclear matters.

The problem can then be summed up as follows: Exclusive United States control of nuclear strategy is politically and psychologically difficult to reconcile with a strategy of multiple choices or flexible response. The European refusal to assign a meaningful military mission to conventional forces in Europe is incompatible with the indefinite retention of large United States forces there. If the United States places a high enough value on conventional defense, it will have to concede Europe a measure of autonomy in nuclear control. Or else it will have to move to an effective sharing of political sovereignty. If the Europeans want to insist on an automatic nuclear response, a reconsideration of our conventional deployment on the Continent will become inevitable. Refusal to face these facts will guarantee a perpetuation of present disputes and increasing disarray within NATO.

NATO'S NUCLEAR DILEMMA

NATO's nuclear dilemma has developed because there is an increasing inconsistency between the technical requirements of strategy and political imperatives of the nation-state. Three factors have produced the difficulty: (1) the need for centralized control of military operations, (2) the desire of each major ally to have substantial influence on common decisions, especially during crises, in defining the *casus belli* and in participating in the planning of the controlled operations foreseen by the doctrine of flexible response and (3) the wish of the major allies to share in the prestige and the political power which control of nuclear weapons confers or is thought to confer.

The dilemma arises because there is no scheme which can reconcile these objectives perfectly so long as the Atlantic Alliance remains composed of sovereign states. The occasional bitterness of the debate is at least in part due to the fact that neither the United States nor its European critics has been prepared to admit that a genuine conflict of interests exists. The only political solution that could resolve this contradiction is unattainable in the foreseeable future: turning over *all* the nuclear weapons of the Alliance to an authority embracing the North Atlantic area—a supranational political and defense community which would be essentially a federal government. In the absence of such an embracing political structure, a clash of interests is inevitable.

This is illustrated by two United States policies: (1) the sharp attack on the national nuclear forces of Britain and France and (2) the various schemes to achieve central command and control over the nuclear weapons of the Alliance within the present framework of NATO.

With respect to national nuclear forces, Great Britain

since 1951 and France since 1958 have been engaged in a program to develop nuclear capabilities under their own control. In 1954, an amendment to the McMahon Act made possible United States nuclear assistance to Great Britain. The provisions of the amended McMahon Act have never been extended to France. This discrimination has been a constant source of irritation in Franco-American relations—and would have been regardless of which government was in power in France.

United States policy, which had been tolerant of the nuclear programs of its Allies, grew increasingly hostile from 1961 onward. The French nuclear program was described as irrelevant and harmful to the Alliance. The same criticisms, if more muted, were applied to the British nuclear program. The tension inherent in an attack on major defense programs of two close allies exacerbated the debate about other aspects of NATO strategic doctrine—particularly the role of conventional weapons.

United States opposition to the British and French nuclear programs was supported by the following major arguments: There‚ was no strategic need for national nuclear forces since all significant targets were already covered by United States strategic forces. National nuclear forces were divisive because their very existence implied distrust of the United States. They were wasteful and would divert resources from the conventional build-up which should be the primary NATO effort. They would promote nuclear proliferation. National nuclear forces would make impossible the flexible response which was the key to United States strategy. They were too small and too vulnerable to concentrate on military targets. And if they attacked population centers, the enemy in rage and frustration would retaliate against the civilian population of the United States.

Regardless of the merits of these arguments, they were certain to lead to a bitter, divisive debate. A full-scale theoretical onslaught on major programs of close allies impelled their governments to elaborate a doctrine to justify them, which, in turn, could not help but stress conflicting interests with the United States. The political impact of United States views thus went far beyond the technical arguments in which they were couched. To ask a government to confess the bankruptcy of a policy which it has pursued at heavy expense for over a decade is to undermine its domestic position and to evoke reactions of hostility. We might ask ourselves how an American administration would respond if an allied government publicly and repeatedly insisted that one of our major programs was "divisive," "dangerous" and "useless."

Apart from the involvement of the United States strategic doctrine in the domestic disputes of close allies, the debate involved a difference in perspective with our Allies even on purely military grounds. Our European critics have identified the doctrine of flexible response with the concept, enunciated by Secretary McNamara at Ann Arbor in 1962, of counterforce operations confined to military targets and designed to disarm the enemy. Many of them considered this concept unrealistic as soon as it was enunciated. To densely populated Europe, the distinction between' military and civilian targets has always seemed rather ephemeral. While not objecting to a "disarming" strategy as *one* possible option, some of our European Allies have seen no compelling reason to subordinate *all* considerations to a very remote contingency.

Even before Secretary McNamara abandoned his counterforce doctrine, United States pronouncements were postulating a scenario for general nuclear war that was somewhat remote. In his presentations to the Armed Services Committee in 1963 and in 1964, Secretary McNamara described only *one* contingency for general nuclear war: a full-scale Soviet nuclear attack on the United States concentrating on military targets. The United States would then respond by attacking Soviet residual forces and other targets.[23]

[23] In his testimony before the Armed Services Committee in January 1964, Secretary McNamara associated the defense of Eu-

But it is not clear what could possibly tempt even a rash Soviet planner into such a course or why the Soviets would then attack American missile sites. As long as the present numerical imbalance between Soviet and American strategic forces remains, the Soviets could not conceivably benefit from launching a blow against the United States strategic forces. Even if every Soviet missile destroyed an American delivery vehicle, the Soviets would have disarmed themselves and would find themselves confronted with a large American force unrestrained by any Soviet threat.

In short, a "disarming" strategy cannot be an optimum strategy for both sides. Soviet military theorists have consistently denied the possibility of the kind of war described by Pentagon officials. This would not be decisive were it not in accord with the realities of the strategic equation; for a war confined to military targets, even if it were technically feasible, cannot be in the interest of the weaker side. As the United States reduced the Soviet retaliatory force, the sensible strategy for the Soviets would be to begin attacking objectives of great value to America, including, perhaps, Europe.

---

rope with *tactical,* not *strategic,* nuclear weapons should the conventional forces prove inadequate. Thus, in his report to the Armed Services Committee on the Fiscal Years 1965–1969, Defense Program and Defense Budget (January 27, 1964), Secretary McNamara said:

> . . . a large-scale Soviet attack on Western Europe . . . would be extremely dangerous to our own security, and would compel us to respond immediately with whatever force was needed to halt the onslaught, *even with tactical nuclear weapons, if necessary* [emphasis added] (pp. 56–57).

And a little further on, when discussing General Purpose Forces, Secretary McNamara said:

> (1) The forces envisioned in NATO plans for the end of 1966 . . . could hold an initial Soviet attack on the central front using non-nuclear means alone. (2) Until these requirements are met, the defense of Europe against an all-out Soviet attack, even if such an attack were limited to non-nuclear means, would require the use of *tactical* [emphasis added] nuclear weapons on our part (p. 58).

Even before the latest casualty estimates by the Pentagon, this situation produced pressures either for European nuclear forces or for a more effective voice in ours. As has been frequently pointed out by Pentagon spokesmen, the Soviet delivery vehicles aimed at Europe far exceed in number those deployed against the United States. It has also been emphasized that even a "controlled" nuclear war would produce casualties in Europe exceeding the scores of millions estimated for North America. In these conditions, it is understandable that some Europeans have come to the conclusion that Europe must have its own means of retaliation in order to discourage the Soviets from using Europe as a hostage in the Soviet version of "flexible response."

In order to meet these concerns, the Kennedy Administration in 1961–1962 offered a number of schemes which sought to combine assurances about the availability of American weapons with undiluted American control. However, these schemes missed the central concern of our Allies which was not technical but political: A centralized military strategy was possible only if the United States was prepared to yield at least some of the freedom of action in the political realm that it was asking its allies to give up in the military field. The issue of nuclear control emphasized that NATO required a mechanism for managing political crises even more than a military staff for planning a war.

This is illustrated by the initial United States proposals for nuclear control, which concentrated on such gestures as "earmarking" and "assignment" of nuclear weapons to NATO. Thus in May 1961 President Kennedy formally offered to "commit to the NATO command five—and subsequently still more—Polaris . . . submarines . . . subject to any agreed NATO guidelines on their control and use."[24] This pledge was declared fulfilled by Secretary McNamara at the Athens ministerial meeting when he announced

[24] John F. Kennedy, address to the Canadian Parliament, May 17, 1961, *DOSB*, Vol. XLIV, No. 1145 (June 5, 1961), p. 841.

that five Polaris submarines had already been "committed" to NATO with more to come.[25] In his report to the House Armed Services Committee of January 1963, Secretary McNamara announced that the United States had "earmarked a fully operational Polaris force to the NATO command."[26]

These measures were largely symbolic. In the absence of a political mechanism for managing crises and developing strategic doctrine, there was a serious question about the practical meaning of the term "assignment." All forces in NATO are under national command in peacetime. NATO headquarters are planning outfits that control the forces "assigned" to them only during specified maneuvers or in war. Each ally retains the right to go to war according to its own constitutional processes. The right to withdraw forces is inherent, and "assignment" does not significantly restrict the independent disposition of NATO forces. This has been demonstrated by the United States withdrawal of forces from Germany for action in Lebanon, by the French withdrawal of its fleet from NATO, by the use of NATO-assigned forces by both Greece and Turkey during the Cyprus crisis and by the withdrawal of British forces from Germany for use in Malaysia. Thus the assignment of American and British strategic units to NATO does not significantly restrict the ability to use these forces for national purposes (or, what is even more relevant, to refrain from using them). The severely criticized escape clauses in the Nassau Agreement concerning national emergencies gave Britain no additional rights; if Britain were to abandon these clauses, by assigning its nuclear forces "irrevocably" to NATO, as has been proposed, this would not materially change the situation for the inconceivable case that it would be prepared to go to nuclear war without the United States.

[25] *New York Times*, May 6, 1962. No more submarines have, in fact, been assigned.

[26] *Hearings on Military Posture,* Committee on Armed Services, House (88th Cong., 1st. sess., 1963), p. 298.

But assuming that "assignment" does imply a higher degree of commitment, what precisely was its strategic significance? Did it mean that there was a stronger obligation to use submarines "assigned" to NATO than SAC in the defense of Europe? What was one to make of the phrase in the communique after the NATO ministerial meeting in Athens in May 1962 which stated that the United States and Great Britain had given "firm assurances that their strategic forces will continue to provide defense against threats to the Alliance beyond the capability of NATO-committed forces to deal with"?[27] Did this mean that there were two "thresholds" in NATO strategy: one between conventional and nuclear war and another between the strategic forces assigned to NATO and the rest of SAC? If so, this would mean either that the counterforce strategy on which the Administration had staked so much would have to be abandoned or that the strategic forces under the control of SACEUR would have to be increased vastly—at least to match the Soviet MRBM's stationed in Eastern Europe. In other words, before determining the significance of a rearrangement of the nuclear forces within NATO there must be an agreed strategic doctrine and a political mechanism for managing crises; this is now lacking.

It has been argued by some that the strategic forces earmarked for NATO can fill precisely this need by encouraging joint Allied guidelines for their use. The significance of this view depends on what is actually involved in an agreement to joint guidelines. Are they to be conceived as a kind of contingency plan for the employment of nuclear weapons, *provided* the governments concerned agree to implement these plans? Or are they to be considered as a delegation of authority to use nuclear weapons in certain specified contingencies without further reference to political authority?

If guidelines are to be interpreted in the former sense— as a form of contingency war plan—they are a useful exer-

[27] Text of communique, *New York Times*, May 7, 1962.

cise in Allied consultation. But in that case it is not clear how the NATO-committed Polaris forces are to be distinguished from other strategic forces in the Alliance. Joint planning could and should take place even with respect to forces not formally assigned to the Alliance.

If, on the other hand, the guidelines are to be a form of delegation of authority, serious problems would arise. It is difficult to imagine any President agreeing to such an unprecedented abdication of constitutional responsibilities. And even if it were taken, it would probably compound the problem. The predelegation of authority would be confined to the most obvious and unambiguous cases. A guideline so conceived will omit more cases than it specifies and thus raise uncertainties precisely about the ambiguous cases that have caused the greatest worries.

The dialogue on nuclear control thus has taken place on two levels which rarely coincided. On strictly strategic grounds, the United States doctrine is more nearly correct than the alternative of its European critics; division of labor within an alliance conceived as a unit *does* promote the most efficient allocation of resources. What the United States overlooked was that NATO is *not* a single political unit, nor is it likely to be one in the foreseeable future. The blind spot of the United States has been its unwillingness to face the political implications of its strategic views: Central command and control over all the nuclear weapons of the Alliance is incompatible with undiluted sovereignty. The United States cannot insist on integration of strategy while jealously guarding its complete freedom of political decision. Using an abstract *a priori* logic, our European critics have deduced their strategic views from their conception of the nature of political sovereignty. There is merit in their political analysis, but they have refused to face the fact that there must be some relationship between a political posture and what is strategically feasible.

Thus, even before De Gaulle's press conference of January 14, 1963, a stalemate in the strategic debate had occurred. Europeans had been reluctant to respond to American pressures for an increase in conventional forces. The frequent, unilateral changes in United States strategic doctrine had shaken European confidence. The United States proposals for sharing nuclear control had not met the real concerns of those Europeans asking either for a greater share in the nuclear decisions or for greater autonomy with respect to their own. In order to escape this impasse, the United States—starting early in 1963—began ever more urgently to press a scheme for a NATO nuclear force, the so-called Multilateral Force (MLF).

Chapter Five

THE ISSUE OF NUCLEAR
CONTROL–THE MULTILATERAL
FORCE (MLF)

Few major innovations of American policy have produced such sharply conflicting emotions as the proposed NATO Multilateral Force (commonly referred to as the MLF). Though its fate is still uncertain, so much American prestige has been invested in it for so long that, whether it succeeds or fails, it will affect the shape of the Alliance. It is therefore important to understand how the MLF was conceived and what it was expected to accomplish.

The MLF, which emerged in February 1963 as America's principal effort to restore the cohesion of NATO, had previously been held at arms length by the Kennedy Administration. After De Gaulle's veto of Britain's membership in the Common Market, the MLF was resurrected and pushed with increasing passion. The United States concentrated on the problem of nuclear control partly because the French challenge seemed to relate political autonomy to nuclear independence, partly because Washington feared the twin specters of a German national nuclear program and Franco-German collaboration in the nuclear field.

The original proposal for a NATO multilateral force grew out of a military "requirement" which had been generated in accordance with the NATO doctrine prevalent in the late fifties. According to this concept, SACEUR was to have the capability to destroy all weapons aimed at Europe. Thus when the Soviet Union began to deploy large numbers of medium-range ballistic missiles in western Russia, two NATO requirements emerged: a modernization program to replace vulnerable tactical aircraft with missiles and an interdiction mission giving NATO the capability to destroy the Soviet MRBM's.

When the issue of counteracting the Soviet MRBM's was raised in 1959, the first impulse of the Eisenhower Administration was to go along with a proposal of SACEUR (then General Lauris Norstad) which envisaged the installation of a mobile land-based version of the Polaris missile in Europe under the double-veto system. Upon further consideration, this proposal was rejected. It was argued that large numbers of missiles constantly moving on European roads might disquiet the populations and thus encourage neutralist tendencies. The double-veto system was believed to provide inadequate safeguards against the ultimate control of nuclear weapons by Germany. Accordingly, a State Department study group headed by Professor Robert R. Bowie proposed that NATO's MRBM requirement be met by Polaris missiles installed on ships (in the early version, submarines). These ships were to be jointly owned, operated and financed by the participants and were to remain under SACEUR's control at all times. To prevent the withdrawal of national contingents, each ship was to be manned by crews of mixed nationality. Each participant was to have a veto. The multilateral scheme was submitted to the NATO Council by Secretary of State Herter in December 1960 for study. A final decision was delayed until the new administration could assess the problem.

There occurred a hiatus of several months while the Kennedy Administration reconsidered NATO strategy. Having concluded that greater reliance should be placed on conventional forces and that control over nuclear weapons should be centralized, the Kennedy Administration did not look with particular favor on the creation of any new nuclear force within NATO. Thus, on May 17, 1961, in a 'speech on NATO's nuclear arrangements, President Kennedy mentioned the MLF only very indirectly. He urged the European allies to meet the conventional goals of NATO before ". . . we look to the possibility of eventually establishing a NATO sea-borne force, which would be truly multilateral in ownership and control, if this should be desired and found feasible by our allies, once NATO's non-nuclear goals have been achieved."[1] In the course of the next year, administration spokesmen invited our Allies to analyze the problem and to develop a satisfactory control plan.

The two conditions put forward by the United States—a prior conventional build-up and European agreement about a control plan—suggested that the MLF scheme was not considered very urgent. Most of America's Allies doubted the need for a conventional build-up. They could not afford both to strengthen their ground forces and to contribute to a NATO nuclear force. Moreover, none of our Allies possessed sea-borne nuclear delivery vehicles. Since a command and control system for even a national nuclear force is far from a simple matter, the probability that they would develop a meaningful control system for a *multilateral* sea-borne force was not great. Indeed there were many in the administration who believed that the problem would be found insoluble. It was expected that the Allies would then ask the President to act as executive agent for the Alliance on nuclear matters.

When this did not happen, the United States in 1962

[1] John F. Kennedy, "The Common Aims of Canada and the United States," speech at Ottawa, May 17, 1961, *DOSB*, Vol. XLIV, No. 1145 (June 5, 1961), p. 841.

continued its gingerly approach to the MLF. In September 1962, McGeorge Bundy spoke hedgingly of a multilateral *European* force.

It would also be wrong to suppose that the reluctance which we feel with respect to individual, ineffective, and unintegrated forces would be extended automatically to a European force, genuinely unified and multilateral, and effectively integrated with our own necessarily predominant strength in the whole nuclear defense of the alliance. Any possible arrangements for assistance and cooperation in such an enterprise would, of course, require full consultation and approval by all appropriate agencies of our Government.[2]

The speech said nothing about what the United States meant by "multilateral," "unified" or "integrated."

A month later Under Secretary of State Ball returned to the theme of a NATO nuclear force. He insisted that it was militarily unnecessary and he continued to stress the priority placed by the Kennedy Administration on the build-up of conventional forces. But he added:

. . . should other NATO nations so desire, we are ready to give serious consideration to the creation of a genuinely multilateral medium-range ballistic missile force fully coordinated with the other deterrent forces of the North Atlantic Treaty Organization.[3]

In the following weeks an American briefing team toured Europe to explain the American concept of a multilateral force, including the provision for crews of mixed nationality. It did not elicit a significant European response.

In December, Secretary Rusk spoke vaguely of a force "not . . . so heavily dependent upon the United States

[2] McGeorge Bundy, "Building the Atlantic Partnership: Some Lessons from the Past," speech on September 27, 1962, *DOSB*, Vol. XLVII, No. 1217 (October 22, 1962), pp. 604–605.

[3] George W. Ball, "NATO and the Cuban Crisis," speech on November 16, 1962, *DOSB*, Vol. XLVII, No. 1223 (December 3, 1962), p. 835.

alone." But he stressed that it was up to the Europeans to formulate a concrete proposal:

We also have expressed our willingness, if our allies wish to do so, to consider a multilateral nuclear force which would not be so heavily dependent upon the United States alone. Now, we have not ourselves put forward a precise plan in this regard. This is something that our friends across the Atlantic would presumably wish to do if they conclude what it is they would like to propose in this field.[4]

At the regular NATO ministerial conference in December 1962, the United States took no initiative with respect to the MLF. A week later at Nassau, however, the United States and Great Britain decided to subscribe part of their national nuclear forces to a NATO multilateral force:

Returning to Polaris the President and the Prime Minister agreed that the purpose of their two governments with respect to the provision of Polaris missiles must be the development of a multilateral NATO nuclear force in the closest consultation with other NATO allies. They will use their best endeavors to this end.[5]

This was one of the many ambiguities in the Nassau Agreement, an exegesis of which absorbed energies on both sides of the Atlantic for many months. Did "multilateral" mean the assignment of national contingents to NATO as Great Britain argued? Or did it involve a commitment to create a mixed-manned, sea-borne force as the United States urged? For a few weeks after the Nassau Agreement, the term multilateral was in fact used interchangeably for either arrangement. Whatever the answer, it is obvious that until De Gaulle's press conference on

[4] Dean Rusk, News Conference on December 10, 1962, *DOSB*, Vol. XLVII, No. 1227 (December 31, 1962), p. 995.

[5] Text, Joint Communique and Attached Statement on nuclear defense systems issued on December 21, 1962, by President Kennedy and Prime Minister Macmillan, *DOSB*, Vol. XLVIII, No. 1229 (January 14, 1963), p. 44.

January 14, 1963, the MLF was far from a high priority goal of American foreign policy.

Whatever the hesitations of the administration, they were resolved by De Gaulle's press conference. Within a week, Secretary Rusk said in a television interview that the United States would proceed with the MLF even without France (though he did not make clear whether he was using multilateral in the American or the British sense).[6] On February 9, the legal counsellor of the State Department, Abram Chayes, explicitly advanced the Multilateral Force as an alternative route to the Grand Design that De Gaulle had sought to block with his veto of Britain's entry into the Common Market.[7]

By March 1963, the United States had dropped the conditions of a non-nuclear build-up and of a prior European agreement on a control plan. Indeed, it now argued that a final decision on the control problem should await the actual creation of the Multilateral Force. Ambassador Livingston Merchant was assigned to carry out the negotiations to bring the Multilateral Force into being. On April 27, 1963, Under Secretary Ball laid down four criteria for the MLF: (1) There must be many participants. (2) The force must not be based predominantly in one country. (3) Through mixed-manning, the components must be made unavailable for withdrawal. (4) The decision-making must be collective. He went on to describe the MLF in glowing terms:

The kind of multilateral force I have described has much to commend it. Not only is it the best means of dealing with the nuclear problem in the present political framework; it is also a means of promoting gradual and constructive evolution within that framework. The multilateral force would offer the great advantage of a further

[6] Dean Rusk, "Today," NBC Television, January 21, 1963, *DOSB*, Vol. XLVIII, No. 1233 (February 11, 1963), p. 206.

[7] Abram Chayes, "European Integration and American Foreign Policy," February 9, 1963, *DOSB*, Vol. XLVIII, No. 1236 (March 4, 1963), p. 321.

opportunity to work toward greater unity in Europe and closer partnership between Europe and the United States.[8]

During 1963 the MLF became the main focus of American NATO policy. The original posture of responding to European wishes was abandoned. American spokesmen ever more insistently urged the MLF as a major contribution to restoring Allied cohesion—indeed as the principal available step. Thus, on October 27, Secretary Rusk, speaking in Frankfurt, said:

Such a multilateral missile fleet would be militarily effective. Its accurate and well-protected missiles would be counted toward the total needs of Western deterrence.

It would strengthen Atlantic partnership by binding the United States and Europe in an inextricable nuclear tie. The missiles and warheads would be jointly owned and controlled; they could not be unilaterally withdrawn.

And it would strengthen European cohesion by providing the presently nonnuclear powers an opportunity to share in ownership, manning, and control of a powerful nuclear force on the same basis as other members of that force.[9]

The full apparatus of American persuasion—official, semiofficial and unofficial—pressed the MLF on our European Allies. In September 1964, Thomas K. Finletter, United States Representative at the NATO Council, went so far as to say: "As goes this fleet, so may go the defense of the West and our efforts to prevent war."[10] There were strong intimations that if the other Allies procrastinated the United States would go ahead with the MLF as a German-American project—a position supported by Chancellor Erhard on October 6, 1964.

[8] George W. Ball, "The Nuclear Deterrent and the Atlantic Alliance," speech April 26, 1963, *DOSB,* Vol. XLVIII, No. 1246 (May 13, 1963), p. 739.
[9] Dean Rusk, "Toward a New Dimension in Atlantic Partnership," speech at Frankfurt on October 27, 1963, *DOSB,* Vol. XLIX, No. 1272 (November 11, 1963), p. 730.
[10] *New York Times,* September 11, 1964.

This onslaught overcame the initial reserve of many of our Allies. After brief hesitation, the Federal Republic agreed to the scheme. While its original motive may well have been to prove that the Franco-German Treaty of Collaboration was not inconsistent with continued loyalty to the Alliance, the Federal Republic soon became nearly as enthusiastic an advocate of the MLF as the United States. Greece, Turkey and Italy agreed in principle to participate. Britain, Belgium and the Netherlands joined the other countries in a study of the technical feasibility of mixed-manning. France refused any degree of participation.

However, the large number of participants in the technical studies was deceptive. United States insistence made it difficult for allied governments to face the issue of the MLF on its merits. The defense ministries of our Allies (except in Bonn), which might be thought to have a vested interest in the MLF, were opposed or lukewarm, while the foreign offices, fearful of the political consequences of a refusal, were pressing it. The skepticism or indifference of the military was countered by the concern that flat rejection might jeopardize the American commitment to the defense of Europe.

Moreover, American negotiating tactics were deliberately designed to avoid difficult political issues. The complex problem of control was sidestepped. During 1964, American diplomacy concentrated on studies regarding the technical feasibility of mixed-manning. Efforts were also made to draft a charter for the operation of the MLF if the governments concerned later agreed to join. The negotiations thus had a curious aspect. Some governments, though indifferent, participated just to keep informed; others did not want to offend their senior ally. The United States and other advocates of the MLF, in turn, took the view that joining the technical discussions implied a commitment in principle to the MLF. The confusions thus engendered were amply demonstrated when, after having taken part in all the technical discussions, Belgium announced in November 1964 that it would not join the MLF after all. In January 1965 Turkey also withdrew from the MLF.

Thus the MLF—ridiculed by many when it first appeared, doubtfully received even under American pressure, perhaps accepted, except in Bonn, with the hope that it would never come to pass—took on increasing substance. By the end of October 1964, discussions had reached the following point: The MLF was to be composed of twenty-five surface ships, each carrying eight A-3 Polaris missiles with a range of 2,500 miles. Each ship was to be manned by crews drawn from at least three nationalities. No nation was to contribute more than 40 per cent of the total. Command of the ships was to be in proportion to the financial contribution. (In practice this would have meant that the Federal Republic and the United States would each contribute 40 per cent, leaving 20 per cent to be divided among the five or six other participants.) The Federal Republic was to be by far the largest European contributor, paying close to 70 per cent of the European share. The control system had not yet been decided, but it seemed certain that an executive body in which all participants were represented would make decisions, at least initially, on the basis of unanimity. The timetable called for signing a treaty on the MLF by the end of 1964, with ratification taking place sometime during 1965. The new British government was expected not to refuse a project that had already advanced so far. It was assumed that the smaller European countries would follow the British lead. France would then be isolated.

But it was unrealistic to expect that so far-reaching a scheme as the MLF could be pushed through without facing the central political issues. The illusion that France would stand idle at the emergence of a project that had the practical consequence of isolating her was shattered. As American pressure increased, French opposition came into the open, and the Federal Republic was caught between the conflicting views of its closest allies. The new

British government began to state misgivings about the
MLF that had been muted by the imminence of elections.
The Secretary General of NATO, Manlio Brosio, announced that in his view so radical a step toward integration as the MLF required unanimous consent, even of
the countries not participating, thus giving France an effective veto. The MLF, proposed to restore Allied cohesion, became instead an additional element of discord.

At this point, President Johnson wisely removed American deadlines to permit a calmer consideration of NATO's
nuclear problem. Whatever its ultimate fate, it is already
clear that many of the extravagant claims made for the
MLF are unfulfillable, and what will finally emerge may
have little relationship to the original project.

THE CASE FOR THE MLF

How did it happen that for nearly two years the MLF
became the focus of United States NATO policy? And why
did the United States stake so much on the issue of nuclear
control?

The MLF became the keystone of United States NATO
policy because, as so often happens, several conflicting
pressures and points of view in our bureaucracy suddenly
coalesced. The immediate impetus, as we have seen, was
SACEUR's requirement for medium-range missiles to counteract Soviet missiles aimed at Europe. This military requirement acquired a symbolic significance because of
German uneasiness about the early versions of the doctrine
of flexible response. Though German demands for reassurance about the continued validity of the American
nuclear guarantee generally concerned the disposition and
use of *tactical* nuclear weapons on German soil, they were
interpreted in Washington as the forerunner of more
sweeping proposals, which the MLF was designed to de-
flect.

Another motive behind the MLF was to prevent other
Allies from following the lead of Britain and France in

developing national nuclear programs. To the extent that national weapons programs were justified by the unreliability of American assistance, other Allies might be moved to develop nuclear arsenals of their own. According to this line of reasoning, the British nuclear program had produced the French effort and the French program would inevitably evoke similar aspirations in Germany.[11]

The MLF was given additional impetus by the reluctance of the NATO nuclear powers to share their planning and strategic decisions with their non-nuclear Allies. The Nuclear Committee of the NATO Council, which was created in April 1962 to provide a forum for the nuclear powers to discuss their strategic policy, remained dormant. Proponents of joint planning hoped to fill this gap through the MLF.

Another pressure for the MLF came from American strategic doctrine. Though the United States Defense Department would have preferred that all nuclear weapons of the Alliance remain under American control, it accepted the MLF as the next best expedient—provided the American veto remained unimpaired. The Pentagon was further attracted by the proposition that the MLF might provide a "safety net" into which the nuclear Allies might jump in order to dispose of their nuclear arsenals.

An opposite view was taken by the advocates of European integration. Their objection to the nuclear programs of France and Britain was less that they divided the Alliance than that they divided Europe. Too weak to encourage self-reliance, too nationally oriented to provide a

[11] Indeed, President Kennedy saw the spread of nuclear weapons to countries that must have been startled to find themselves listed as possible candidates for the nuclear club. Thus, in his television interview of December 17, 1962, President Kennedy said: "The question is whether the United States should join in helping make France a nuclear power, then Italy, then West Germany, then Belgium. How does that produce security when you have 10, 20, 30 nuclear powers who may fire their weapons off under different conditions?" (The CBS Television Network, Transcript of an Interview with President John F. Kennedy, December 17, 1962, p. 13.)

focal point for European loyalties, these programs prevented both European integration and the "dumbbell concept" of Atlantic partnership. It would be different with a
European nuclear force. According to the European integrationists, both in the State Department and overseas,
a European nuclear force would have the advantage of
promoting European unity; and it would be strong
enough to become a respectable partner for the United
States. The MLF was accepted by Jean Monnet's influential Action Committee for a United Europe for precisely
the opposite reason that the Pentagon resigned itself to it:
The European integrationists (and their allies in the State
Department) saw in the MLF the kernel of a separate
European nuclear force. They supported the MLF because
they wanted a new basis for uniting Europe, which would
provide a bridge for eventual British participation.[12]

These motives might have canceled each other out had
it not been for President de Gaulle's press conference excluding Britain from the Common Market. Many American
policymakers reacted with a sense of personal outrage and
began to cast about for some suitable response. They chose
the MLF partly because the French challenge seemed to
base itself on nuclear autonomy, partly because the MLF
happened to be the one "integrationist" project available
which had a strong group of supporters within the government. In other words, conversion of the United States
government from aloof receptivity to passionate advocacy
of the MLF was less the result of positive conviction than
reaction to French intransigence. Nothing had changed
between December 10, 1962, when Secretary Rusk stated
that it was up to the Europeans to formulate a plan with
respect to the MLF, and January 21, 1963, when he first

[12] For a splendid historical account of the MLF see Alastair Buchan, "The Multilateral Force: An Historical Perspective," Institute for Strategic Studies, Adelphi Papers, Number Thirteen (October 1964).

For the best statement on behalf of the MLF see Robert Osgood,
The Case for the MLF; A Critical Evaluation (Washington: Washington Center of Foreign Policy Research, 1964).

committed the United States to pressing it—except De Gaulle's veto of Britain's entry into the Common Market. The MLF was an attempt to implement the Grand Design without France and, if necessary, against it.

Once the United States committed itself to the MLF, the official arguments on behalf of it went something like this: The issue of nuclear control is the fundamental problem before the Alliance and the one in which American leadership has been most explicitly challenged. The cohesion of the Alliance therefore requires that it be "solved." Only three solutions are conceivable: American hegemony, which is psychologically unacceptable; nuclear proliferation to other NATO countries, which is politically divisive and strategically dangerous; and the MLF which will give the Federal Republic equal status while supplying a new impetus to European integration and strengthening Allied cohesion.

There were, however, several difficulties with this policy. The first was the lack of clarity about our real objectives. The MLF became the focus for many diverse hopes, and its supporters had many contradictory motives. It was supposed to revitalize NATO, yet reduce the role of France in Europe. It was to prevent nuclear proliferation and yet satisfy alleged German desires for a share of nuclear control. It simultaneously sought to meet requirements of the Pentagon for central control over nuclear weapons and the hopes of many Europeans for the emergence of a European nuclear force. Perhaps these aims were not irreconcilable. But because an explicit consideration of them was avoided in favor of the technical problem of mixed-manning, the debate in the winter of 1964 was mortgaged by many previous evasions and ambiguities, some of them deliberate.

These inconsistencies became all the more serious because the issue of nuclear control was inherently divisive. A project which involved giving Germany access to nuclear weapons was bound to bring on almost instinctive reactions of disquiet, which were magnified by the hints from Washington and Bonn that, if necessary, the United States and the Federal Republic might establish the MLF bilaterally. French hostility compounded the uneasiness of almost all the other Allies. To be sure, if the need was urgent the United States might well have been justified to vindicate its leadership position by pressing on despite Allied doubts. A great deal, therefore, turns on the answer to two related questions: How valid was the analysis which produced the MLF? How good was the remedy? An answer to these questions is all the more important because while removing original time limits, the administration has continued to maintain that the MLF remains the best solution to NATO's nuclear problem.

THE MLF—WRONG PROBLEM, WRONG ANSWER

The military case for the MLF has usually been put in terms of the MRBM "requirement" developed by SACEUR in the late fifties. However, this "requirement" reflects many of the unsolved problems of NATO doctrine. Existing NATO doctrine assumes that all the missiles necessary to eliminate the Soviet MRBM's should be under SACEUR's command. But should a counterforce mission deep into Soviet territory really be a top priority task of SACEUR? Indeed does it make any strategic sense when missiles on both sides are numbered in the hundreds and can be either hardened or made mobile? In any event, the MLF as originally conceived is much too small to deal with the Soviet MRBM's by itself. Those who cite the SACEUR "requirement" on behalf of the MLF encourage later pressures for increasing its size so that it can conduct effective counterforce operations. This would require many more missiles than the 200 projected in initial MLF plans.

If, on the other hand, the task of neutralizing the Soviet MRBM's is to be given to the MLF in conjunction with SAC, it becomes relevant to inquire why it is necessary to have *two* nuclear forces in the Alliance in *both* of which the United States has the final say. Since SAC would be the key element in any coordinated strategy, the MLF is at best a cumbersome and costly device to accomplish what remains a necessity in any event: to give our Allies greater access to *American* strategic planning. In other words, if joint planning is confined to the MLF, it will be inadequate; if it is extended to cover all relevant strategic forces, the MLF is unnecessary.

However, the military case for the MLF has never been decisive. Successive SACEUR's have been at best lukewarm about the project. And until six weeks before it emerged as a principal objective of American NATO policy, our highest officials had declared the MLF militarily unnecessary.

The key argument on behalf of the MLF has always been political. Specifically, it was supposed to help prevent nuclear proliferation by providing a framework within which our nuclear Allies could abandon their nuclear programs. It was to discourage other Allies from entering the nuclear field. Above all, it was to give equal status to the Federal Republic in nuclear matters.

The first objective has been negated by the refusal of France and, to a lesser extent, of Great Britain to abolish their national forces. As for the other Allies, none except the Federal Republic has either the resources or the motivation for a national nuclear program. The issue then becomes whether the MLF is a good device for absorbing Germany's nuclear ambitions.

There is no doubt that the vitality of the Atlantic Alliance depends importantly on the long-term orientation of the Federal Republic. The Federal Republic must be treated as an equal partner and must be able to participate fully in developing common policies. It is another question whether access to nuclear weapons should have been made the criterion of equality. It will never be known whether a subconscious desire for the possession of nuclear weapons did exist in Germany or what form it could have taken if it had. Was there a nuclear problem in Germany or did the United States create it—in the words of the former Defense correspondent of the London *Times* —by the passionate advocacy of its solution?

The trouble with self-fulfilling prophecies is that in retrospect it is impossible to demonstrate whether what happened was predicted or caused by the prophecy. The fact is that once the theory of a German appetite for nuclear weapons had become established, every German proposal was interpreted to become consistent with it. Thus, in 1960 Chancellor Adenauer stated that French and British possession of nuclear weapons should not give these countries a privileged position within NATO. The advocates of the MLF used this to demonstrate a veiled German desire for nuclear weapons. It is more likely that Chancellor Adenauer was concerned lest the Directorate proposed by President de Gaulle exclude the Federal Republic. It was a demand for political equality, not necessarily for nuclear weapons.

A similar interpretation was put on the strategic views of former Defense Minister Franz Josef Strauss. He sought more information about the nuclear stockpiles in Germany, a guarantee that these would not be withdrawn without the consent of NATO and a degree of unspecified joint control over weapons fired from German soil.[18] But Strauss' stated concern was with the tactical nuclear weapons already in the NATO stockpiles and of a range not suitable for a retaliatory strategy.

Whatever the afterthoughts of Adenauer and Strauss, the question remains whether it would not have been wiser to take their statements at face value rather than gear our policy to guesses about their unstated desires. The spread of nuclear weapons to Germany was much more complicated than simply extending the British and French precedents. It was a grave error to act as if Germany by a unilateral decision could enter the nuclear field. No country

[18] See, for example, the *Frankfurter Allgemeine Zeitung,* April 21, 1962.

faced greater obstacles in developing a national nuclear program. In the treaty which established the Western European Union and made German rearmament possible, the Federal Republic renounced the production or testing of nuclear weapons on its territory. There is a curious inconsistency between the proposition that the Federal Republic wanted nuclear weapons so badly that it might break that treaty and the argument that another treaty could then restrain this desire.

Moreover, the issue was hardly urgent. At least until the elections of 1969, it would have been impossible to mobilize domestic support within Germany for a national nuclear program. Any German government would have had to hesitate before taking a step which might have irrevocably ended all hopes for reunification. German restraint would have been all the more indicated because any attempt to develop German national nuclear weapons would have awakened latent distrust all over Europe. It is doubtful that NATO could have survived if the Soviet Union had used the existence of a German national nuclear program as a pretext to unleash a series of crises. No European country would have run major risks so that Germany might have nuclear weapons under national control.

For all these reasons it is probable that German nuclear demands would not have been articulated for the better part of a decade—if then. This interval could have been used to foster European political unity and an Atlantic political structure. The former would have diminished the significance of the nation-state; the latter might have allayed fears in the field of security. Concurrently with these longer term measures, it would have been essential to give Germany fuller access to political decision-making in the Alliance.

Such policies would have been far wiser than to become an advocate for German claims in the nuclear field which the Federal Republic could not have articulated for itself. They would have dealt with the real pressures behind the spread of nuclear weapons within the Western Alliance. Was the French nuclear program—begun by De Gaulle's predecessors—really inspired by the example of Great Britain as so many of our policymakers seem to believe? It is likely that the experience of Suez, with its dramatic demonstration of how American and European policies and interests might diverge, was a more powerful catalyst than speeches in the House of Commons. The fact that we gave Britain a special status in East-West negotiations did more to emphasize the political utility of Britain's nuclear arsenal than the claims of British defense ministers. Thus whether the Federal Republic did in fact feel a sense of discrimination would depend above all on its *political* role. A scrupulous concern for German interests—especially in the conduct of East-West negotiations—and an intimate system of political consultation might well have met the demands likely to be advanced by any foreseeable German government in the sixties.

Instead, a vicious circle was created. The United States put forward a proposal based on a theoretical conception of *German* desires that the Germans felt obliged to accept because they did not want to thwart *American* wishes. What was originally intended as a device to tie the Federal Republic to NATO and the United States to Europe became an end in itself.

Regardless of whether the MLF grew up in response to German nuclear appetites or whether it stimulated them, it is unlikely to absorb whatever nuclear aspirations exist in Germany. Its primary role will be to shift the debate from the issue of the ownership of nuclear weapons to the issue of control of a force in which the Federal Republic is the largest European shareholder.

A great deal depends, therefore, on the solution of the complex issue of control of the MLF. During the MLF negotiations, strangely little attention was paid to this problem. The United States took the view that since the Multilateral Force does not yet exist the issue of nuclear control need not be faced until later. Official spokesmen have also implied that the United States would be willing to consider a modification of the initial control arrangements, including giving up the veto.

Both of these arguments raise serious questions. Physical operation of the MLF will offer next to no insight into the problem of political control. Knowledge of how to operate a missile-carrying ship is irrelevant to the issue of how a coalition of sovereign states decides to enter a nuclear war. The passage of time will serve only to buttress the bargaining position of countries which will have made a major financial contribution to the MLF and whose interests with respect to its control arrangements are likely to diverge from ours.

The complexity of the issue of nuclear control is demonstrated by the three kinds of nuclear forces that will exist in NATO if the MLF comes into being. They are: (1) National nuclear forces such as SAC, the French *force de frappe* and, depending on its ultimate disposition, perhaps the British deterrent—these would remain under exclusive national control. (2) Nuclear forces "assigned" to NATO that, depending on the meaning attached to the word "assignment," will be available to NATO for planning purposes even though they are also subject to national decision. (3) The MLF, which, at least initially, can be activated only by unanimous consent.

An MLF in which each contributor has a veto will not fundamentally change the situation with respect to nuclear control in NATO. No country presently *unable* to initiate nuclear war would be able to do so, and no country *able* to go to nuclear war could be prevented from doing so. No country can be made to enter nuclear war through membership in the MLF.

In case of disagreement with our European Allies, one of two things would happen. If we decided to resort to nuclear weapons against their wishes, the MLF would be inactive; but we could use SAC and the Polaris submarines assigned to NATO. If the situation were reversed—that is, if our Allies wished to use nuclear weapons and we disagreed—neither the MLF nor SAC could operate. In return for an expenditure of upward of three billion dollars our Allies would obtain a veto over some three per cent of our nuclear force while we retain complete freedom of action with respect to the remainder. Can anyone seriously believe that this can be a permanent state of affairs?

A force that multiplies safety catches and is too small for its mission is certain to face pressure (1) to turn it into a useful military instrument by increasing its size at least to the level of the Soviet MRBM's in Western Russia and (2) to dilute the unanimity principle to avoid paralysis in times of crisis. These pressures are likely even among allies initially indifferent or hostile to the MLF. Defense ministers will be forced to justify continuing expenditures. They will feel obliged to make the MLF a significant institution.

There have already been hints of things to come. The German Defense Minister, Kai-Uwe von Hassel, has stated that the veto of all the participants, while acceptable initially, will have to be reconsidered once the MLF has come into being.[14] In the United States, two possible solutions have been proposed: (1) eventual surrender of the American veto and (2) the less radical suggestion that the United States retain its veto while the smaller contributors give up theirs.

Can the United States seriously consider giving up the veto? Robert R. Bowie, who originated the concept of the MLF and who has been one of its most influential defenders, has written:

We should be ready to concede to a multilateral force the same degree of ultimate autonomy as has already been granted the British national force. The final outcome might take the form of either (1) an integrated NATO force in which the United States, *without a veto, would be one member,* [emphasis added] or (2) an integrated European force (without the United States as a member),

[14] Interview in *Christ und Welt* (October 23, 1963), p. 7.

closely coordinated with United States forces, but under ultimate European control.[15]

It is not easy to see how so fateful a decision as the use of nuclear weapons can be abdicated to a majority vote of even very close allies. The Constitutional provision that a declaration of war requires the consent of two-thirds of the Senate may well prove insurmountable. The Congressional debate on such a proposition could not avoid discussing the circumstances in which a nuclear war might break out. This would force the administration to define contingencies in which in its judgment the use of nuclear weapons would *not* be appropriate. The doubts generated by such a debate would do more damage than any benefit it could possibly bring.

For precisely what would giving up the veto actually imply? Does it mean that when requested by a majority of our Allies we would agree to go to war with the small part of the total nuclear arsenal of the Alliance represented by the MLF while SAC remained inactive? Or does it mean that we would be prepared to go to war with our entire nuclear arsenal? The former interpretation would be utterly contrary to the strategic doctrine elaborated so persistently by Secretary McNamara and his associates. To enter nuclear war with only the MLF, which is a small part of the total nuclear force of the Alliance and one not exceptionally well-suited to discriminating targeting, would make no military sense. It would prevent a strategy of flexible response. And Soviet retaliation against a blow by a force in which we participate will surely not take into account our negative vote on the control body.

But if the second interpretation is correct—that we would be committed to go to war with our *entire* strategic force—then why must a special multilateral force be set up? If we are prepared to limit our sovereignty to this ex-

[15] Robert R. Bowie, "Strategy and the Atlantic Alliance," *International Organization*, Vol. XVII, No. 3 (1963), p. 728.

tent, it would be better to create a political control body for the Alliance as a whole and agree to go to war on the basis of majority vote.

Difficult as it will be to decide on a control mechanism for entering nuclear war, the political control over the actual military operations of the MLF will be even more complex. Who is to be responsible for changing planned targets (retargeting, in strategic jargon) or for determining the scale of individual attacks? How is the MLF to fit into wartime negotiations? How does one go about ending hostilities—on the basis of one vote or unanimity? With whom would the Soviet Union deal when nuclear operations are to be stopped? To evade these questions until irrevocable decisions are made is to invite endless controversy later on.

A final problem of control is raised by that aspect of the MLF which attracts many of its advocates: The international status of the crews produced by mixed-manning. If each national contingent is to remain responsive to national direction, the only problem is one of communications and the difficulty inherent in control by the threat of mutiny. If, however, the crews became international in outlook and if their loyalties came to transcend national ties—as the proponents of the MLF urge—serious control problems may develop in time. The unauthorized use of nuclear weapons by national military units—about which sensational novels have been written—is restrained by long traditions of civilian supremacy and by habits of obedience. International crews separated for long periods from their societies may be less subject to such inhibitions. To start integration in the nuclear realm before a corresponding political framework exists may thus create a dangerous imbalance.

What about the other claims being made by the advocates of the MLF? Will it eventually develop into a European nuclear force? Will it promote European integration? Secretary Rusk has praised the MLF because of its potential contribution to European cohesion.[16] Deputy Assistant Secretary J. Robert Schaetzel has argued that:

The multilateral force would also inevitably make easier the eventual development of a European nuclear force, should this be the desire and within the grasp of the Europeans.[17]

The then Vice President Johnson said much the same thing:

The movement to Atlantic partnership·makes this [MLF] possible. The movement to European unity makes this desirable—as a first step toward a greater European voice in nuclear matters. Evolution of this missile fleet toward European control, as Europe marches toward unity, is by no means excluded.[18]

The Action Committee for a United Europe, headed by Jean Monnet, has endorsed the MLF as the precursor of a European nuclear force.

Two problems are raised by the prospect of transforming the MLF into a European force: (1) the relative role of Germany and (2) the relationship of the United States to the force.

The problem of Germany is acute because participants in the MLF have been promised influence in the control body and command over ships in proportion to their financial contribution. Thus, if there is to be a European point of view within the MLF, its spokesman is likely to be the Federal Republic.

Such a prospect is not in the interest of NATO, of Euro-

[16] Dean Rusk, "Toward a New Dimension in the Atlantic Partnership," *DOSB*, Vol. XLIX, No. 1272 (November 11, 1963), p. 730.

[17] J. Robert Schaetzel, "The Nuclear Problem and Atlantic Interdependence," *Atlantic Community Quarterly*, Vol. 1, No. 4 (Winter 1963–64), p. 567.

[18] Lyndon B. Johnson, address at Brussels on November 8, 1963, *DOSB*, Vol. XLIX, No. 1275 (December 2, 1963), pp. 853–854. See also Robert R. Bowie, speech before the Western European Union Assembly, December 3, 1963, *op. cit.*, pp. 127–128.

pean cohesion, of the Federal Republic or of international
stability. It would push the most exposed ally into the
forefront of every dispute. It would make the Federal Republic, which already has the largest conventional army,
the most significant nuclear power in Europe as well. This
would again raise fears that a decade and a half of far-
sighted German policy have only begun to erase. It might
fuse anti-American, anti-German and anti-nuclear feelings into a dangerous wave of neutralism.

Some of the advocates of the MLF argue that the
prospect of German domination will make Britain and
France more eager to join. This may be the case. But it is
possible that Britain and France will in time move away
from an alliance that threatens to turn into a special German-American arrangement. Even if the assumption proves
correct, however, such a process of solving NATO's nuclear
problem would be extremely worrisome. It would be better for the long-term stability and cohesiveness of Europe
for the Federal Republic to join an institution in which
France and Britain are the senior partners, than for Britain
and France to be obliged to seek membership in a grouping to which Germany is the largest European contributor
and in which ultimately it may play the same role as
France does in the Common Market. History has been al-
tered by smaller nuances.

Apart from the fear of German domination, the MLF
is a poor chrysalis for a European nuclear force. Such a
force could grow out of the MLF in only one of two ways:
(1) by an American decision to withdraw from the MLF
or (2) through a European request that we leave it. Either
course would be divisive in the extreme. It is one thing
for a European nuclear force to develop from the present
national programs which have existed for many years. It
is quite another for a European force to come about
through a United States withdrawal, voluntary or forced,
from a joint Atlantic enterprise. Such an act might raise
serious doubts about the continued validity of America's
commitment to the defense of Europe.

In short, to leave open the two most important and interrelated problems of the MLF—that of control and that of evolution of the force—will magnify tensions later. If the MLF comes into being, the United States may be haunted for years by the inconsistencies of its arguments on behalf of it. To the Federal Republic, the MLF has been represented as a device to give non-nuclear countries an increased participation in nuclear matters. To Soviet and European critics, the MLF has been advocated as decreasing, if anything, the role of its members in the decision to go to nuclear war. Thus Gerard C. Smith, then Special Assistant to the Secretary of State for the MLF, said on April 22, 1964:

Any wartime decision to fire the missiles would be by multilateral agreement, rather than by bilateral agreement as in the case of these earlier strategic missiles. *The MLF will thus increase the number of states with fingers on the safety catch, rather than on the nuclear trigger* [emphasis added].

There would be no increase of risk of compromise of weapons design data under MLF. Multilateral custodial procedures would assure that individual countries had no greater access to information about how to design and manufacture weapons than at present under the NATO atomic stockpile.[19]

The dilemma of how to reconcile the requirement of central control over nuclear weapons with the sovereignty of our Allies is real. But for the long-term vitality of the Alliance it would have been better to face this issue head-on than to present different versions of the control problem to different audiences. If there *is* a German demand for nuclear weapons—as the advocates of the MLF have alleged—it is unlikely to be satisfied by "increasing the number of states with fingers on the safety catch, rather than on the nuclear trigger." If other countries do wish to enter

19 Gerard C. Smith, "The Nuclear Defense of NATO," speech on April 22, 1964, *DOSB*, Vol. L, No. 1299 (May 18, 1964), p. 785.

the nuclear field, they are not likely to be put off by a device which creates the illusion of participation while giving "no greater access to information about how to design and manufacture weapons than at present." The MLF cannot at one and the same time satisfy demands for nuclear sharing and assuage concerns about nuclear proliferation.

Originated to fulfill SACEUR's military requirement, pressed as a counter to a French challenge, the MLF stands in danger of compounding every problem it was supposed to solve. It has prevented a reconsideration of the strategic missions that gave rise to the military requirement. Rather than heal the rift in the Alliance, the MLF is likely to multiply divisions. There is something absurd about trying to prevent the spread of nuclear weapons by bringing the non-nuclear countries of NATO into the nuclear field, often with only their reluctant assent. It makes no sense to attempt to revitalize NATO with a project which, because of the opposition of France and other Allies, will have to be set up *outside* of NATO. It is contradictory to advocate European political unity while urging a scheme which is certain to produce a rift between France and the Federal Republic.

To be sure, France cannot be given a veto over every measure to strengthen the Alliance. But a direct clash is justified only when a disputed scheme commands wide support and will in fact bring about a structure which enhances the long-term vitality of the Alliance.

There is reason to doubt that the MLF meets either of these requirements. Though the proponents of the MLF have tended to blame all objections on the manipulations of short-sighted men, the opposition of France, the indifference of most other NATO Allies and the split within the Federal Republic cannot be simply shrugged off. Outside the Federal Republic there is not one country whose agreement to the MLF represents anything more than acquiescence in American pressure.

Proponents of the MLF often compare their project to

the Schuman Plan, which, despite heavy initial criticism, laid the basis for European economic integration. However, while many constructive innovations have had to withstand criticism when first proposed, not everything that is criticized is necessarily constructive. The Schuman Plan promoted Franco-German cooperation in areas where long-term interests were parallel. The longer the Coal and Steel Community lasted, the more obvious were the benefits of common action.

The opposite is likely to be the case with the MLF. Once established, the conflicting motives of the participants will become increasingly apparent. There is a latent difference of opinion between the Federal Republic and the United States and Great Britain about the size of the force as well as about its composition, specifically about whether land-based missiles should supplement the sea-based MLF. It is likely that the Federal Republic regards the MLF as the first installment in meeting SACEUR's requirement for medium-range missiles while the United States and Britain consider it a final satisfaction of existing needs. Though this will not become apparent in the early stages of the project, it is bound to lead to difficulties later on.

Another potential dispute derives from the fact that the Federal Republic favors the Multilateral Force partly to increase its share of nuclear control. Most other countries—especially Great Britain—will participate, if at all, in order to *prevent* an increase of German control. This difference can be obscured in the early stages of the MLF; it, too, will become more and more acute as time goes on.

Finally, an extremely divisive debate in the Federal Republic can be avoided only if the MLF treaty contains a "European" clause providing for the possibility of transforming the MLF into a European nuclear force once European political integration is further advanced. The Italian government (whose parliamentary support for the MLF is dubious in any event) has taken a similar position. Great Britain, on the other hand, will not agree to such a prospect; indeed, its participation in any new nuclear arrangement is conditional on a British veto over any structural changes. It is one thing to create an institution whose evolution is likely to strengthen common objectives; it is quite another to stake so much on a device where conflicting interests have been kept latent only by avoiding consideration of the key issues.

The MLF may therefore strengthen the very tendencies it seeks to combat. In its advocacy of the MLF, the United States has granted almost all of the propositions of its European critics. It has agreed that possession of nuclear weapons is a criterion of equality. It has granted that ownership of some strategic forces is essential for participation in strategic planning and political decisions. It has admitted that influence in the Alliance somehow depends on access to a strategic nuclear arsenal. It has differed only about the nature of ownership and the way control should be exercised. But since the control procedures of the MLF patently favor United States hegemony, they can be used by the nationalists and extremists as a proof of American bad faith. If the Federal Republic finds itself at odds with the United States about control, or with its other allies about the evolution of the force, a serious backlash could develop.

The MLF may backfire even with respect to its primary objective of preventing Franco-German nuclear collaboration. Having made access to nuclear weapons the test of equality, we have given an incentive to the Federal Republic to seek alternative arrangements if the MLF fails or if its control arrangements prove unsatisfactory. Disappointment could then justify a Franco-German nuclear collaboration for which prior to the MLF no significant support existed within the Federal Republic.

It was to render a poor service to the Federal Republic to seek to restore Allied cohesion by a scheme which involved access by Germany to nuclear weapons. If the MLF succeeds, the Federal Republic will be embroiled with France. If it fails, leaders who have staked a great deal on following the American lead will be discredited. Participation by Germany in a nuclear fleet has resurrected instinctive fears all over Europe. Within Germany, pro-American and pro-French factions have rent the governing party, the Christian Democratic Union. The MLF thus threatens internal German stability and creates the danger that the Federal Republic will become isolated internationally.

Advocates of the MLF often argue that it is easy to pick holes in any existing nuclear control plan but much harder to offer a constructive alternative. To be sure, if the issue of nuclear control is, in fact, the cause of Allied tensions, the MLF proponents have a point. However, the issue of nuclear control is a symptom, not a cause, of NATO's difficulties. There exists no neat solution for it so long as NATO is composed of sovereign states. Nor does the MLF "solve" it. The basic problem in the Alliance is political and not strategic. There is something incongruous about NATO's absorption in technicalities of mixed-manning while it lacks a common policy toward the Communist world, flounders dividedly in the former colonial areas and has yet to concert a strategic doctrine. To devote so much energy to the problem of who pushes the button in the remote contingency of nuclear war while neglecting the issues which confront the Alliance daily comes close to being escapism. Insofar as the German conversion to the MLF was not the result of American missionary zeal, it reflected above all a desire to establish a claim not to be excluded from further East-West negotiations and to create another organic link between the United States and Europe.

The MLF is at best a circuitous way to achieve these goals. In fact, it reverses the correct priorities. Political unity must *precede,* it cannot follow, nuclear integration. To pursue nuclear multilateralism while foreign policy remains national must emphasize divergent interests. The imagination and dedication expended on the MLF would, therefore, have been better spent in strengthening political cohesion. Our allies are not likely to be convinced that their interests will be taken seriously during the improbable eventuality of general nuclear war when no consensus exists for the conduct of day-to-day diplomacy and for crisis situations. Rather than take the detour through the MLF, it would have been wiser to aim directly for coordination of policy by setting up a body to develop common policies for many unsolved problems of the Alliance in East-West relations, strategic doctrine, trade policy, arms control or relations with the emerging nations. If France had refused to participate, the disruptive intent would have been obvious. France would have stood apart from an effort which commanded a real consensus. Moreover, a future French government could participate in such a group more easily than in the MLF, in which French membership could well be precluded by financial considerations alone. If a political steering body for the Alliance had then decided to include the Federal Republic in the ownership of strategic weapons, the political context would have been entirely different. It would have represented the common view of all Allies rather than the pressure of one. Regardless of the ultimate fate of the MLF, a political body to coordinate Alliance policy and to manage crises remains essential.[20] If it should be argued that the Atlantic Alliance will never be able to develop a common political program, the emptiness of nuclear multilateralism becomes apparent. Nations that cannot agree on common negotiating positions are not likely to be able to concert a common strategy for an apocalypse.

Even in our bilateral relations with the Federal Republic, the strengthening of political consultation should have had priority. If we had created institutions to give the Federal Republic access to our strategic and disarmament planning and the conduct of East-West negotiations in general, these could have been used as a brake on eventual Franco-German nuclear collaboration much as the Franco-German Treaty turned out to be one of the factors

[20] For an elaboration of such a policymaking body, see Chapter 8.

thwarting the MLF. By reversing the process, we brought
on what we feared most. We whetted German nuclear
appetites without giving satisfaction to the political concerns. It is questionable whether it is in our interest to discourage Franco-German intimacy, but at least it should
not be based on disillusionment with the United States.

The MLF, as originally conceived, is not likely to be
realized. So much opposition exists that even the most
passionate advocates will have to modify the scheme. It
may be useful, however, to inquire what lessons can be
drawn from the experience.

The most important one is not to try to solve political
problems with technical expedients. Confronted with a political and philosophical challenge in De Gaulle's exclusion of Britain from the Common Market, American
policymakers reacted by staking everything on a scheme
of nuclear control which they had previously treated with
indifference. They then spent two years negotiating its
mechanical aspects. In the process, the deeper causes of
NATO's disarray were neglected. The ends and means became confused. At its best, the MLF was irrelevant to the
fundamental problems of NATO. It would have repeated
within its framework many of the disputes which it was
supposed to overcome.

In Washington, this was obscured because one small
group in the government had become so deeply committed
to the MLF that it acted as a lobby rather than an organ
for calmly weighing alternatives. In the words of one
acute observer, the MLF proponents engaged in "a public
relations campaign to gain official, political and academic
support, of an energy and ruthlessness unknown since
Harriet Beecher Stowe. . . ."[21] This has made it difficult
to determine whether what appeared in Washington as
European opinion did not really reflect European acquiescence in the passionate advocacy of one segment of
our bureaucracy. The result was a whole series of mis-

[21] Alastair Buchan, "Is This NATO Crisis Necessary?" *The New
Republic*, Vol. 151, Nos. 6–7 (August 8, 1964), pp. 19–21.

judgments. European support for the MLF was grossly overestimated. Despite the repeated criticisms of the MLF by British Labor leaders when in opposition, it was expected that the new British government would agree to a treaty setting up the MLF within two months of coming into office. The divisive impact of the threat of a German-American nuclear partnership was misjudged. The capacity of the German political structure to withstand strain was completely misconceived. Throughout, some American officials acted as if getting agreement to the MLF was an end in itself. By using whatever argument was convenient to this purpose, a number of partially contradictory promissory notes were handed out.

The pressure of a relatively small group of officials in the State Department gave our Allies a misleading impression of American unanimity and commitment. The Pentagon had accepted the MLF only on the assumption that ultimate American control would remain unimpaired. The group in the State Department that originated the MLF proposal and pressed it on our Allies was much more sympathetic to the ultimate emergence of a separate European nuclear force. Indeed, it occasionally urged the MLF as a means to this end. Although the cohesiveness of our society depends on understating conflicting views, it is dangerous to engage in major international innovations unless we are clear about our ultimate direction.

All this suggests the need for a reexamination of some governmental procedures. We need a planning focus less geared to immediate crises and more capable of developing concepts responsive to fundamental trends. There should be less reliance on the accidents of bureaucratic pressures. Our own aims must be clear before we commit our prestige. We should not use the process of negotiations to make up our own minds. Not to reveal what we intend to do is a question of tactics; not to know is to mortgage the future.

Fortunately, partly because of the initiative of the new British government, partly because of President Johnson's removal of previous time limits, an opportunity exists to take a new approach to the issue of nuclear control. The wise, if abrupt, decision of President Johnson to reduce the pressures for the original MLF project and Britain's initiative have smoothed the way for a new study of the entire problem. This should enable us to determine the real wishes of our Allies before irrevocable decisions are taken. In any reassessment, we must, of course, keep in mind that in many countries, notably in the Federal Republic, leaders have staked their careers on our previous proposals. Though another approach to the issue of nuclear control would have been preferable, future policy must consider that simply to abandon the MLF now would have a different significance than earlier. Moreover, some of the objectives that the MLF has sought to realize *are* important. For example, the goal of political equality for all members of the Alliance is crucial. Means must be found to achieve those objectives of the MLF project essential to Allied cohesion. The controversy about the MLF will have served some useful purpose if it permits the Alliance to return to fundamentals: the definition of common purposes and an answer to the question of what the members of the Alliance really want in the nuclear field.

Chapter Six

THE NUCLEAR PROBLEM—
WHERE DO WE GO
FROM HERE?

STRATEGIC WEAPONS

The nuclear problem in the Alliance has four components: (1) The United States would like to establish central control over the nuclear weapons in the Alliance. The ideal solution from the point of view of the Pentagon is to deprive all Allies of the physical capacity to act autonomously in the nuclear field. (2) Two of our Allies, Great Britain and France, have national nuclear weapons programs. (3) It is desirable to prevent the spread of nuclear weapons within the Alliance and elsewhere. (4) The MLF negotiations have established or confirmed (depending on the point of view) the claims of non-nuclear Allies to participate in nuclear control and, perhaps, to some form of ownership of nuclear weapons.

No program could perfectly reconcile all these objectives, partly because each Ally has two somewhat contradictory aims with respect to nuclear policy, partly because there is an inherent inconsistency between the attempt to establish central control over nuclear weapons and the jealousy with which each major Ally, including the United States, has heretofore guarded its sovereignty.

The two contradictory aims of the Allies sometimes tend to cancel each other out: Each Ally wants to avoid being forced into nuclear war against its will, and it wants to be certain of nuclear support when its existence is at stake.

What our Allies understand by nuclear support is less clear. They want the *appearance* of nuclear support so that the Soviets never challenge their vital interests. Whether they are actually prepared to face the consequences of nuclear war is ambiguous. Their tendency to base NATO's military policy entirely on deterrence suggests that many of them may be above all concerned with their veto if nuclear war seemed imminent. They may be more interested in not being forced into nuclear war against their will than in being able to force us into a nuclear war against our will.

The ambivalence of our Allies underlines the incompatibility between central control over nuclear weapons and undiluted sovereignty. If no conflict of interest among the Allies were conceivable, the concern with either veto or triggering ability would not exist. But as a sovereign state is the final judge of its interests, absolute reassurance is unobtainable. No one can predict with certainty how hard-pressed leaders will react under the unprecedented stresses of imminent nuclear war—not only with respect to the decision to use nuclear weapons but also with respect to the many nuances of bargaining during crises. The single-mindedness with which the United States has always guarded its freedom of decision is as significant a symptom of this dilemma as France's excessively theoretical claims to independence.

American proposals—including the MLF—have largely avoided this problem. The United States, starting from the technically unexceptionable premise that the conduct of nuclear war should be centrally controlled, has tried hard to create a structure in NATO which deprives our Allies of the physical capacity to act independently. We have been less ready to face the inevitable corollary: Those nations which are being asked to entrust their nuclear defense to the United States will urge, in return, a commensurate surrender of American sovereignty in the political field. To insist on centralized strategy while diplomacy remains national guarantees mounting disputes.

France, on the other hand, has expressed the implications of sovereignty clearly and correctly, but it has neglected the technical requirements of nuclear strategy. In the face of the risks of a nuclear holocaust, no country can have complete freedom of decision—least of all a nation with a nuclear force strong enough to start a nuclear war but far too weak to finish it. While the United States has overemphasized the technical aspects of central command and control, France and those Europeans agreeing with her have pushed the legal implications of sovereignty to a point where they clash with the technical realities of the nuclear age.

We react bitterly when Europeans suggest that no one can foresee how even the most solemn commitments will be interpreted in the stark circumstances of a nuclear showdown. But when we argue *against* the nuclear forces of Britain and France, we seem to understand the problems produced by sovereignty very well. Then we tend to reverse the field and use the arguments which our nuclear European Allies invoke against us and thereby generate suspicions where none had been articulated before. Thus J. Robert Schaetzel, Deputy Assistant Secretary of State, explained why even a joint Franco-British nuclear force which shared command and control responsibilities with other European countries would still not meet the need as he saw it:

An agreed European control mechanism would still not answer the basic question of these non-nuclear countries: In the moment of crisis would the nuclear powers of the arrangement—the powers which owned and operated the nuclear forces—in fact consult and collaborate on an equal basis with their associate members?[1]

Carrying Schaetzel's argument one step further, it may be relevant to ask why, if our European Allies cannot rely upon formal commitments among themselves, they should have absolute trust in the United States, which is 3,000 miles away and has a recent history of isolation.

The debate about nuclear control has reversed the real priorities. It has created the impression that differences about political purposes can be resolved by a technical expedient in the military field. Allies that cannot agree on a common diplomacy on much less vital questions are asked to accept unitary direction in the stark and catastrophic contingency of nuclear war. Instead of attempting to unify foreign policy and long-range planning, the dominant schemes of nuclear control leave these to existing processes of consultation while putting all energies behind the creation of technically integrated nuclear forces.

The opposite course would be much wiser. Focusing attention on the conduct of nuclear operations causes the Allied debate to be beset by confusions and evasions. Discussions about nuclear war are inherently unreliable because no government can be certain about its actions when the lives of its entire population are quite literally at stake. To pretend that a voting formula or any other essentially legal construction will oblige a government to go to nuclear war when its convictions dictate otherwise is to ignore the most fundamental reality of the nuclear age: In the past a nation's reputation for reliability often seemed more important to it than its fear of the consequences of war. No serious person can pretend that the possibility of wiping out entire populations has not changed this relationship.

Thus in the nuclear age alliances will hold together only

[1] J. Robert Schaetzel, "The Nuclear Problem and Atlantic Interdependence," *The Atlantic Community Quarterly*, Vol. 1, No. 4 (Winter 1963–64), pp. 565–566.

if their members grow so intimate politically that they consider their vital interests virtually indistinguishable. If this condition is met, the physical arrangement of nuclear forces is relatively unimportant. If a political consensus does not exist, arguments about the conduct of nuclear war only accentuate the underlying difficulty when they do not confuse it.

Indeed, to the extent that debates about nuclear control magnify existing political disputes, they achieve the opposite of what they attempt to promote. They may erect a façade of Allied unity which will prove brittle under stress. The discussions about the MLF and even about the British substitute—the Allied Nuclear Force—illustrate this. Some countries—especially Great Britain and almost certainly the United States—favor these new constructions only if they guarantee a perpetuation of the American veto. Others—notably the Federal Republic and probably Italy—will agree to them only if they contain a "European" clause, that is if the new nuclear force can in time become European and free of the American veto. This difference in approach can be overcome only through formulas which evade the real issue and permit the partners to maintain often conflicting constructions. In short, any new nuclear force, when it becomes serious, will repeat within its framework all the debates which it is designed to resolve. The amity its creation would seem to produce would be more apparent than real.

Thus the major focus of Allied debate should shift away from the creation of new nuclear forces to building the political consensus which alone can give military forces their meaning. This seems to be the direction indicated by Secretary McNamara's proposal at the NATO Defense Ministers' meeting in June 1965 for a select Committee within the Alliance to deal with nuclear matters.

Up to that time, the United States had been reluctant to shift its emphasis for three reasons: (1) the desire to suppress the national nuclear forces of Britain and France,

(2) the corollary that autonomy in the nuclear field for some of our Allies—or for a European force—would jeopardize our security and (3) concern that the Federal Republic might harbor a sense of discrimination if France and Britain remained the sole Allies in possession of nuclear weapons.

The desire to suppress the national programs of France and Britain has had the paradoxical result that we have been prepared to bring the non-nuclear countries of NATO into the nuclear business—as long as they accepted an American veto—in the hope that this might thwart the efforts of our nuclear Allies. We have been less concerned about the proliferation of nuclear know-how which the MLF is bound to bring than about eliminating the already existing centers of nuclear decision within the Alliance. We have preferred establishing yet another nuclear force —provided it was subject to an American veto—rather than concede in theory the autonomy which France and Britain already possess in practice.

The debate engendered by this policy has been more conductive to self-righteousness than to sober thought. By placing so much stress on the actual conduct of nuclear operations, we have forced our Allies into inherently misleading justifications of their nuclear programs. They have projected the remote nightmare of the failure of the Alliance into the present; we in turn have confused their fears with their preferences.

But the real concern behind pressure for European autonomy goes deeper. Europeans have had too much experience with nuances of interpretation which can all but nullify formal commitments; indeed, at some point, all of them have felt obliged to leave some ally to his fate. The concern for a European role in nuclear affairs expresses a desire to obtain a measure of insurance against the unforeseeable events of which European history is so full. The problem posed by American strategic doctrine is that it seeks to gear the structure of the Alliance to a contingency—the outbreak of general nuclear war—which our

Allies consider tantamount to their end as functioning societies. Their primary concern is therefore to prevent this contingency by complicating the predictability of nuclear operations. The thrust of their efforts is to increase their influence *before* hostilities start, during day-to-day diplomacy and in crisis management.

As for the argument that the British and French nuclear programs jeopardize our own security because they may force us into a nuclear war against our will, this is carrying logical extrapolations to extremes. France and Great Britain must know at least as well as we—though we can hardly expect them to advertise this fact—that using their nuclear forces independently against the Soviet Union would be a desperate last resort. The French and British nuclear programs are not a strategic preference but an attempt to provide insurance against a disastrous contingency within Europe and against nuclear developments in other parts of the world. Taking out fire insurance does not indicate a liking for fires. On the contrary, it may prevent a remote possibility from turning into an obsession and thus free energies for more constructive tasks.

Even from the United States point of view there are important reasons for modifying our heretofore doctrinaire opposition to other centers of nuclear decision within the Western Alliance. It is, of course, highly desirable that the spread of nuclear weapons be arrested. It is less clear that this objective is furthered by concentrating our pressures against our closest Allies. There is no evidence that the nuclear program of Communist China was in the slightest influenced by the example of Great Britain or that its willingness to end its nuclear efforts depends in any sense on the actions of our European Allies. The same is true of the possible nuclear programs of India, Israel or Egypt. When the real danger of nuclear proliferation is the spread of nuclear weapons into the hands of anti-Western countries, it is not clear that the first remedial step should be the elimination of the nuclear programs of our closest Allies. Would it not be wiser to concentrate our anti-proliferation policy on countries which may join the nuclear club in the future? Is it really in our interest to be the only Western country possessing nuclear weapons? Is it not likely that in that case all pressures around the world will eventually concentrate against us while our European allies sink into the irresponsibility of the impotent?

To be sure, two national nuclear forces are not the ideal way to share nuclear responsibility within the Alliance. A united European force coordinated with that of the United States would be preferable. But policy must work with the material at hand. It cannot choose the theoretical at the expense of the attainable. For the immediate future, the issue is whether a European force should develop—if at all—out of the existing European nuclear programs or whether it should grow out of a new structure, such as the MLF. To be sure, the MLF may well wreck any prospect of a European nuclear identity because of the divisions within Europe which it will inevitably produce and also because countries having once left the nuclear field are not likely to reenter via the supranational route. But if it *should* lead to a European nuclear force—as some of its proponents urge—the MLF will have shifted the nuclear balance within Europe toward presently non-nuclear countries, which are much more vulnerable to pressures than Britain and France. Thus the MLF is either a poor starting point for a European force or will bring into being the kind of European nuclear force that would create the greatest long-term difficulties.

On both sides of the Atlantic serious individuals oppose a European nuclear force because they fear that it would lead to a reckless European policy and to an eventual withdrawal of the United States from Europe. But what exactly is the danger posed by European autonomy in the nuclear field? Is the problem the essentially technical one of coordinating legally autonomous forces in a common strategy? Or is the concern deeper? Are we really worried lest, for whatever reason, Europe may feel so desperate or

behave so irresponsibly that it would be prepared to go to
nuclear war against our wishes and in the full knowledge
that this would mean the end of its existence as a functioning society? If divisions in the Atlantic area ever reach
this point, the Alliance will have come to an end whether
or not a European nuclear force exists. If our Allies
should feel forsaken, they would sooner or later reenter
the nuclear field or else withdraw into sullen neutralism.
A wise United States policy will not invest American
prestige in forcing our Allies into a structure which makes
autonomous action *physically* impossible. Rather it will
create a relationship which grants physical autonomy
while reducing the political desire for it.

With such an attitude, the coordination of technically
autonomous nuclear forces should not prove an insuper-
able problem. Indeed it is likely that nuclear autonomy is
the least divisive form of European unity. In the economic
field, competition between Europe and the United States
involves, at best, indirect risks. In the political area, the
temptations for independent action are great and the
penalties small. In military matters—and particularly in
the nuclear field—the closest association between Europe
and the United States is in the self-interest of both sides.
Whatever their formal autonomy, it is inconceivable that
our Allies would *prefer* to go to war with the relatively
small nuclear forces available or in prospect for them and
without the support of our necessarily preponderant
arsenal. Close coordination between Europe and the
United States in the nuclear field is dictated by self-
interest; and Europe has more to gain from it than the
United States.

This is not to say that the United States should actively
promote a European nuclear force. On the contrary, the
United States should show more restraint in seeking to influence internal European arrangements and exert its influence in shaping Atlantic relationships. It does mean,
however, that we should not seek to destroy those elements from which a European force could emerge by

pressing for an alternative—the MLF—which will in time cause much greater difficulties and which involves a much greater degree of nuclear proliferation. No final solution is possible so long as the Alliance remains composed of sovereign states. Any interim arrangement should therefore be consistent with the most constructive evolution of European and Atlantic relationships.

This suggests that any new Allied construction in the nuclear field should be based on the existing nuclear forces; it should emphasize political unity rather than military structures; and it should leave open the evolution of European autonomy in the nuclear field.

Would such a course discriminate against the Federal Republic and thus alienate her? It is to render a poor service to responsible Germans to encourage pressures which in the name of German equality confuse the issues. Germany's role in the Alliance is not furthered by devices which are either misleading or irrelevant. For example, it is not clear what is achieved by pressing for the mixed-manning either of British submarines or of British airplanes—as is the tendency with respect to the so-called Allied Nuclear Force. If Britain retains control over its nuclear forces, disguising this fact will multiply distrust later on. If Britain is to leave the nuclear field, it is not easy to see in what way German security is enhanced. It is possible to argue that an autonomous British nuclear force does not add to deterrence; it is not plausible that it could impair it. Subjecting the British nuclear force to multiple vetoes eliminates its chief significance: that of adding an element of uncertainty to an aggressor's calculations. Is it really in the Federal Republic's interest to encourage it to strain its relations with France for this objective—all the more so as the practical consequence could well be to enhance the long-term role of the French nuclear force?

Some argue that as long as the nuclear forces of the Alliance remain national, no assurance exists that these forces will not be withdrawn in times of crisis. But every

existing scheme—ANF, MLF or a mixture of the two—
would leave the major part of the United States strategic
forces under national control, and this is surely the key
element of any strategy. In order to avoid this problem,
there have been experiments with such formulas as "irrevocable assignment." But it is not healthy for the Alliance to waste energies on legalistic clauses which obscure
reality. Assignment—as we have seen—is always hypothet-
ical. Assigned forces can be used only if there is a decision
to go to war by the national government to which they
belong according to its constitutional processes. And no
sovereign government is going to be forced to go to war
against its will—no matter what the arrangement of nuclear forces and regardless of the label under which they
are grouped. A nuclear structure depending initially on the
coordination of national nuclear forces is no protection
against situations in which the Alliance has already collapsed. But neither is the MLF, which could be paralyzed
by a single veto. There is no technical or legal expedient
which can serve as a substitute for political unity or which
could protect the Alliance against failure to achieve it.

The real test of any new structure as far as the Federal
Republic is concerned is its ability to provide full *political*
equality. Participation in vital negotiations should not depend on the possession of a national nuclear arsenal. The
Federal Republic must have a real opportunity to contribute to the formulation of positions in such fields as
disarmament while they are still fluid. In other words, political unity must precede nuclear integration. To reverse
the process is to sow the seeds of unending disputes.

Thus until either Atlantic or European political cohesion progresses further, the nuclear policy of the Alliance
should be three-pronged: (1) There is need for a political
mechanism to plan long-term policy, to manage crises and
to control the nuclear weapons of the Alliance. This may
require the establishment of an Executive Committee of
the NATO Council composed of the United States, Britain,
France, the Federal Republic, Italy and a rotating repre-

sentative of the smaller countries.[2] (2) The military advice to this Committee should come from a group of senior officers from the United States, Great Britain, France and the Federal Republic of Germany. It might be useful to charge the NATO Standing Group with this task. In that case it would have to be expanded to include the Federal Republic, and its seat would have to be transferred from Washington to Paris. (3) The existing strategic nuclear forces in the Alliance, including that part of the United States force earmarked for the defense of Europe, should be coordinated—either through an Allied Nuclear Force or some other arrangement—in a way which leaves open the evolution of a European force. The Federal Republic should be given an equal voice with its nuclear allies in the targeting and deployment of these nuclear forces. In bringing such a force into being, the Alliance should strive to reduce existing rifts rather than magnify them. The participation of France is more important than theological debates about the relative merits of integration and coordination. The joint planning of technically autonomous nuclear forces is more significant than the façade of "earmarking," "assignment" and other devices which confuses all issues.

The United States has obvious interests with respect to the European components of such a structure. The following criteria seem most important: (1) European forces should be well protected so that they do not invite preemptive attack or have to be used precipitately because of their vulnerability. (2) These forces should possess an effective command and control system so that they are at all times responsive to political direction. (3) They should be a part of a strategy that includes the possibility of flexible response. (4) They should be coordinated as part of a common NATO strategy.

As for the Command Structure, the sensible arrangement from a military point of view would be to place all

---

[2] The functions of this Committee are described in Chapter 8.

weapons above a certain range (say 300 miles) under a separate NATO Strategic Command. From a strictly military point of view, SACEUR (The Supreme Commander Europe) will have his hands full conducting the land battle. He should not, at the same time, be responsible for what amounts to a segment of general nuclear war.

At the same time, some of our Allies, especially the Federal Republic, see in the control of nuclear weapons by SACEUR a guarantee against nuclear disengagement. These allies seem to feel that since SACEUR is located in Europe he will be more sensitive to European needs than Washington. In these circumstances a reconstruction of the Command should await the elaboration of political mechanisms to restore confidence. However, the attempt to freeze the existing command structure in order to avoid undesirable political changes demonstrates the need for a recasting of the processes of political consultation. If a political consensus continues to be lacking, difficult problems—such as arms control—will always arise at a moment of maximum embarrassment. Distrust will grow. A military commander cannot possibly be used to paper over this problem indefinitely. Its solution must be sought by developing a political program for the Alliance as a whole.

Within the framework outlined here, the Alliance could finally address itself to the tasks which must be undertaken rather than spend energy on legalistic debates about who has a right to do what in circumstances that no one can describe. With some insurance available for the improbable contingency that the United States might interpret its interests differently from those of Europe, our Allies are likely to come to conclusions very similar to ours about the desirability of a strategy which provides multiple options.

Such an arrangement provides the greatest flexibility with respect to the future. If European political integration progresses, the European contingents in the Allied nuclear structure can merge into a European nuclear force. If desired by the European members, the Western European Union could be given official status in the various political and military bodies from the beginning. If integration proceeds more slowly, the major Allies can contribute individually to the planning of Allied nuclear policy. In either case, the United States will remain closely linked to Europe through a structure which leaves the Europeans free to develop their own initiatives. An Allied nuclear structure in which an American contingent is an integral part and which controlled all the weapons relevant to its mission would be a better symbol of the indivisibility of Atlantic interests than an MLF whose strategic role would be, at best, marginal. By ending the debate about integration as against coordination, we would maximize the possibility of obtaining eventual French collaboration.

For this to be achieved a change in attitude on both sides of the Atlantic is needed. The United States would have to abandon its futile insistence on maintaining physical control of all the nuclear weapons in the Alliance. Some of our Allies would have to stop extolling the theoretical virtues of autonomy and begin dealing with the problem of how autonomous nuclear forces can achieve a coordinated strategy. We have often been dogmatic in defending the theoretical virtues of "integration." But our Allies—especially the French—bear a heavy responsibility for the current state of affairs because they have never spelled out concretely what they mean by their alternative of coordination. If abstract and doctrinaire attitudes are avoided, the solution of current disputes is far from hopeless. Arguments about the right of independent action in the nuclear field are acute only when they are theoretical. Any crisis serious enough to cause the Allies to consider the use of nuclear weapons is also likely to reveal the underlying community of interest. It is this community rather than American physical control which is the best guarantee of the cohesion of the Alliance.

TACTICAL NUCLEAR WEAPONS

One of the consequences of the obsession with the MLF has been that many issues requiring urgent attention have been swept under the rug in order to maintain the momentum behind the Multilateral Force. One of these problems concerns the role and control of tactical nuclear weapons.

Tactical nuclear weapons have had a checkered history in NATO strategy. They were first introduced into the NATO arsenal in the middle fifties to offset what was then believed to be a permanent numerical superiority of Soviet manpower. As a result, thousands of nuclear weapons were shipped into Europe. They included almost everything from artillery pieces with ranges of about fifteen miles to Pershing missiles with ranges up to 700 miles (in the improved versions). The term tactical was defined to include all weapons placed under the authority of SACEUR even though some of the longer-range weapons would be indistinguishable from those controlled by SAC. From its beginning, the tactical nuclear establishment on the Continent raised formidable problems of coordination that remained dormant only because the dominant American strategic doctrine predicted that any nuclear war was likely to be massive and all-out.

The advent of the Kennedy Administration in 1961 changed this. Committed to a strategy of flexible response, the new administration began to evaluate the suitability of the nuclear establishment on the Continent for discriminating military operations. Its conclusions were skeptical: Early in the Kennedy Administration, the then Deputy Secretary of Defense Gilpatric rejected the notion of tactical nuclear war with the argument that it was impossible to build any limit into a nuclear war.[3] Deputy Assistant Secretary of Defense Alain Enthoven insisted that once

[3] Roswell L. Gilpatric, Press Conference on June 6, 1961, *New York Times,* June 7, 1961.

the dividing line between conventional and nuclear weapons is crossed, no obvious "fire-break" exists short of large scale thermonuclear war.[4] Secretary McNamara spoke deprecatingly of a limited nuclear war below some "ill-defined threshold of strategic exchange."[5] These views were given urgency by the problem of exercising political control over the nuclear weapons stationed on the Continent. Controlling a few hundred strategic weapons during military operations is difficult but soluble. Controlling thousands of weapons of many different ranges and characteristics in the confusion of combat is another matter.

At the same time, while skeptical about the utility of much of the tactical nuclear arsenal in Europe, both the Kennedy and Johnson Administrations have muted their doubts in order not to complicate further the disputes over the role of the conventional weapons and the MLF. Indeed, tactical nuclear weapons have been used as a means to reassure the Europeans about the continued validity of our nuclear guarantee and to insure German support for the MLF. As a result, the tactical nuclear establishment on the Continent has been substantially increased since 1961—by some 60 per cent according to Secretary McNamara's announcements. The thousands of nuclear weapons on the Continent thus exist in a shadow land. To many of our Allies, they have become a touchstone of the American commitment, while American planners regard them with extraordinary ambivalence. To build up the tactical nuclear establishment without clarifying its mission would seem to emphasize the worst features of all available options.

The question whether so much reliance should have

[4] Alain Enthoven, "American Deterrent Policy," *Survival,* Vol. V, No. 3 (May–June 1963), p. 96.

[5] Robert S. McNamara, "Major National Security Problems Confronting the United States," speech made before the Economics Club of New York, New York City, November 18, 1963, *DOSB,* Vol. XLIX, No. 1277 (December 16, 1963), p. 917.

been placed on tactical nuclear weapons ten years ago must not obscure the need to deal with the current situation, which is dominated by the following facts: (1) On the Continent there exists a large and growing arsenal of tactical nuclear weapons without a clearly defined mission. (2) The United States is solemnly committed to maintain this arsenal in Europe. (3) Our European allies see in the tactical nuclear establishment on the Continent a token of our nuclear commitment to Europe and a guarantee of a more or less automatic nuclear response once hostilities reach a certain scale. Its size and deployment therefore transcend purely military considerations. (4) The Soviet army is equipped with tactical nuclear weapons; hence, the decision to use nuclear weapons is no longer entirely up to the West. (5) NATO ground forces are inadequate to withstand a full-scale Soviet onslaught. Even the proposed build-up of NATO ground forces to thirty divisions would leave the West numerically inferior to a fully mobilized Soviet army—and this does not take into account the inevitable disadvantage of a coalition when confronting a single state. (6) The tactical nuclear establishment in Europe is extremely vulnerable. Because strategic weapons are relatively secure, fears that they will tempt a disarming, pre-emptive blow are usually exaggerated. But the classic pre-emptive situation does exist with respect to the tactical nuclear arsenal in Europe. As now deployed it is capable of inflicting severe damage; it is, in turn, highly vulnerable to a first strike. This may well add to deterrence; at the same time, it increases the probability of escalation should war occur.

There exists yet another inconsistency between NATO's military deployment and our strategic doctrine: Pentagon officials have indicated a clear preference for resisting even a major Soviet attack by conventional weapons. At the same time, they have announced repeatedly that if a conventional defeat were imminent, we would resort to tactical nuclear weapons. Considering the extreme vulnerability of the tactical nuclear establishment on the Continent and the fact that the Soviets would not attack without expecting to win, these two propositions tend to cancel each other out. If there is large-scale aggression—an admittedly improbable contingency—the Soviets have every incentive to seek to neutralize NATO's tactical nuclear arsenal by launching an attack against it.

All this suggests that it is imperative to reconsider the mission and deployment of the tactical nuclear arsenal on the Continent. Some argue that all nuclear missions—including the so-called tactical ones—can be performed by the strategic forces, which are more easily controlled and more suitable for discriminating operations. They maintain that any use of nuclear weapons would bring about so much confusion that the situation in the combat zone would appear relatively unimportant. Finally, some officials have implied that the nuclear arsenal in Europe is militarily unnecessary. Secretary McNamara has on occasion seemed to share this view.

The notion that all tactical missions can be performed by strategic forces must be assessed in terms of three problems: (1) the probability of uncontrolled escalation if battlefield weapons are used, (2) the suitability of strategic forces for tactical operations and (3) the feasibility of conducting nuclear operations confined to a battlefield.

The problem of escalation has two aspects: escalation within the theater of operations and escalation into general war. As long as NATO's tactical nuclear establishment is so vulnerable, the danger of escalation of *any* military operations within Europe is enormous even if they begin with conventional weapons. The precondition of any effective use of tactical nuclear weapons—as of strategic weapons—is to enhance their invulnerability.

The probability of escalation to general war depends on the vulnerability of the opposing retaliatory forces. If the strategic forces are extremely vulnerable, any use of nuclear weapons is likely to expand very rapidly. In that case, any large-scale military operation—even a conventional one—in an area as vital as Europe would involve risks out of proportion to any conceivable gain. The doctrine of massive retaliation will remain valid.

When retaliatory forces grow increasingly invulnerable, as Secretary McNamara has postulated, the pressures against rapid escalation would probably be great. There may be no *logical* stopping place once nuclear weapons are being used. There is, however, a very crucial *psychological* obstacle to automatic escalation. When mutual invulnerability guarantees catastrophic destruction and offers no prospect of great military advantage, neither side can be very eager to let escalation proceed automatically. Both sides are likely to look for excuses to limit, not expand, military operations.

This is not to say that in case of a full-scale Soviet attack on Europe our responses should be confined to battlefield weapons. On the contrary, there are important reasons for making sure that the Soviets are under no misapprehension that a full-scale attack on Europe could be confined to Europe. If the Soviets have shown a willingness to conquer Europe, the war is by definition no longer local. It cannot end with the *status quo ante*. If the Soviets come to believe that their territory would be spared but we would devastate Europe by confining the use of nuclear weapons to the combat zone, they may have an incentive for aggression. Such a strategy, even if it succeeded in stopping the attack, would eliminate Europe as a factor in international politics; it would guarantee that any other threatened area would surrender.

Nevertheless, even though a full-scale attack on Europe would inevitably bring the strategic forces into play, there is a problem of relating their action to local operations. Strategic forces are not designed to affect a local situation *directly*. Whether used demonstratively, punitively or in discriminating counterforce operations, their purpose is to force the aggressor into ordering an end to his local attacks, not to blunt the attacks themselves.

But is it wise to neglect the local outcome? It is at least possible that once strategic weapons are used, however discriminatingly, all other considerations could become submerged in the desire to end a spiral toward ever greater devastation. If the aggressor has made major advances, the ensuing confusion and panic may well enable him to consolidate his gains.

This suggests that, together with an agreed doctrine for the use of strategic forces, the Alliance requires a nuclear capability to deny an aggressor a significant territorial advance. Tactical weapons used early in the face of a full-scale attack could perform this role. If a standstill in military operations can be forced, a major objective of the defense will have been achieved. Aggression would have no object if it were certain to result in a stalemate.

Thus the nuclear components of NATO must have two aims: (1) they should seek to force a standstill of the initial onslaught and (2) they should be able to inflict sufficient punishment on the aggressor so that he is forced into negotiations. The aggressor must not believe that our response will shift all the risks of nuclear devastation to the victims of aggression. But there must also be a local response capable of preventing a *fait accompli* and an attempt to negotiate on the basis of it.

To achieve these objectives, the tactical nuclear establishment on the Continent must be adapted along the following lines: (1) its mission must be redefined, (2) its vulnerability must be reduced and (3) its deployment must be changed.

The current number of tactical nuclear weapons in Europe suggests an intention to conduct a self-contained tactical nuclear war with battlefield weapons used as a more efficient explosive to defeat the opposing forces. But a prolonged use of battlefield weapons according to purely military criteria would surely obliterate the combat zone, and this cannot be in the interest of any threatened country. Thus the mission of the tactical nuclear weapons should not be considered in isolation from the other, primarily strategic, operations which will be taking place. This makes it necessary to redefine some traditional military missions. For example, given the range of modern weapons, air superiority can be obtained—if at all—only by deep penetration of hostile territory on a scale indistinguishable from general nuclear war.

At the same time major efforts should be made to enhance the invulnerability of the tactical nuclear weapons remaining on the Continent and to improve their command and control procedures. Tactical nuclear weapons present particular difficulties of command and control. The strategic arsenal can be fitted with electronic devices which make it possible to subject each weapon to political control. But individual control, even if technically feasible, presents different problems when thousands of weapons of very different ranges and characteristics are involved. No communications system could withstand such a strain.

During the Presidential campaign of 1964, it was proposed that one way of solving this problem would be to delegate authority to a military commander, specifically to SACEUR. This was justified with the argument that communications between Washington and Paris might be interrupted. But such a scheme would create more problems than it solves. For one thing, no other member of the Alliance would be prepared to make such a delegation of authority. Also, SACEUR would be extremely ill-advised to resort to nuclear weapons without making sure that SAC is alerted. If communications are adequate for that purpose, they should also be adequate for political control to be exercised. Moreover, the real communications bottleneck is not between Washington and Paris, but between NATO headquarters and the field commanders. But if authority to initiate the use of nuclear weapons were delegated to field commanders, this would mean that nuclear war could be started by officers least familiar with the strategic context and most subject to immediate pressures which may or may not be symptomatic of the overall situation. Field commanders do not have access to strategic intelligence about the Soviet Union or to plans

for general war. Thus the initial decision to use tactical
nuclear weapons will have to be made by Washington
(or by the Executive Committee of the NATO Council described below). Once the decision is taken, they will have
to be released by category of range, yield and geographic
location. This underlines the urgent need for an agreed
NATO strategic doctrine.

Another subject requiring careful reexamination is
NATO deployment. Currently it is an uneasy compromise
between the desire to retain a conventional option and
the reality that nuclear weapons have become an integral
part of the equipment of all military units. This reflects a
real dilemma. To fight a conventional war, military units
must concentrate; to be effective during nuclear operations, they must disperse. Units deployed for conventional
operations present tempting targets for nuclear attack
and may thus invite it. Units deployed for nuclear war are
too dispersed to resist an attack with conventional weapons. In all likelihood, it will be impossible to shift from
one mode of deployment to another *during* military operations, particularly if the opponent has introduced nuclear weapons first. But current NATO deployment involves
precisely this danger. Units are concentrated as if the
likely attack would be conventional. At the same time,
even their forward echelons are equipped with nuclear
weapons. This concentration coupled with the ambiguity
of NATO doctrine and the vulnerability of tactical nuclear
weapons gives an aggressor a high incentive to use nuclear weapons first.

It has become increasingly clear that NATO will not raise
sufficient troops for a purely conventional defense of Europe—all trends, in fact, are in the opposite direction. It
is therefore crucial that deployment on the Continent take
into account the realities of NATO in the next decade.
NATO's conventional forces are suitable for two major
roles: (1) to act as a screening force to determine that
a full-scale attack is, in fact, taking place and thus to discourage sudden seizures of NATO territory and (2) to fur-

nish a reserve to resist aggression on the flanks of NATO or in areas outside of Europe where the Alliance might agree on joint action.

NATO deployment should reflect this. There should be a screen of conventional forces deployed forward and organized for purely conventional combat. The size of this screen would depend on the total NATO forces available and on a military estimate of what is required to force a major Soviet concentration before aggression can have any chance of success. The remainder of NATO's divisions—deployed behind this screen—should be organized for nuclear war. With such a deployment, it would be obvious to any aggressor that once operations reached a certain magnitude nuclear war would be inevitable. At the same time, NATO deployment and weapons design would reduce the incentives for pre-emption. In addition, there should be a strategic reserve organized to intervene rapidly either in a land battle in Europe or in distant theaters. However, no arrangement of military forces will, of itself, solve the problems of the Alliance. The ultimate challenge lies in the political field. It is whether NATO can develop common purposes and whether it can devise a political structure that combines community with flexibility.

PART FOUR

Political Prospects

Chapter Seven

EAST-WEST RELATIONS
AND THE FUTURE OF GERMANY

There is a curious disproportion between the energy devoted to nuclear control and that spent on the issue of the future of Germany. This is no accident. Nuclear control, for all its complexity, has the advantage of seeming concrete. Solutions permit technical analysis. Absorption in this problem can therefore serve as an escape from issues that are intangible and much less amenable to mechanical remedies. Yet it is probable that over the next decade the cohesiveness of the Alliance will be tested more severely by the problem of German unity than by the issue of who presses the button for nuclear war.

Basic to any policy regarding the future of Germany is a common conception of East-West relations.

EAST-WEST RELATIONS

East-West relations have been a cause of disagreement within the Alliance at least since the death of Stalin. In the early years of NATO our European Allies feared above all that we might return to our traditional isolationism. They, therefore, suppressed whatever doubts they might have had about the American understanding of the Communist threat. If anything, they had an interest in exaggerating the extent of the immediate danger. Stalinist intransigence did the rest. America's commitment to the defense of Europe grew absolute. In American thinking, the danger of Communist aggression became as ominous as our nostalgia for our historic aloofness from international affairs was great.

After the death of Stalin, the previous Allied unanimity about the nature of the Communist threat evaporated.[1] Under the impact of periodic Soviet peace offensives and the schisms within the Communist world, differences in the Allies' approach to the Communist challenge became apparent. Great Britain, Italy and the Scandinavian countries tended to treat every Soviet peace offensive as the beginning of a new era of international cooperation. Each sign of Communist moderation was hailed as a basic change in the Soviet system. In these countries the predominant view was that Soviet ideology had become transformed into a Marxist form of moderate nationalism.

In the Federal Republic and in France after the advent of De Gaulle, the attitude has been quite different. The Federal Republic, divided by Communist intransigence and repeatedly subjected to Communist pressures, has seen in Soviet peace offensives merely a variation of tactics, not a major shift in objectives. Supported by France, the Federal Republic has been uneasy about East-West negotiations and fearful that any settlement would legitimize, at least indirectly, the division of Germany. In 1962, Paris and Bonn disagreed with the United States about the utility of the exploratory talks regarding Berlin. They have been unhappy about most of the schemes advanced at the Geneva Disarmament Conference. France rejected—as the Federal Republic would have liked to do but did not dare—the limited Nuclear Test Ban Treaty.

[1] Throughout, there had been significant opposition groups in each country which maintained that the threat was exaggerated or even that NATO was provocative.

United States policy has oscillated between these conflicting views. American pronouncements include many of the phrases about Soviet intransigence characteristic of the early days of NATO. Our actual policy has tended toward bilateral dealings with the Soviets. Seeking to straddle the conflicting views of its Allies but not reconciling them, the United States has retained the liturgy of the Cold War while adopting a good deal of the practice of those urging a policy of relaxation of tensions.

As a result, much of the Allied debate about East-West relations has concerned not the content of a program for negotiation but the nature of the Soviet system. Those who assume that there has been a change in Soviet policy tend to stress the impact of modernization on Soviet purposes. To them a great deal depends on establishing good personal relations with Soviet leaders and on bringing about a general atmosphere of goodwill. Those who insist on the unchangeable nature of Soviet hostility postulate a Soviet society immune to the erosion of time —an achievement which would be unprecedented in human history.

But the desirability of easing tensions should never be in dispute. The only sensible debate can concern the question of how peace can be achieved and then made secure. The issue is not whether tensions should be artificially maintained, but what their cause is and how they can best be ended. Is the Cold War the result of personal malice or does it have deeper causes? Is a lasting detente reached by improving the atmosphere first and moving from there to specific settlements? Or is a relaxation of tensions reliable only if it is tied from the very beginning to a settlement of outstanding issues? Above all, what exactly is to be understood by a settlement? These are the questions which the Alliance must answer for itself if it is to determine whether a given peace offensive represents a change of tactics or a change of policy.

Peace offensives, of course, are not new in Soviet his-

tory. Peaceful co-existence has been avowed since the
advent of Communism in Russia. It was stressed particularly between 1924–1939; between 1941–1946; at the
time of the Geneva Summit Conference of 1955; again
on the occasion of Khrushchev's visit to the United States
in 1959; and following the Cuban missile crisis in 1962.
On each occasion the reason for the detente was some
internal or external strain on the Soviet system. In 1924,
it was the struggle between Stalin and Trotsky, which was
followed by the forced collectivization of agriculture and
the purges; in 1941–1946 it was the German invasion;
in 1955 it was the succession struggle after the death of
Stalin; in 1959 it was part of a Soviet attempt to push the
Allies out of Berlin; since 1962 it has been caused by the
shock of the defeat in Cuba and the internal strains on
the Soviet system.

On each occasion the period of relaxation ended when
an opportunity for expanding Communism presented itself. The period of tranquillity after 1924 was followed
by the annexation of Bessarabia, the Baltic States and
one third of Poland, as well as an attack on Finland.
World War II led to the creation of the satellite orbit in
Eastern Europe. The spirit of Geneva gave way to an attempted penetration of the Middle East and a crisis over
Berlin. And, the spirit of Camp David was succeeded by
another Berlin crisis which did not end until the installation of Soviet missiles in Cuba.

During each previous Soviet peace offensive, many in
the West—including some who thought of themselves as
staunchly, sometimes almost religiously, anti-Communist
—hailed a fundamental change in Soviet attitude. This
demonstrates the extent of the American consensus that
conflict is usually the result of individual malice rather
than of structural causes. The corollary is that East-West
tensions can be ended by a simple change of heart on the
part of Communist leaders. In 1933 a noted historian
wrote:

The former crusaders of world revolution at any cost have exchanged their swords for machine tools and now rely more on the results of their labor than on direct action to achieve the ultimate triumph of the proletariat.[2]

When Stalin abolished the Comintern in 1943, the late Senator Tom Connally from Texas commented: "Russians for years have been changing their economy and approaching the abandonment of communism and the whole Western world will be gratified at the happy climax of their efforts."[3] In 1956 Secretary Dulles was impelled by the spirit of Geneva to say: "The Soviet leaders are scrapping thirty years of policy based on violence and intolerance."[4] This is matched by Secretary Rusk's statement early in 1964: "They [the Communists] appear to have begun to realize that there is an irresolvable contradiction between the demands to promote world Communism by force and the needs of the Soviet state and people."[5]

Each of these assessments turned out to be mistaken—except Secretary Rusk's, which cannot yet be judged. The reason is not obscure. Any system has its own dynamism that shapes its leaders and affects what is considered reasonable in internal discussions. There is need for an assessment of those factors in the Soviet system that produce belligerence and those that encourage accommodation. These are delicately balanced. It should be the goal of Western policy to give a maximum spur to the peaceful trends.

[2] Michael T. Florinsky, *World Revolution and the USSR* (New York: The Macmillan Co., 1933), p. 216.

[3] *New York Times,* May 23, 1943.

[4] U.S. Department of State Press Release, No. 92, February 25, 1956.

[5] Secretary Rusk, "Why We Treat Different Communist Countries Differently," address to the Full Citizenship and World Affairs Conference of the International Union of Electrical Radio and Machine Workers at Washington, D.C., on February 25, 1964, *DOSB,* Vol. L, No. 1290 (March 16, 1964), p. 393.

Two factors encourage intransigence in the Communist world: the qualities of the men who rise to leadership positions and the ideology on which the Communist system is built.

Any comparison of the composition of the Presidium of the Communist Party of the U.S.S.R. at the beginning of any decade with its membership at the end of that decade illustrates the precariousness of high office in the Soviet system.[6] Turnover is rapid; the penalties for failure in the inevitable leadership struggle are drastic. Loss of position involves public disgrace, usually for the former leader's family as well, and complete separation from all erstwhile colleagues or from any public activity.

Even more poignant than the fate of the top leadership is that of the middle and lower echelons. The top leaders at least have the consolation that the enormous risks they run are on behalf of their own ambitions; those on the lower levels may find themselves submerged as a result of events totally out of their control. Loyalty may turn into a source of personal danger; subordinate officials

[6] The fate of the first groups of post-Stalin leaders has been described as follows by Severyn Bialer in "Twenty-four Men Who Rule Russia," *New York Times Magazine*, November 1, 1964, p. 27:

Two (Beria and Bagirov) were shot. Six (Malenkov, Molotov, Kaganovich, Bulganin, Saburov and Pervukhin) were denounced and expelled from leadership and have disappeared from public life. One (Voroshilov) was publicly denounced, expelled from the leadership but admitted to Khrushchev's banquet circuit. Two (Ignatiev and Melnikov) gradually disappeared from public life following censure.

Three are no longer in positions of leadership but are still members of the Central Committee and occupy positions of secondary importance. These are Aristov, the Ambassador to Poland; Mikhailov, the Ambassador to Indonesia, and Pospelov, the director of the Institute of Marxism-Leninism. One (Ponomarenko) was removed from the Central Committee without censure and occupies a fourth-rate post. Only two (Mikoyan and Suslov) outlasted Khrushchev and are now in the front ranks of the post-Khrushchev leadership.

will often share the fate of the leader even though they may have had no real alternative.

All this creates an atmosphere of suspicion—even of conspiracy—in the Communist leadership groups. There is no legitimate succession. Power goes to those skillful and ruthless enough to seize and hold it. It becomes its own justification because it brings control of the only source of legitimacy: the Communist Party apparatus. In the past, no attempt at collective leadership has lasted. One leader has eliminated all rivals and has not felt restrained by ties of loyalty or by past obligations. Stalin had all the individuals who helped him into power executed. Khrushchev disgraced Kaganovich, whose protégé he had been, and turned on Marshal Zhukov six months after being saved by him from a conspiracy of his own colleagues. Brezhnev and Kosygin owed their careers to Khrushchev; they nevertheless overthrew him and started a campaign of calumny against him within twenty-four hours of his dismissal.

Only an enormous desire for power can impel a man to enter such a career. Anyone succeeding in Communist leadership struggles must be single-minded, unemotional, unsentimental and dedicated. Nothing in the experience of Soviet leaders would lead them to prize peace as an end or to accept protestations of personal goodwill at face value. Their own career—indeed their survival—has been advanced by the ability to dissemble. Khrushchev's success, as Brezhnev's after him, depended on his ability to hide his ambition until it was too late for his rivals to organize against him. Suspiciousness is therefore inherent in the domestic position of Soviet leaders. It is unlikely that their attitude toward the outside world is more benign. There is no reason for them to treat foreign statesmen more gently than their own colleagues or to expect more consideration from them.

The Soviet system tends to produce leaders who identify their survival with the elimination of all possible rivals. Domestically this means that the power of potential competitors must be broken. Internationally it implies that opponents must be neutralized if at all possible. The motives of Soviet leaders may well be defensive. The problem is that they feel secure only when all conceivable rivals have been reduced to impotence. Wary of even his closest colleagues, the type of man who rises to a position of leadership in the Soviet Union will identify security less with goodwill than with a balance of forces and will be tempted to engage in constant probes designed to reduce the power and influence of countries whose size or structure makes them possible competitors of the U.S.S.R. This does not make crises inevitable or settlements impossible; Soviet leaders, whatever their experience, are cautious and patient. But if peace were to depend on their pronouncements alone, it would not be very secure.

Soviet tendencies to exert maximum pressure and to emphasize the importance of a balance of forces are reinforced by Communist ideology. To be sure, Communist leaders do not follow the teachings of Marx or Lenin literally; they could not, even if they wished, because these writings are too contradictory and too dependent on tactical considerations. However, if ideology does not guide the day-to-day actions, its basic categories shape the Communist sense of reality. It is considered to be the guarantee of the ultimate victory that will make all sacrifices worthwhile. It is the means for establishing discipline within the world Communist movement by providing criteria of legitimacy for the settlement of disputes. While the growing gap between ideology and reality is one of the latent weaknesses of any Communist system, in the immediate future ideology continues as one of the prime obstacles to a basic accommodation.

Communists believe that Marxism-Leninism supplies an invaluable tool in understanding historical trends and the relation of forces existing at any particular moment. According to it, "subjective" factors, such as the personal convictions of statesmen, matter less than the "objective" factors they reflect. These objective factors include the social and economic conditions of society, the nature of the economic process and, above all, the class struggle. Communists consider that Marxism-Leninism enables them to distinguish between appearance and reality, to avoid the "subjectivism" inherent in an excessive reliance on personality and the "adventurism" that risks a historical movement on one throw of the dice.

Belief in the predominance of "objective" factors explains why Soviet leaders, whenever they have had to make a choice between Western goodwill and a territorial or political gain, have unhesitatingly chosen the latter. The friendship of the West built up during the heroic efforts of World War II was ruthlessly sacrificed to the possibility of establishing Communist-controlled governments in Eastern Europe. The spirit of Geneva did not survive the temptations offered by the prospect of penetrating the Middle East. The spirit of Camp David ended with another ultimatum on Berlin. The many overtures of the Kennedy Administration were rebuffed until the Cuban missile crisis demonstrated that the balance of forces was not in fact favorable.

The Soviet reliance on "objective" factors is one of the reasons that negotiations with the Soviets have often been so frustrating. Communist negotiators cannot admit that they could be swayed by the arguments of opponents whose understanding of the basic laws of historical development is, by definition, inferior to their own. They cannot reciprocate "concessions" because they believe that concessions are made to reality, not to individuals. They may change their position, but they will go to great lengths to demonstrate that they did so of their own volition and at their own pace. For them a great deal depends on avoiding what seems basic to most Western negotiators: the give-and-take of a bargaining process. Their attitude toward Western negotiators is very similar to that of Western psychiatrists toward their patients: no matter what is said, they think that they understand their Western counterpart better than he understands himself. This is one of the reasons that exercises in personal diplomacy—even at the highest level—have been so futile. No Soviet leader could make an agreement based on the proposition that he has been impressed by the personal qualities of a capitalist statesman. Settlements are possible; but to be meaningful in Soviet eyes they must reflect "objective" conditions and not a personal relationship.

The ritualistic belief in the importance of the class struggle causes Soviet leaders to adopt a posture of irreconcilable philosophical hostility toward the non-Communist world. Even while advocating political co-existence, the Communist Party of the U.S.S.R. declared:

The C.P.S.U. [Communist Party of the Soviet Union] resolutely opposes peaceful coexistence in the province of ideology. These are elementary truths, and it is time for everyone who considers himself a Marxist-Leninist to master them.[7]

Thus peaceful co-existence is never advocated for its own sake. It is justified primarily as a tactical device to overthrow the West at minimum risk. In replying to Chinese charges that it was abandoning world revolution, the Communist Party of the U.S.S.R. proposed the following test for the policy of "peaceful co-existence":

Does the policy of peace and peaceful co-existence favor the development of the revolutionary class struggle in the capitalist countries, the upsurge of national liberation movements?[8]

In yet another reply to their Chinese tormentors, the Soviet Communist Party affirmed:

[7] "The Soviet Reply to the Chinese Letter," open letter from the Central Committee of the Communist Party of the Soviet Union as it appeared in *Pravda*, July 14, 1963, pp. 1–4; *The Current Digest of the Soviet Press* (hereafter referred to as *CDSP*), Vol. XV, No. 28 (August 7, 1963), p. 23.

[8] "Another Statement Answering Chinese on Test Ban," statement of the Soviet Government as it appeared in *Pravda*, September 21, 1963, pp. 1–2, and September 22, 1963, pp. 1–2; *Izvestia*, pp. 1–2 and 1–3; *CDSP*, Vol. XV, No. 38 (October 16, 1963), p. 12.

We fully support the destruction of imperialism and capitalism. We not only believe in the inevitable death of capitalism, but are doing everything possible for it to be accomplished through class struggle as quickly as possible.[9]

Moreover, "peaceful co-existence" is advanced by Soviet leaders not as a new insight, but as the continuation of Leninist tradition. This proposition has elicited the following exasperated comment from George F. Kennan:

. . . people in Moscow are not likely to strengthen belief outside Russia in . . . their attachment to liberal and tolerant principles of international life . . . by pleading that such an attachment flows inevitably from the nature of the social and political system prevailing in the Soviet Union. It is possible to conceive that the Soviet attitude in such questions may have changed; it is not possible to accept the proposition that it did not need to change in order to meet the requirements of peaceful co-existence. . . .[10]

These factors, which almost overnight could produce again an expansionist Communist foreign policy, must be balanced against restraints that, over a period of time, may become dominant. First, there is the power of modern weapons. Ideological hostility comes up against the stark risks of nuclear warfare. Soviet leaders must be acutely aware that, if they press intransigence beyond a certain point, they run the risk of hazarding what they have built up at so much sacrifice over four decades. Whatever the strategic theory of the West—even if it is not an ideal one—Soviet planners will not be easily convinced that the danger of escalation in any direct confrontation is not enormous. The West would have to behave extraordinarily foolishly before the Soviets risk an overt military challenge. To be sure, in some circumstances aggression does

[9] "The Soviet Reply to the Chinese Letter," *op. cit., CDSP*, Vol. XV, No. 28 (August 7, 1963), p. 20.
[10] George F. Kennan, "Peaceful Co-existence: A Western View," *Foreign Affairs*, Vol. 38, No. 2 (January 1960), p. 174.

not need to take the form of direct military action, and this accounts for the persistence of the so-called "wars of national liberation." However, if the West conducts itself with reasonable prudence, the traditional methods of military pressure can be made increasingly unattractive. Then agreements may be possible to implement one interest which the two great nuclear powers must have in common: to prevent a nuclear holocaust. It is significant that one of the principal arguments advanced by Soviet leaders on behalf of peaceful co-existence is that nuclear war is too dangerous. It is in the West's interest to see to it that it remain so.

Another factor which acts as a restraint on Soviet foreign policy is the instability of the leadership group. A great deal of the energy of Soviet leaders is absorbed in internal maneuvering. It is a symptom of weakness that, over forty years after seizing power, the Soviet Union has not solved the problem of legitimate succession. Each ruler has felt secure only by villifying his predecessor.

In almost half a century of Soviet rule, the reputation of only the first leader (Lenin) has outlived his tenure in office. In the short term, the patience and capacity for endurance of the Russian people may support such a style of government. At some point, however, cynicism and demoralization are likely to set in. Sooner or later, the Communist leaders will be asked by the younger generation how a system which constantly invokes the universality of its maxims can produce leaders who, by the account of their successors, are so fallible and so corrupt; how an ideology which prides itself on its mastery of "objective" forces could have as its pervasive aberration—again by its own account—the "cult of personality."

The difficulty of settling domestic disputes is closely related to the inability of Communist countries to deal with each other. Communist ideology does not admit the possibility of conflict among Communist states. Since national rivalries are thought to be the result of class conflict, they are expected to disappear wherever Socialism has triumphed. In the absence of any provision for the settlement of disputes, Communist leaders try to deal with disputes among Communist states as they conduct their own internal struggles: by seeking first to ostracize and then to destroy their opponents. But among sovereign states, such tactics cause disputes to harden into irremediable schisms. Each schism, in turn, demonstrates that a supposedly universal orthodoxy can be interpreted in various ways. This must, in time, erode confidence in the universality of Communist ideology as well as the discipline of the world Communist movement.

Thus, events of the past decade have had a profoundly disruptive impact on the unity of the world Communist movement. The enormous tactical flexibility of Communist parties in the past has been due to two factors: belief in the scientific truth of Communist ideology and the existence of Moscow as the center of Marxist infallibility. Belief in scientific truth supplied the inward assurance; the pre-eminence of Moscow provided the discipline without which tactical flexibility easily degenerates into opportunism.

The unity produced by these factors has been undermined by three developments: de-Stalinization, the Sino-Soviet split and the manner in which Khrushchev has been overthrown. De-Stalinization raised the question of the relationship between the scientific truth of the dominant ideology and the murderous cult of personality of Stalin. How could a system that was supposed to end forever man's oppression produce an even more pervasive tyranny than the one it replaced? How could belief in scientific truth be reconciled with slave labor camps and a police state? Even if the Russian people did not ask such questions, Communist cadres must have been assailed by doubts which must have been reinforced when Khrushchev was overthrown in his turn and denounced for "hare-brained schemes."

The Sino-Soviet split was the catalyst for the overt fragmentation of the Communist world. The causes of this rift are many and complex. There is the rivalry of two empires along the most extended land frontier of the world. Competition for a dominant role in the underdeveloped countries plays a part. But what makes the dispute insoluble is the conflict over the leadership of the world Communist movement. While the actual manifestations of the rift may be patched up from time to time, its underlying cause seems beyond repair. A movement that claims to represent a universal truth cannot tolerate two centers of orthodoxy. As long as Peiping rejects the doctrinal preeminence of Moscow, the most important reason for discord will persist—whatever temporary adjustments may be made.

The mere assertion of Peiping's independence on doctrinal matters was bound to alter the nature of Communism. Once the Soviet Union's doctrinal infallibility was challenged, the pattern of relationships within the Communist world changed irretrievably. The East European governments, beset by economic difficulties, saw an opportunity to solidify their sometimes tenuous hold by appealing to the national feelings of their populations. The Soviet Union was no longer in a position to command their loyalty but had to compete for it. In the face of Albanian and then Rumanian defiance, the previous monolithic unity of the Communist world has been eroded. Convinced Communists must be demoralized by the disarray; technicians see in the Sino-Soviet split an opportunity for striking the maximum bargain for their country.

Khrushchev's fall has also had unfortunate consequences for the cohesiveness of the Communist world. Communist leaders, whatever their attitudes toward Khrushchev, must have realized that they were jeopardizing their own position by tying themselves too closely to whoever might be in power in Moscow. Since foreign Communist leaders share many of the characteristics of their Soviet colleagues—including a highly developed sense for personal power—the instability of the Kremlin hierarchy impels them to protect themselves by a measure of autonomy. They must try to safeguard their position against possible future upheavals in Moscow. The initial hesitation of the Communist parties around the world in endorsing Khrushchev's ouster can be partly explained by this.

Personal ambition thus reinforces the dominant trends in East European countries. Two decades of Communist rule have, if anything, intensified traditional nationalism. Communism has been able to gain a measure of popular acceptance only where its leaders emphasize national and not Communist concerns. The autarchic organization of Communist economies compounds these tendencies. It encapsules each state in a system of total planning, which complicates relations even with Communist neighbors. A particularly virulent form of nationalism results.

All of this suggests that the current period of relaxation of tension has been initiated by the Soviets not because a few individuals have overcome the opposition of some unnamed Stalinists, but because conditions require it. To the West the challenge presented by this detente can be defined as follows: When the Communist world faces internal difficulties, should we bask in the relative calm of the Communist tone, or should we use the opportunity to press for the settlement of issues that produced the tension in the first place?

Domestic considerations impel many Western leaders to present themselves to their electorate as the architects of a lasting peace. The temptation is, therefore, strong to treat a more conciliatory Communist tone as a permanent conversion to a peaceful course and to gear everything to personal diplomacy.

Such attitudes will cause the West to squander its opportunities, as has happened so often in the past. The prospects for peace are not served by leaving the Soviet leadership with the impression that any action, no matter how belligerent, can always be reversed by a change of tone. Negotiations will prove empty if they are confined to vague protestations of goodwill. If a detente is not to be part of another cycle leading to renewed tensions, it is essential that negotiations be concrete and programs specific.

Above all, the West must conduct its policy without illusions. The same pressures that have produced a relaxation of tensions can also tempt Soviet leaders to enter upon another period of hostility. There is always the danger that the Kremlin will try to restore the unity of Eastern Europe by fostering a crisis centered on Germany. Even as it is, the East European governments almost invariably support Soviet foreign policy, particularly in the underdeveloped world. Events in other continents can have a backlash in Europe. The Soviets could be drawn into an intransigent course as a result of situations over which they have no direct control. The weakening of central authority in the Soviet Union may enable various bureaucracies to operate relatively autonomously, including those with a vested interest in fomenting upheavals. The spiritual malaise of Communism could be reversed if an unchecked collapse of Western influence and power around the world seems to demonstrate the validity of the basic tenets of Leninism.

Even the split between the largest Communist countries represents danger as well as opportunity. It means that henceforth the West will confront not alternating periods of hostility and conciliation but both at the same time. It can also happen that the two Communist giants may try to outbid each other in giving so-called liberation movements an anti-Western cast—the situation in the Congo is a good example.

Moreover, to the degree that the Soviet Union is certified as the more conciliatory Communist country, a "respectable" form of Communism begins to intrude into the domestic scene of several of our Allies. One of the major achievements of the postwar period in Europe has been the isolation of the Communist parties. Under the impact of many factors, this isolation is beginning to break down. In Italy, for example, the "opening to the Left" has resulted in new-found strength for the Communist Party. In

France, the demoralization of the traditional parties by De Gaulle and the change in tactics by the Communist Party has opened up prospects of a Popular Front for the first time in thirty years.

Similar factors influence the approach of Communism in the new countries. Until de-Stalinization, ambitious leaders were restrained from joining the Communist camp because this action reduced them to the status of satellites. With the growing disarray in the Communist world it will seem increasingly possible to combine nationalism and Communism. Many in the West draw comfort from this. But it is important to distinguish between a national Communist government in Eastern Europe and a similar regime in, for example, Latin America or Africa. A national Communist regime in Eastern Europe is an improvement over the previous condition of absolute Soviet control. A similar regime in Latin America or Africa would inevitably become a center of anti-Western policy.

If the West is to act purposefully in this situation, it must develop a common policy and a specific program. The temptation for bilateral approaches is great. Each national leader, depending on his temperament, has visions of appearing as the arbiter of a final settlement or of adding Communist pressures to his own as a bargaining device within the Alliance. This sets up a vicious circle. Since leaders generally do not reach eminence without a touch of vanity and since some stake their prestige on their ability to woo their Soviet counterparts, they tend to present their contacts with the Soviets as a considerable accomplishment. But the real issues have gone unresolved because they are genuinely difficult; hence they are usually avoided during summit diplomacy in favor of showy but essentially peripheral gestures. The vaguer the East-West discourse, the greater will be the confusion in the West. Moreover, each leader faces two different audiences: toward his own people he will be tempted to leave the impression that he has made a unique contribution to peace; toward his allies he will be forced to insist that he will make no settlement in which they do not participate. Excessive claims are coupled with reassurances to uneasy allies which are in turn tempted to pursue bilateral diplomacy.

Such a course is suicidal for the West. It will stimulate distrust within the Alliance. The traditional Western balance of power diplomacy will reappear manipulated by the Kremlin. Any Soviet incentive to be responsible will vanish. The Soviet leaders will be able to overcome their difficulties with the assistance of the West and without settling any of the outstanding issues. Since in the Kremlin —as in the West—there must be many who consider the status quo preferable to change, the result is likely to be diplomatic paralysis obscured by abstract declarations about peace and friendship.

A great deal depends, therefore, on two related policies: (1) the willingness of the members of the Alliance to subordinate short-term advantages to a long-term conception of the future and (2) their ability to develop a concrete and common program. A united West would have unusual opportunities for negotiation. The disarray in Eastern Europe should permit the West to adjust its policies to the degree of autonomy shown by the various East European countries. Measures to discipline the arms race could be considered in a new atmosphere. The problem of East-West trade policy urgently requires a comprehensive solution. All these approaches presuppose some consensus in the West about the shape of international affairs over the next decade or so.

Central to any long-term policy is some conception of the future of Germany. No other issue illustrates so dramatically the need for unity and for purpose, for an agreed Allied policy as well as for concrete proposals.

THE FUTURE OF GERMANY

The position of the Federal Republic after De Gaulle's press conference of January 14, 1963, and the

Franco-German Treaty of Collaboration has become increasingly complicated. After the initial period of shock, the United States undertook an assiduous wooing of the Federal Republic. One motive behind the MLF was to prevent West Germany from accepting a possible French offer of nuclear cooperation—an offer which has not yet been made and, given De Gaulle's awareness of the European equilibrium, might never have been extended. In order to tie Germany to us, successful efforts were made to have German arms purchases funneled to the United States. The culmination of this process was an agreement between Secretary McNamara and Defense Minister von Hassel signed on November 14, 1964, which in effect made the German armed forces dependent on the United States for their military equipment.

In the political field the United States, while welcoming Franco-German rapprochement, has made clear that it does so only as long as this does not lead to a new power grouping—a condition inherently impossible of fulfillment. Thus, George McGhee, U.S. Ambassador to Bonn, has said:

. . . It is true that the signature of the Franco-German Treaty came as a surprise to many Americans, particularly in the light of what had already been accomplished without a formal treaty. . . . Fears which have been expressed that the Franco-German Treaty might be used as a vehicle . . . for a new power alignment in Western Europe have so far proved groundless. It is in the interest not only of Germany and France but of Europe and the whole Atlantic community that they remain so.[11]

American pressure and high-handed French actions have placed the Federal Republic in an extremely uncomfortable position. Germany, though courted on all sides, runs the risk of finding itself isolated. Every gesture by the Federal Republic toward one of the protagonists evokes

[11] George McGhee, "Some Thoughts on Current Issues," July 16, 1964, *DOSB*, Vol. LI, No. 1310 (August 3, 1964), pp. 140–141.

so much pressure by the other that a compensatory move must then be made. In order to assuage American outrage over the Franco-German Treaty, Chancellor Adenauer agreed in principle to the MLF. When the negotiations over the MLF threatened a Franco-German rift, Chancellor Erhard felt obliged to re-cement Franco-German ties. Because of its understandable insecurities, Germany requires, above all, a calm and steady senior partner. The frequent changes in American policy on strategic doctrine, nuclear control and the emphasis to be given to various partners must radicalize German political life, whatever the merit of individual United States positions. French policy has been consistent but it has confronted the Federal Republic with choices which it is unprepared to handle. As a result, the Franco-German rivalry threatens to split the pro-Western elements in Germany into pro-American and pro-French factions. Over a period of time, the beneficiaries must be the nationalists or the quasi-neutralists. Thrown on its own resources by the rivalry between France and the United States, the Federal Republic has been forced to become increasingly conscious of its own national aspirations.

Thus Germany is growing more vulnerable to Soviet cajolery or Communist blackmail—a trend further magnified by American hints that Germany should be more flexible toward the East. As long as Germany could avoid a direct confrontation by pleading the pre-eminent role of some other relationship—the Western Alliance or the Franco-German Treaty—these dangers were minimized. The combination of De Gaulle's abruptness and America's short-sighted reaction to it threatens to bring about what each of the rivals should fear most: a Germany increasingly absorbed in its own unfulfilled national aims and aware of the bargaining position conferred on it by its central position and growing power.

All this threatens to upset the delicate balance on which Germany's integration into the Atlantic Alliance was built. It exposes the Federal Republic to dangerous pressures and temptations. Germany has emerged as the balance wheel of the Western Alliance. The most exposed Western ally, 17 million of whose people are Communist hostages, has become the focal point of all disputes. Its internal structure may not be equal to this strain. There are signs already that the conflict may tear apart the governing party, the Christian Democratic Union, which largely forged the pro-Western orientation of the Federal Republic. This will liberate tendencies in the other parties that are now restrained by their desire to present themselves as responsible trustees of a well-established consensus. France, in turn, seeing that the Franco-German Treaty by which it has sought to limit the Federal Republic's freedom of action has had the practical consequence of enhancing Germany's national role, may be tempted to seek reinsurance by improving its relations in Eastern Europe. Thus the current situation contains a series of time bombs.

The most serious potential conflict between the Federal Republic and its Allies—and the lever which the Communist countries may hope to use to pry Germany loose from its Atlantic ties—concerns reactions to the division of Germany. The problem is complicated by three factors: (1) NATO is an alliance of status quo countries; yet one of its principal members seeks a basic change in the status quo. (2) None of Germany's allies shares her national aspirations with equal intensity. (3) Germany's past has left a legacy of distrust that creates special obstacles to its international role. These divergences would be difficult enough for a cohesive Alliance to reconcile; the rivalry between France and the United States threatens to make them insoluble.

These problems become particularly severe whenever there appears to be some relaxation in East-West tensions. To most of the members of NATO, detente comes as a welcome respite. To the Federal Republic, it implies the danger of a tacit acceptance of the status quo. Most of the Allies do not find the status quo intolerable, whereas the

Federal Republic considers consolidation of the East German regime a sacrifice of basic national aspirations.

This is why German leaders are always extraordinarily ambivalent during periods of detente. They welcome relief from pressures against Berlin; but they are uneasy lest all other aspects of the German situation become frozen too. They make a distinction between "peripheral" settlements which they welcome and "central" agreements which they oppose unless they bring some visible progress on the German question. If this progress is delayed too long, there will be increasing pressures for purely German initiatives. The Alliance may soon have to choose between developing a common, active policy on German reunification or seeing the Federal Republic pursue the goal independently.

Many in the West find both possibilities disquieting. Remembering two world wars and the atrocities of the Nazi period, they are uneasy about the prospect of having international tensions focus on Germany for the third time in fifty years. But the West must rise above its memories, keeping in mind that the disasters of this century arose in part because Germany strove to assert its own narrowly conceived interests against both East and West. Ten years after the decision to restore Germany to a respected place in the international community, it is unfair to invoke Germany's past transgressions in discussions of policy alternatives. It is possible to argue that other choices should have been made a decade ago. Today, the sole hope for having Germany be a responsible member of the Atlantic Community is to treat her like one.

The fate of the 17 million people in East Germany is one of those intangible issues that can remain quiescent for many years, only to erupt suddenly and dramatically. Although few West Germans expect to achieve unity rapidly, fewer still are prepared to accept their country's division as permanent. Growing prosperity in the Federal Republic tends to magnify the uneasy feeling of guilt and responsibility. Any determined, perhaps demagogic, group could suddenly bring the issue to the fore. Coupled with setbacks in other fields, this could severely shake the political stability of the Federal Republic. A so-called Rapallo policy—a change of fronts toward the East—is extremely unlikely; but the consequences for the West would be serious enough if Germany thought that its national aspirations were being thwarted by the Alliance. The Soviet Union would then be able simultaneously to use a national appeal to Germany and an appeal based on the fear of Germany to the other Western countries.

Any policy on Germany must deal with three problems: (1) relations with the Soviet Union, including the complex of issues involved in any relaxation of tensions, (2) relations with the East Germany satellite regime and (3) relations with the East European governments. In all three respects the interests of the Western Allies and of the Federal Republic are potentially divergent; at the very least they must be carefully synchronized.

With respect to the detente, German concerns are often met with the argument that almost any measure that eases tensions also promotes German unification. According to this theory, once a policy of co-existence is firmly established, Eastern Germany may grow dispensable in Soviet eyes. As the Soviet Union begins to pursue more national policies, the ideological impetus for maintaining a Communist regime in Eastern Germany may decline.

However, it is dangerous to arouse German expectations that are not likely to be fulfilled. Arguments that a detente automatically furthers the cause of German unity must be balanced against others which, on the whole, seem more likely. A statesman can always escape his dilemmas by making the most favorable assumptions about the future. A wise policymaker will also consider the consequences if his hypothesis should turn out to be wrong. The Soviet Union, even if it becomes less committed ideologically, is unlikely to relinquish its hold on Eastern Germany simply as a result of an improvement in the international atmosphere. On the contrary, to the degree that a detente with the West exists, Soviet leaders may well calculate that concessions on the unification of Germany become unnecessary. The German concern that a detente may freeze the status quo in Germany is, therefore, not wholly unjustified.

Granting that the problem of German unification cannot be left to the more or less automatic operation of a detente, the question becomes how German unity is to be promoted: Is it a task for the Alliance as a whole or should the primary initiative come from the Federal Republic? Many leaders in both Washington and London seem to favor a more active role for the Federal Republic. They wish to avoid constant criticisms and to induce the Federal Republic to assume greater responsibility for its future.

But toward whom is the Federal Republic to assume these responsibilities? It would be highly desirable for the Federal Republic to participate more actively within the Alliance in formulating common policies on Germany's future. Some Western officials go further, however. They argue that the Federal Republic should take the lead in dealing with the East, principally with the East German satellite. They are convinced that increased contacts between the two Germanys will promote the erosion of the East German regime. According to this school of thought, the superior cohesiveness and strength of the Federal Republic will give it by far the stronger bargaining position. At a minimum, such negotiations may make life more bearable for the East German population. In time, the East German regime would become more humane, comparable perhaps to the Kadar government in Hungary.

Such reasoning has caused Western proposals for reunification gradually to move toward enhancing the status of the East German regime. In 1955, the Western plan still called for unification through free election. In 1959, a new plan called for a technical commission composed of twenty-five West and fifteen East Germans to engage in preliminary negotiations for a year. Decisions were to be taken by a majority of three-fourths, giving East Germany an effective veto. In the schemes of 1962, the composition of these commissions had become equal and the time limit of one year had been removed. Also in 1962, the West proposed an International Access Authority to Berlin, in which the East German regime was given equal status with the Federal Republic.

This policy has in recent years found support even in the Federal Republic. The West ·German government has accepted—albeit reluctantly—the principle of technical commissions in which East and West Germany would enjoy parity. Others in Germany have begun advocating a "policy of little steps" toward the East German regime. By this they mean agreements between the two German states leading to expanding cultural and perhaps economic ties. They argue that contacts between the two Germanys will carry the "bacillus of freedom" into the East and thus "infect" the East German satellite with Western values.

But enhancing the status of Eastern Germany is a dangerous course. It could lead to a situation where two German states will be competing for adherents all over the world; it could defer indefinitely any hope for unification. It is risky also because the bargaining position of the Federal Republic is precarious. In all such contacts, humanitarian concerns will outweigh political considerations. Even if these negotiations do not succeed in luring Germany out of its formal Western ties, they may produce a serious political split in the Federal Republic.

Germany's allies should not contribute to the already considerable confusion among three partly incompatible objectives: improvement of conditions in Eastern Germany, consolidation of the East German regime and progress toward German unification. Ameliorating conditions in Eastern Germany is desirable for humanitarian reasons. At the same time, it is likely to help the East German regime consolidate itself and thus make unification more remote except on East German terms. As the respectability of the

East German regime grows, the moral cost to the Soviets of maintaining the division of Germany is diminished. As the East German regime gains stature, its pressure on the Federal Republic will almost surely mount.

This process is likely to be gradual. While the East German regime is striving to establish its international status, its demands may be moderate. But once it is recognized —or even if its international status is substantially enhanced—it will have major incentives to seek to undermine the Federal Republic. It will, in fact, be driven to do so by its precarious position. National feelings in Eastern Germany, unlike those in Eastern Europe, are hostile to the existing government. In Poland, Hungary and Czechoslovakia patriotism can lead to the conclusion that the national interest is best served by liberalizing the existing governments. They seem to have become permanent; no focus for alternative loyalties exists. In East Germany, by contrast, national aspirations clash with the existence of a Communist regime. A prosperous, democratic West Germany acts as a powerful magnet. Thus the East German regime has every incentive to seek to weaken the Federal Republic, and it can use its own population as a hostage.

The superiority of West Germany's bargaining position —which is postulated by some American policymakers— may, therefore, be an illusion. On the contrary, German political leaders may find themselves facing a growing dilemma. In return for easing the fate of their population, the East Germans can demand concrete political gains. Confronted by popular pressures and moved by humanitarian impulses, no German government will find it easy to be dispassionate in deciding at what point an accumulation of seemingly marginal concessions has produced an irreversible trend. In turn, every West German concession to the German Democratic Republic will strengthen those in the West who favor recognition of that satellite regime. The result is more likely to be the indefinite continuation of two hostile, competing German states than progress toward unification.

To be sure, if German political leaders are determined to pursue this course, there is nothing we can do to prevent it. But we should make certain that the West cannot be blamed for the probable consequences. And we should do nothing to promote policies that may lead to a growing demoralization of the Federal Republic. In 1962, an "opening to the Left" in Italy was supposed to isolate and weaken the Communist Party. Instead it has undermined the center and opened the way to respectability for the Communists. The same role could be played in Germany by the policy of "technical contacts" or of "little steps" and with much more dangerous results.

Those in Washington and London who believe that the so-called "flexible" Germans will always follow their lead may, moreover, be in for some unpleasant surprises. The German version of flexibility could become indistinguishable from traditional nationalism. This mood was expressed by Berlin's Senator Hoppe at a convention of the Free Democratic Party. Criticizing the Western powers for insisting on their special prerogatives in West Berlin, Senator Hoppe said:

Our elementary national interest is paramount. We cannot be satisfied with safeguarding the status quo. Faith in the strength of the West, in its political superiority, in the inventiveness of the free world all can be maintained and strengthened only if we exercise initiative in that which we are free to act on in accordance with our national interests.[12]

Erich Mende, Vice Chancellor and FDP Minister for all-German affairs, later supported Hoppe. Unless relations are handled with great delicacy on both sides of the Atlantic, such an attitude carries within it the seeds of serious misunderstandings.

Finally, as German activity toward the East increases, the

[12] *Spandauer Volkszeitung,* September 13, 1964. I am indebted to Hans Speier, author of a forthcoming book on Germany, for calling my attention to this quotation.

fear of another Rapallo may create a vicious circle. Germany's Western neighbors will draw closer together; they may also seek to anticipate the Federal Republic by speeding up their own contacts with Moscow. This cannot be in the interest of either Atlantic or European cohesion; in the long run it will prove disastrous for the Federal Republic as well, because it may lead to its eventual isolation.

Only a united Atlantic Alliance facing jointly the issue of Germany's future can minimize the danger of a sharp conflict between Germany's national goals and its Atlantic ties. The effort to devise a common German policy is essential not only in order to retain Germany as a willing member of the Alliance, but also for the peace of Europe as well. It is against all probability that a large and dynamic country can be kept divided indefinitely in the center of the continent that gave the concept of nationalism to the world. As long as two German states exist, they are bound to interact with each other. If they consider that their social and political systems are incompatible, each will be driven to try to subvert the other. Since they contain the same basic population and a similar tradition, each has unusual scope for doing so. The Soviet formula that the two German states should settle their own future is a short-sighted, if clever, move to consolidate the status quo. It guarantees that sooner or later events will move beyond the control of either East or West—and perhaps of the Germans themselves. The permanent division of Germany into hostile, competing states is inherently dangerous. If Germany's neighbors to the East understand their own interests, they will realize that the present course may have the gravest long-term consequences.

If German unification is to be a central concern of the Alliance, a clarification of objectives is necessary. While the Federal Republic should not be urged into bilateral dealings with the East, it should be given every encouragement to make a major contribution to the formulation of an *Allied* position on Germany. When Foreign Minister Schroeder proposed to the NATO Ministers' Conferences of May and December 1964 that the three Western powers make new diplomatic overtures on behalf of German unification, he deserved a more positive reaction than he received. To be sure, the Western Allies were probably correct in their view that any proposal acceptable to the Federal Republic would not prove negotiable with the Soviet Union. But negotiability is only one criterion for diplomacy and not always the decisive one. If we can discuss only those items which the Soviets have declared negotiable, the agenda of any conference will be determined by them. On the issue of Germany, in particular, one purpose of Allied negotiations should be to demonstrate that, if no progress toward unification is made, the onus for it rests on the Soviets.

While the Allies should show greater understanding for the anguish of a divided country, the Federal Republic has to face the fact that German unity can become an active policy only if it is embodied in a concrete program. Heretofore Bonn has demanded support for German unification, but it has recoiled from encouraging a specific scheme to achieve it. It has feared that any proposal might involve provisions about Germany's frontiers and about limitations on German arms which would amount to unilateral concessions. Understandable as these concerns are, they run the risk of turning the issue of German unity into a largely rhetorical enterprise. Serious negotiations on German unity presuppose the willingness of the Alliance to develop a specific set of proposals.

A precondition of any negotiating program is an agreed strategy toward Eastern Germany. Specifically, should the West seek to ameliorate conditions in the so-called German Democratic Republic by increasing contacts with it or by isolating it? The latter course seems the most promising and the one most consistent with a long-term policy on German unification. This presupposes, however, an orchestration of the policy of the Allies with those of the Federal Republic toward the countries of Eastern Europe. Today the East German regime is being widely supported in Eastern Europe at least in part because of the historical fear of Germany and the memory of the Nazi occupation. The East European countries are much less committed to the existence of a Communist regime in East Germany than to a divided Germany, which may seem to them the best guarantee of their security. Though they cannot admit it, a unified Communist Germany might worry the East European states hardly less than any other powerful unified German state. There is reason to believe that the East German regime is despised in Eastern Europe; but this attitude cannot be fully exploited so long as the Federal Republic is not able to pursue a more active policy in Eastern Europe.

Heretofore, the Federal Republic has refused to maintain diplomatic relations with any government that recognizes the East German satellite. Recently the Federal Republic has sought to avoid the issue of the Hallstein Doctrine by establishing trade missions in Eastern Europe. One possible method for ameliorating the Hallstein Doctrine with respect to Eastern Europe would be for the Federal Republic to announce that in order to promote a final settlement it would establish diplomatic relations with all of Germany's neighbors, enabling it to bring about direct contact with Poland and Czechoslovakia. Such a policy will not in itself lead to unification. Nor will it make the East European countries abandon their preference for a divided Germany. It will, however, contribute to the isolation of East Germany and hence promote its demoralization. It is likely to reduce the already small East European incentive to support Soviet or East German pressures against exposed Western positions such as Berlin.

Regardless of how successful the West is in coordinating its approach to Eastern Europe and Eastern Germany, a specific plan for the unification of Germany will have to be developed. Any new approach to the problem of German unification should seek to escape the process whereby every succeeding Western plan has moved closer to the Soviet position. If every new Western proposal incorporates additional features of the Soviet proposals, no incentive for accepting any particular program exists. Imperceptibly the Soviet framework for German unity becomes established: that it be negotiated directly by the two German states, which is another way of saying that the East German satellite would be consolidated.

It is important that all concerned recognize that no plan on German unity can avoid a consideration of the difficult and sensitive problem of Germany's frontiers. This tragic issue has its origin in 1945, when the Potsdam Agreement placed the territories east of the Oder-Neisse line, which had been German for centuries, under Polish administration pending a final settlement in a peace treaty. Poland then proceeded to expel the 13 million Germans living there and to replace them with Polish settlers, mostly from Polish territories taken over by the Soviet Union. The Federal Republic has refused to accept the Oder-Neisse line as final. This is partly to retain a bargaining lever for an eventual peace conference, partly because of the pressure of the refugees from the disputed territories, most of whom now live in the Federal Republic.

The problem posed by the Oder-Neisse line is one of the human tragedies of our time. The reluctance of the Federal Republic to renounce territories which had been German for centuries is understandable. Moreover, there is something cynical about the insistent East European demand that the Federal Republic accept the eastern frontier of the East German satellite regime which, in turn, is recognized by all East European countries. The Eastern European countries obviously want to have it both ways: they prefer to keep Germany divided along the Elbe; but they also insist that the Federal Republic recognize the eastern frontier of the Soviet puppet regime on the Oder-Neisse. These inconsistencies complicate a meaningful discussion.

Nevertheless, even granting all these obstacles, the perpetuation of German claims to the territories east of the Oder-Neisse line complicates progress on the issue of unification. It provides the Soviets with a convenient excuse for maintaining their hold on Eastern Germany; it cements Soviet relations with Eastern Europe. Reluctance to cede a claim to territories that no longer contain any German settlers contributes to perpetuating foreign rule over 17 million Germans between the Elbe and the Oder-Neisse line. The refusal to face the issue of the Polish border guarantees that the frontier of free Germany will remain on the Elbe.

To be sure, it is an important tactical question at what point the Federal Republic should renounce its claims. It is possible to sympathize with the reluctance to offer such a painful sacrifice gratuitously. But it is essential to recognize that acceptance by Germany of its eastern frontiers will have to be part of any responsible program for unification. Unification is impossible so long as it is considered an inevitable prelude to a new set of pressures in Eastern Europe.

Thus three factors must be reconciled in any plan for Germany's future: (1) the German desire for self-determination, (2) the East European concern for security and (3) the Soviet concern lest a unified Germany impair its own security and shake its international position. These objectives are, of course, incompatible to some extent. A great deal depends on whether it proves possible to convince those most concerned that to strive for absolutes will lead first to stagnation and ultimately to crisis.

For present purposes it is not necessary to offer a detailed program; rather, the primary need is to agree on a new concept. One possible course would be to separate the issue of self-determination from that of unification for an interim period, say fifteen years. Pressure for immediate unification consolidates all opponents of Germany in Eastern Europe and *sub rosa* in Western Europe as well. Self-determination, on the other hand, is a moral imperative commanding wide consensus. If rejected by the Communists, it would place them at least morally on the defensive.

Such a proposal could take the following form: The Western countries, including the Federal Republic, could declare that, while the unification of Germany remains the ultimate goal, their immediate aim is to enable the population of East Germany to choose the form of government it prefers. The Western Allies could, therefore, declare their willingness to acquiesce in the existence of an East German state provided its government emerges from a process of free elections. For a period of fifteen years the territory now called the German Democratic Republic would have a status similar to that of present-day Austria. A loose confederation could be established between the two German states, but East Germany would be independent, neutral and demilitarized. For a period of ten years, the existing economic obligations of the present German Democratic Republic to the East European countries, including the Soviet Union, could be maintained. After that period, these links would depend on normal negotiations with the government then in office in East Germany.

A commission composed of the European neutrals, Sweden, Switzerland, Austria and perhaps Finland, would monitor the free elections and the demilitarization provisions of the treaty. After a period of fifteen years, there would be a plebiscite supervised by the same commission to determine whether East Germany wanted to continue as a separate state in loose confederation with the Federal Republic or whether it preferred unification. In either case, East Germany would remain demilitarized. Both German states would recognize the existing frontiers of Germany, including the Oder-Neisse line. After the neutral commission certified that the government of East Germany was freely elected, Berlin could become the capital of that state as well as the seat of the organs of the German confederation. No further reason to maintain Berlin as a separate political entity would exist.

After a freely elected government has been installed in East Germany, Soviet troops would be withdrawn from that country. Within the Federal Republic foreign troops would retire a distance roughly equal to that between the Elbe and the Oder. The number of West German troops in that belt would be limited. The Federal Republic would renounce access to the ownership of nuclear weapons.

Even if there were agreement in principle, many details would remain to be worked out: for example, the precise definition of demilitarization or what international undertakings would be consistent with the neutral status of the new state. But once the direction of an "Austrian" solution for East Germany is taken, the advantages would be plain: while Germany would have to defer full unification for fifteen years, the German states that emerged would no longer be antagonistic. There would be opportunity for conditions within Germany to be equalized gradually. A foreign regime detested by the population would be removed. The East European states would gain the security of a divided Germany for fifteen years and a demilitarized belt along their borders for the indefinite future. The East European economies could adjust to the loss of the East German partner over a ten-year period. The Berlin problem would be solved. Germany's frontiers would be settled both juridically and psychologically because the generation that was expelled from Eastern Europe would have largely disappeared by the time Germany was unified. Arms control schemes for Europe could be considered in a new atmosphere.

The price, of course, would be high. The Federal Republic would have to defer its hopes for immediate unification in return for agreement on a terminal date to the division of Germany. The Soviet Union would have to be prepared to give up the hope of a Communist Germany. The East European governments would have to change their policy of acquiescing in what seems most expedient to their senior partner. The Western Allies would have to overcome inertia and place the problem of Germany high on their agenda.

But the rewards would be great. Such a program would

end a situation that is bound to become more dangerous the longer it lasts. It would allow a more objective analysis of arms control in Europe. The construction of Europe could be placed on a sounder basis. Even were such a program rejected initially by the Soviets, it would change the framework of negotiations. Rather than begin with enhancing the status of the East German regime, as is the case with current schemes, the new program would focus attention on its oppressiveness as the principal obstacle to unification. By taking a stand on the issue of self-determination, the West would have a platform most likely to command international support. By separating self-determination from unification, an interim period for adjustments and a framework for meeting legitimate security concerns of Germany's neighbors are provided.

Nevertheless, it is improbable that any negotiating formula will advance German unity. Even the most reasonable program is likely to be rejected by the East. The long-term hope for German unity therefore resides in the unity of Europe. As nations lose their former significance, the fear of any'one state will diminish. A united Western Europe moreover will be a powerful magnet for the countries of Eastern Europe. If an all-embracing European structure ever comes to pass, the existing dividing lines may seem less crucial.

This is why the existing rift in the West is so unfortunate. The practical result of the Franco-American rivalry is that each ally is tempted to add the Federal Republic to its side by holding out vague hopes and grandiose schemes for the achievement of Germany's maximum objectives. German leaders will be torn by the conflicting demands of their allies and their own national aspirations. The West, which has so often been rent by internal struggles, stands in danger of repeating its historic folly. Paris may have thought that by committing the Federal Republic to a treaty of special friendship it was braking temptations of nationalism and providing for the construction of Europe. Washington's attitude toward the Treaty of Collaboration was motivated by a desire to combat Third Force tendencies. These competing efforts stand in danger of producing what they seek to prevent; the attempt to use Germany as a balance wheel will complete the fragmentation of the Atlantic Alliance.

The best hope to prevent a latent nihilism in Germany from again menacing the West is to give the Federal Republic a stake in something larger than itself. The future of the Federal Republic depends on two related policies by the West: (1) recognition of the psychological and political dilemmas of a divided country and (2) the ability to make the Federal Republic part of a larger community. These policies are interdependent; to pursue one without the other is to defeat both. It is to the construction of this larger community that we must now turn.

Chapter Eight

WHAT KIND OF ATLANTIC PARTNERSHIP?

Two solutions are usually offered for enhancing Allied cohesion: (1) an improvement in the process of consultation and (2) the development of a united Europe with federal, supranational institutions as the precondition for an Atlantic partnership.

THE PROBLEM OF CONSULTATION

The inherently difficult problem of coalition diplomacy is magnified under present conditions by three factors:

1. The firm commitment of the United States and the U.S.S.R. to the existing balance of power provides their allies with increasing scope for purely national actions.

2. The internal workings of modern government are so complex that they create a variety of obstacles to meaningful consultation. Nations sometimes find it so difficult to achieve a domestic consensus that they are reluctant to jeopardize it afterward in international forums. The American tendency to confine consultation to an elaboration of its own blueprints often reflects a desire to avoid

complicating still further our own increasingly complex decision-making process.

3. As governments have found in their own domestic experience, access to the same technical data does not guarantee unanimity. In an alliance of states very unequal in size and strength, differences are almost certain to arise. And they are likely to be intensified because the histories of the states vary widely and because of a technology of unprecedented destructiveness and novelty.

The American historical experience causes our policy-makers to be reluctant to admit that the process of consultation may have objective limits. United States society, with its large area of consensus, encourages the belief that all problems are soluble through goodwill and a willingness to compromise. A rationalistic streak produces a conviction that there are single, universally valid answers to most problems and that agreement is sure to emerge if the interested parties gather around a table. This creates a temptation to conduct Alliance diplomacy as if it were analogous to the domestic policy of stable societies.

However, the most difficult issues of coalition diplomacy are more complicated. Differences in history, geography and domestic structure become relevant. The analogy to domestic policy breaks down.

In stable societies, domestic decisions tend to be accepted because there is a consensus on legitimacy. Those who are overruled generally consider maintenance of domestic order more important than any particular grievance; if they do not, domestic policy acquires some of the characteristics and sanctions of foreign policy and, in extreme cases, leads to civil war. In stable societies those who are overruled retain the hope of winning another round later or of influencing the implementation of the decision. In democracies, there exists the possibility of changing the government with the next election.

In a coalition of sovereign states, these safety valves are not available. Legitimacy resides in the individual governments. Decisions require their consent—this is the essence of sovereignty. Even when they agree to be bound by majority vote—a rare occurrence in coalitions and not the case with NATO—their sovereignty implies the right to renounce the treaty. In short, those who dissent and are prepared to insist on their sovereignty cannot be bound indefinitely.

If fundamental differences among sovereign allies persist, the partners are torn between the desire to maintain the appearance of unity and the attempt to vindicate their views. The need to present a façade of harmony has at least three consequences: (1) It puts a limit on the sanctions that can be applied to a recalcitrant ally. (2) One of the few pressures available is to mobilize domestic pressures against an obstructive partner, thus multiplying resentments. (3) Because misgivings are sometimes subordinated to an appearance of amity, the real views of the governments cannot always be deduced from their formal statements. Simultaneously—and somewhat contradictorily—a premium is placed on intransigence. Ruthless allies can use their partners' desire for harmony to impose a desired course. But if this happens too frequently, there is a dangerous build-up of frustration that cannot be smothered indefinitely by declarations of friendship. This has been happening in the Atlantic Alliance.

Consultation, therefore, is far from a panacea. It is least effective when it is most needed: when there exist basic differences of assessment or of interest. It works best in *implementing* a consensus rather than in *creating* it. Nevertheless, an improvement in the consultative process should be one of the primary objectives of the Alliance.

Many American schemes for strengthening NATO have taken the form of making our predominant position psychologically more acceptable; we try to create a structure which physically prevents any ally (except the United States) from acting autonomously. This tends to turn our Allies into advisors in an American decision-making process. It then becomes relevant to inquire whether such a system serves the long-term political vitality of the Alliance.

The effectiveness of any process of consultation is tested by the answers to the following questions: Who has a right to be consulted? Whose voice carries weight? Who has technical competence? These three questions do not necessarily have identical answers. Many agencies in our own government have a right to be heard, but not all have the same influence. When some Europeans ask for a greater voice in our decisions in return for giving up some of their military autonomy, the issue they raise is: compared to whose voice *within* the United States government? That of the Arms Control and Disarmament Agency? Or the Joint Chiefs of Staff? Or the State Department? Or the Commerce Department? In our interdepartmental disputes, the outcome is clearly affected by the constituency that the agency or department represents. The weight given to advice is related to the competence that it reflects and this in turn depends on how seriously a given department takes its role.

These considerations apply even more strongly in an alliance of sovereign states. The challenge is not only to provide a forum for the expression of a point of view—important as this is—but also to bring about a framework which encourages the emergence of responsible attitudes. Setting up lines of communication without paying corresponding attention to what flows through them is to evade the key problem. If the United States insists on retaining a dominant position and complete freedom of action—if integration becomes in practice an exegesis of American schemes—we will probably find that the political will of Europe will eventually be broken. Before a government makes a major effort to acquire the competence necessary for developing a serious point of view, it must be convinced that its views matter not only by the grace of a senior ally but also because of structural necessities.

American policy has not always been sensitive to the

psychological prerequisites for effective consultation. It generally holds that influence in the Alliance is apportioned as in a stock company: the partner with the largest number of shares in a common enterprise is supposed to have the greatest influence.

Influence is, of course, an intangible quality. However, to measure it entirely in terms of contribution to a common effort is much too mechanical. President de Gaulle, with his disconcerting habit of cutting through slogans to the underlying reality, has put his finger on the fact that as long as NATO is an alliance of sovereign states, a too literal conception of "integration" can easily lead to an evasion of responsibility. Difficult decisions can be avoided, and failure can be blamed on other allies. Even a major effort may not result in a corresponding increase in influence. In an alliance of sovereign states, a country's influence requires that its effort be considered essential and that its partners do not take it for granted. In determining an ally's real—as opposed to his formal—role, one can do worse than inquire what its choices are in case of disagreement. To combine technical integration with insistence on sovereignty can in time erode the moral basis of joint action.

Heretofore, American policy has assumed that the chief obstacle to close United States-European cooperation on a global scale is that the resources of the European nation-state are inadequate for the requirements of the modern age. According to this school of thought, the political integration of Europe will solve the problem of Allied consultation. A united Europe will be prepared to share world-wide burdens which a Europe of national states is reluctant to assume. Under Secretary of State Ball has expressed the American view as follows:

The problem will never be fully solved until Europe gets on further with the achievement of its own unity—until it organizes itself on a scale commensurate with the requirements of the age.

There are quite obvious reasons for this. The undertaking of world responsibility requires a world view. The discharge of such responsibility under post-colonial conditions must be based on the command of vast resources for defense and foreign aid—and on the will to use them. Western Europe collectively has more than enough resources, but a fragmented Europe cannot efficiently mobilize them in support of a common effort and a common view.[1]

The nature of world responsibility is rarely defined; it is assumed to be self-evident. Thus, United States Ambassador to Germany, George McGhee, spoke as follows:

This [Atlantic partnership] entails increasing contributions in formerly remote areas like Vietnam and Central Africa from countries which, like Germany, have only recently acquired the ability to contribute.[2]

American policy seems to consider that its goals in these areas are in the common interest and, therefore, beyond challenge; what it desires is a sharing of the cost.

But is it really true that willingness to assume global responsibilities is related to availability of resources? The American national experience would seem to contradict this assumption. Through the greatest part of its history, the United States possessed the resources but not the inclination to play a global role. Conversely many European states maintained overseas commitments when their resources were much smaller than they are today.

For many European countries, the combination of decolonization and two world wars has been traumatic. Having been forced to relinquish their overseas possessions, they no longer consider that their security is *directly* affected by what happens in, for example, Southeast Asia.

[1] George W. Ball, "NATO and World Responsibility," *The Atlantic Community Quarterly*, Vol. 2, No. 2 (Summer 1964), p. 216.

[2] George C. McGhee, "Some American Thoughts on Current Issues," speech on July 16, 1964, *DOSB*, Vol. LI, No. 1310 (August 3, 1964), p. 138.

Rather than run the risk of nuclear destruction on behalf of a distant area from which they have been recently ejected, they prefer to shift the risks and the burdens to us. They are reasonably sure that long before upheavals in other continents threaten the safety of Europe, the United States will have entered the fray. In other words, they treat America's extra-European concerns in much the same way that the United States looked at Europe's quarrels until 1941.

This problem is not eliminated by drawing distinctions —often moralistic in tone—between "responsibility" and "interest." Under Secretary Ball, echoing similar statements by Secretary Rusk, has argued that:

We Americans have few national interests—in the narrow sense—outside our own territory but we have assumed vast world responsibility. . . . The willingness to accept world responsibility—as distinct from the preservation of national interests—is, in our observation and experience, not universal among the NATO membership.[8]

Aside from the fact that our European Allies are likely to consider a "disinterested" foreign policy as both mercurial and unsteady, the distinction misses the central point. The chief reason for the reluctance of most of our Allies to assume world responsibility is precisely that in the past decade they have been obliged to give up their global interests. Sharing our burdens would give impetus to Atlantic cooperation only if our Allies have the same view as we of what is at stake outside of Europe and if they believe that the United States would curtail its commitments but for their assistance. Neither condition is met today. The very commitment of the United States to a global role—our often-invoked sense of world responsibility—reduces the incentive of our Allies to share in it, much as the commitment of Britain and France to the European balance of power permitted the United States

---

[8] Ball, "NATO and World Responsibility," *op. cit.*, p. 215.

to evade the problems of security in the period before 1941.

Thus, European unity is not a major cure-all for Atlantic disagreements. In many respects it may magnify rather than reduce differences. As Europe gains structure, it will be in a better position to insist on differences whose ultimate cause is structural rather than personal. Phrases like "indivisible interest" are correct when applied to the defense of Europe or East-West relations; they come close to being platitudes in other parts of the world. A wise Alliance policy will not gear everything to the expectation that common positions can be developed on a global basis; it will also take account of the fact that the interests of Europe and America are not identical everywhere.

This fact is relevant to any assessment of the degree of integration of Atlantic policy which it is in our interest to promote. Over the next decades the United States is likely to find itself increasingly engaged in the Far East, in Southeast Asia and in Latin America. Our European Allies will almost certainly consider that their vital interests are not at stake in these areas. If Atlantic policy is completely centralized, it may grow stagnant. The Alliance will be able to agree only on doing nothing. Or else, it will engage in a series of pretenses. The behavior of our Allies toward American requests for assistance in Vietnam is a good example. The Soviets may use our involvements in other continents as a pretext to blackmail Europe. This, combined with the lack of interest among Europeans in the issues involved, may strain the Alliance beyond the breaking point.

Looking beyond the immediate future, it is not difficult to visualize an increasingly powerful China fomenting the already strong tendencies toward turmoil in other parts of the world. If we insist on remaining the sole trustee of policy everywhere, including Europe, the strain on our resources and ingenuity may well be too great. The day will come when we will consider a measure of autonomy in Europe a blessing rather than an irritant. In this century no one could have foreseen at the beginning of any decade what the world would look like at its end. Things have not grown less complicated or more predictable. Those centers of initiative which still exist should not be discouraged. It is not always the least responsible allies that wish to reserve some measure of control over their destiny.

If we face the fact that the interests of Europe and the United States are not identical everywhere, it may be possible to agree on a permissible range of divergence. Each partner will regain a measure of flexibility. The temptation for Soviet adventures might be reduced. Europe could assume greater responsibility for its defense and its future. Put positively, the Atlantic Alliance will have to decide whether to emphasize immediate convenience or long-term political vitality. At any given point of time, centralization of decisions guarantees the greatest degree of coordination. Critics of such schemes can always be put on the defensive by being accused of fomenting distrust. In the long term, however, excessive concentration of decision-making in the hands of the senior partner may deprive our Allies of the incentive to be responsible and it may create profound fissures when a conflict of interest becomes apparent.

This suggests that the vitality of the Alliance would be served by an Allied structure which makes possible a variety of coordinated approaches on some issues. For responsible attitudes to emerge, participants in a consultative process must do more than simply advise. Influencing another country's actions—however benevolent the dominant partner may be—will be demoralizing in the long run. If coalition diplomacy becomes largely an exercise in affecting essentially American decisions, most of our Allies will lose the incentive to make responsible judgments. The type of leader comfortable with such a relationship may be only too ready to shift the burden of difficult choices to our shoulders; this very quality may make him unreliable when he is most needed in times of crisis. For decisions to be meaningful, our Allies must consider them their own, not ours.

Paradoxically, some autonomy in political decisions for Europe is psychologically important for the cohesion of the Alliance. Though this proposition will be granted by most American policymakers in the abstract, they tend to resist independence when it takes the form of challenging our judgments. A decade and a half of hegemony have accustomed us to believing that our views represent the general interest. The difficulty with which decisions are reached in our government produces temptations to turn Allied consultation into an effort to implement essentially American conceptions.

Nevertheless, the future well-being of the Alliance depends on our willingness to adjust the pattern of relationships which grew up after the war. Though historically we are the children of Europe, with respect to the postwar evolution we are somewhat in the position of a father toward a grown-up son. He can always take the attitude that, since their interests are identical, he will continue to control all the resources. He can challenge the son to name circumstances in which their interests might differ. He can tell him that no legitimate request will ever go unheeded. Such an attitude will either drive the son to open rebellion or, if accepted, will break his spirit.

Since the war Europe has been first nurtured and then protected by us. Now we require wisdom and delicacy in handling the transition from tutelage to equality. Grandiose schemes of great technical complexity may magnify inward insecurities. What is needed is a recognition that it is in the long-term interest of the United States to share responsibilities even more than burdens. This will involve a painful loss of some of our former pre-eminence—a process to which no nation has ever adjusted easily. The assertions of European self-will which we find so irritating today can be the growing pains of a new and healthier relationship which ultimately is important for us as well.

In too much of the current dialogue we offer our good intentions as a guarantee of the validity of our actions. But the nature of our intentions is not at issue. It is important for us to realize that our style and our commitment which have been responsible for so many constructive measures can also dissolve the identity of others. Our optimism makes us press for final answers to any problem. These often take the form of abstract models in which other nations are considered interchangeable entities. Our pragmatism produces a willingness to try everything once and a restless quest for ever "new" remedies. Thus, sudden changes in our policy are not uncommon—witness the checkered career of the MLF. Decisions within our government are influenced by a combination of bureaucratic pressures in which the immediate often predominates over the long-term.

All of this can make our impact undermine the sense of responsibility of even close allies. Most societies lack the cohesiveness for the restless quest for novelty which seems natural to us. The constant adjustment of policies to differing pressures can be demoralizing for countries whose margin for maneuver is more limited. What appears as open-mindedness to us may be seen as unsteadiness by others. The fluctuations in our German policy from impatient aloofness in 1961 to ardent wooing in 1963 to a more distant policy in 1965; the changes in the MLF from indifference to passionate advocacy to aloof goodwill in the space of three years; the frequent alterations of our strategic doctrine; the tendency of our bureaucracy to conduct their internal battles by lining up support in foreign capitals—all suggest that it is necessary even for the stability of our own policy to have self-confident partners with a strongly developed sense of identity. Reluctant as we may be to admit it, we could benefit from a counterweight to discipline our occasional impetuosity and to supply historical perspective to our penchant for abstract and "final" solutions. The real case for European autonomy is not burden-sharing but the establishing of a psychological balance between us and Europe.

For centuries one of the most difficult problems of Western political thought has been how to reconcile unity with respect for diversity. Overemphasis on either unity or diversity destroys the delicate balance of creativity. Excessive stress on unity leads to a deadening conformism; exalting diversity as an end produces a relativism hostile to great conceptions and, on the political level, an overconcern with national peculiarities. To strike this balance is the big unsolved problem before the Western Alliance.

THE GRAND DESIGN AND EUROPEAN INTEGRATION

Since the war and with increasing emphasis since 1961, the United States has argued that the most effective structure for Atlantic cooperation is a partnership between the United States and a united, supranational Europe. "When one partner possesses over 50 per cent of the resources of an enterprise and the balance is distributed among sixteen or seventeen others, the relationship is unlikely to work very well."[4] Real partnership, according to American spokesmen, is possible only among equals.

As a result, American pronouncements have often assumed that before Europe could be an effective partner of the United States it would have to unify. This concept of Atlantic partnership, strongly urged also by such wise Europeans as Jean Monnet, has been described by the image of "twin pillars" or "dumbbell." Former Secretary of State Herter has written:

I believe the present Administration [the Kennedy Administration] . . . holds the . . . view, which has come to be termed the "dumbbell" concept—meaning that an

[4] George W. Ball, "Toward an Atlantic Partnership," speech to the World Affairs Council of Philadelphia, February 6, 1962, *DOSB*, Vol. XLVI, No. 1184 (March 5, 1962), p. 366.

economic and political alliance is stronger if it has been agreed to by partners of equal weight on both sides.[5]

The European side of this partnership is to be a United States of Europe organized on federal lines with supranational institutions.

There is no doubt that the dumbbell concept represents one form of Atlantic partnership. But an excessive, almost doctrinaire commitment to it runs the risk of treating a symbol as the only possible reality. This may cause us to beg the key questions by the very terms in which we state them.

The single-mindedness with which the dumbbell concept has been pursued obscures three questions: Is it true that partnership is possible only among equals? What has been the real progress toward European political integration? To what extent is it in the American interest to promote one form of European unity to the exclusion of other possible plans?

Given the nature of America's relations with the rest of the world, it seems strange that partnership should be said to be possible only among equals. The assertion that we can deal effectively only with countries of equal strength is not conducive to inspiring confidence among the great majority of the nations of the world which are weak.

Granting that a strong and united Europe is on balance in our best interest, we must nevertheless inquire whether it is wise—either from the point of view of Europe or of the United States—to insist that there is only one reliable method of bringing about that unity: that of federal, supranational institutions. In the aftermath of De Gaulle's abrupt rejection of Britain's membership in the Common Market, it has become almost a commonplace that the willful act of a single individual interrupted what would otherwise have been a smooth advance toward political integration. According to this view, once Britain would

[5] Christian Herter, "Atlantica," *Foreign Affairs*, Vol. 41, No. 2 (January 1963), p. 301.

have entered the Common Market, an "outward-looking"
Europe would have emerged. Progress toward supranational political institutions would have been continuous.
In the opinion of the "integrationists" in Europe and in the
State Department, European unity would have been promoted by a "community spirit," which in turn was to be
fostered by supranational commissions. Expert judgment
unaffected by considerations of national interest was to
move European political integration forward, step-by-
step, toward a final culmination in which the supranational authorities would be dominant. All this is said to
have been destroyed by De Gaulle's abrupt exclusion of
Britain from the Common Market.

However, no man could have single-handedly brought
about the consequences ascribed to De Gaulle. Significant
underlying factors must have been operating to obstruct
the idealized progression envisaged by the European integrationists on both sides of the Atlantic. It was always
somewhat unrealistic to imagine that the methods by
which economic integration had been achieved could be
applied automatically to the political arena. The "community" approach—which equates method and purpose—
works best when the objective is clear. It answers the question of how a common objective can be realized. It is
much less useful in *defining* this objective.

In the aftermath of World War II, this was obscured
because Europe had been so shattered by the war that
immediate needs were overwhelming. Leaders did not
think that their problem was to choose among different
objectives; on the contrary, the task of meeting minimum
necessities absorbed all their energies. Most countries on
the Continent had governments so weak or were so eager
to overcome a past—or both—that an abdication of some
of their sovereignty seemed a respite from overwhelming
uncertainties. For many in Europe, economic activity became a means to avoid facing nearly insoluble moral or
political issues. And the economic imperatives were so

urgent that the governments were only too glad to turn them over to supranational experts.[6]

As Europe recovered economically, political confidence returned as well. Inevitably this strengthened the national state, the traditional repository of European loyalties. This process took place with varying intensity in each country. Germany and Italy, partly to escape their past, were more ready to submerge themselves in a federal Europe than Britain and France. Smaller countries accustomed to the protection of some major power had less difficulty with the supranational concept than those that had been major powers themselves. France and Great Britain—with the longest history as national states—have consistently aimed for a confederal, rather than a federal, solution; that is, a structure that preserves the identity of the states and in which decisions will be made, at least initially, on the basis of agreement among governments. Four years before De Gaulle came to power, the abortive European Defense Community demonstrated the obstacles faced by a supranational approach to political integration.

But if De Gaulle cannot fairly be charged with being the sole obstacle to European integration on the federal model, he is responsible for confusing the debate about the future of Europe in at least two ways: (1) The controversy between the federalists and the confederalists has become a test of attitudes toward De Gaulle. The line-up is not a reliable guide to the real views of the participants because many who strongly oppose De Gaulle's style and domestic policy are in agreement with him about the organization of Europe. (2) Some of the most ardent advocates of Britain's entry into the Common Market are also dedicated proponents of a federal Europe, which is as unacceptable in London as in Paris. Thus opponents of European integration have often combined forces with

[6] For a splendid discussion of the problem of Europe's identity see Stanley Hoffmann, "Europe's Identity Crisis: Between the Past and America," *Daedalus*, Vol. 93, No. 4 (Fall 1964).

dedicated advocates of it to advance sweeping schemes
certain to be vetoed by the French President.

This confusion has been magnified by the role of the
United States. Our strong support of supranational, federal institutions has contributed to the stalemate in European discussions. While not sufficient to bring about our
preferred solution, our influence is strong enough to block
approaches with which we disagree. Moreover, despite
our ardent support for European unity, our impact has
often been the contrary of what was intended. While
affirming the need for European integration, we have un-
intentionally tended to undermine a European sense of
identity.

During the long period of American predominance, a
group of experts comfortable with the existing relationship
has grown up on both sides of the Atlantic. Having worked
well together for many years, they tend to see problems
from the same perspective. Though they generally favor
European integration, they consider the quest for European autonomy inherently divisive. According to them, if
United States policy is wise, European autonomy will be
unnecessary. If United States policy is mistaken, an independent European policy would only magnify the problem. Thus, both in Europe and the United States, many
who urge European integration balk at the prospect of an
autonomous European policy—which is one of the likely
results of European integration.

This attitude is particularly noticeable in the field of
defense. Were Europe thrown on itself, it would probably
unite sufficiently to assure its security. It clearly has the
potential to do so. But, having been sheltered by American power for nearly two decades, many Europeans are
concerned that the emergence of an autonomous Europe
in the area of defense will undermine the American
guarantee and force them into assuming direct responsibilities. American pronouncements sometimes encourage
this concern. The threat to withdraw American forces has
been used to obtain European support for American

strategic preferences. Proposals such as the MLF have the practical consequence of preventing the emergence of a European point of view on nuclear matters. These American attitudes have inhibited a European quest for autonomy; they have also caused some advocates of European identity in the defense field to give their case an anti-American cast.

These tendencies are reinforced by the fact that some Europeans prefer an Atlantic structure based on the existing NATO states to a united Europe. The smaller countries in particular fear that European integration will result in the hegemony of powerful neighbors. They see no advantage in European autonomy. Since they must follow the lead of a dominant country in any event, they prefer the hegemony of an ally 3,000 miles away and with a tradition of using its power with restraint. Consequently, these countries are a ready-made constituency for schemes to perpetuate the relationship between Europe and the United States that developed after the war.

In short, American policy has been extremely ambivalent: it has urged European unity while recoiling before its probable consequences. We have sought to combine a supranational Europe with a closely integrated Atlantic Community under American leadership. These objectives are likely to prove incompatible. Indeed, the United States will have to reconcile itself to the fact that no matter what structure emerges in Europe, a difference in perspective with the United States is probable, particularly about policies outside of Europe. A wise policy will try to mitigate the impact of this difference; it will not be able to remove it.

This latent difference could well be accentuated by the manner in which European unity is achieved. History teaches that the more abrupt the political transitions, the more drastic have to be the efforts to reestablish some sort of cohesion. A Europe that grows out of the collapse of all traditional loyalties must have as its primary problem the discovery of some specific purpose for its existence.

Too doctrinaire an approach to European unity could produce either a collapse of political will or, more likely, a new and virulent form of nationalism, perhaps even more intense than the nationalism of *patries*. A Europe constructed largely on theoretical models might be forced into an anti-American mold because its only sense of identity could be what distinguished it from America.

It is hard to understand why many European federalists believe that a European parliament would mitigate this danger. The decline in the role of the European national parliaments has been apparent for decades. In no European country—not even Great Britain—does parliament exercise an effective control over the formulation or the conduct of foreign policy. Party discipline has become so pervasive that in European parliaments the majority almost always ratifies the decisions of the cabinet. And where the party system is ineffective—either because the parties are weak or because there are too many of them—the result is paralysis of government rather than parliamentary control. These conditions are likely to be magnified by all-European elections. The need to establish a consensus comprising Schleswig-Holstein and Sicily, Scotland and Bavaria will surely tempt demagogic appeals.

In any event, the real issue is not the institutions but the composition of a united Europe. An effective Europe cannot be built without the whole-hearted support of Great Britain. As long as Britain stands on the sidelines, uncertain about its direction and undecided about its European role, any solution will be partial. Symbolic and substantive measures will be confused. Many in Europe will be wary of British proposals because they fear that they are intended to undermine a European sense of identity. This is most noticeable in the field of nuclear control, but it applies in all other areas of policy as well. "Atlantic" and "European" conceptions will be viewed as alternatives rather than as complementary. This will produce a schism in many countries, most obviously in the Federal Republic. As long as Britain does not make a commitment to the unity of Europe, the thrust of most current policies will be either to isolate Britain or to isolate France.

To be sure, Britain was prevented from entering the Common Market by a French veto. But it is also clear that Britain's ambivalence contributed to this outcome and that it has been uncertain about its relations with Europe for the entire postwar period. Exclusion from the Common Market cannot prevent a major British contribution to the political construction of Europe if Britain is prepared to exercise leadership. Until Britain is ready for this role, debates about the relative merits of federalism and confederalism are academic.

This suggests that the future of a united Europe depends more on developments in London, Paris and Bonn than on strictures from Washington. The United States should therefore leave the internal evolution of a united Europe to the Europeans and use its ingenuity and influence in devising new forms of *Atlantic* cooperation. The passionate commitment of so many American policymakers to a single formula of European integration, that of supranationality, could in fact bring about results quite contrary to those intended. Many European federalists have been devoted adherents of Atlantic partnership; Jean Monnet, their most significant figure, has been a staunch and remarkable friend of the United States. By contrast, President de Gaulle's career is filled with examples of abrupt and unilateral tactics designed to exalt the status of France, occasionally at our expense. It would be one of history's frequent ironies if the structure for Europe proposed by Monnet would generate the greatest pressures for the kind of policy generally described as Gaullist, while the structure advocated by De Gaulle turned out to be best suited for flexible Atlantic arrangements. Our bent for structural remedies sometimes blinds us to the fact that institutions produce their own momentum, which cannot necessarily be foreseen from the intentions of their founders.

While the United States should welcome any unified

Europe that reflects the desires of Europeans, it is doubtful that either our national or Atlantic interests require
our passionate commitment to a supranational structure
for Europe. A very schematic and rigid conception of Atlantic partnership can easily fail to do justice to the rich-
ness and variety of relationships possible within the
Atlantic context. Is each European country always inherently closer to its European neighbors than to the
United States? If we separate the question into political,
military or economic components, is the answer always
uniform and does it always point in the same direction?
Would it not be wiser to retain some flexibility?

There may be various roads to European unity. The
one traced by the Fouchet Plan—calling for institution-
alized meetings of foreign ministers and subcabinet officials—is not the least plausible, and indeed it is the one
most consistent with British participation. It has the advantage that it would produce some immediate progress
without foreclosing the future and thus would put an end
to the process of demanding the desirable in order to defeat the attainable. It would also permit a more flexible
arrangement of Atlantic relations than the "twin pillar"
concept now in vogue. A confederal Europe would enable
the United States to maintain an influence at many centers
of decision rather than be forced to stake everything on
affecting the views of a single, supranational body.

European history demonstrates that stability in Europe
is unattainable except through the cooperation of Britain,
France and Germany. Care should be taken not to resur-
rect old national rivalries in the name of Atlanticism. The
United States should not single out one ally as its special
partner. The attempt to force allies to choose between us
and France—a tendency which, despite all disavowals, is
real—must magnify the European nationalism that French
policy has already done so much to foster.

Our concern thus returns to the somewhat out-of-scale
figure of President de Gaulle. Conceivably he is as petty
and as animated by remembered slights as some of our

commentators suggest. It is also possible that a man so conscious of his historic role has larger purposes. In a period of detente with the Soviet Union, it should not be impossible to conduct a serious conversation with a traditional ally. President de Gaulle has repeatedly expressed his willingness to coordinate strategy rather than to integrate it. It is a welcome sign of progress that, at the NATO meeting of December 1964, Secretary McNamara and French Defense Minister Messmer agreed on a procedure to begin exploring what this means with respect to strategic nuclear forces.

But a more fundamental dialogue is needed. Irritation with De Gaulle's tactics does not change the fact that in his proposal of 1958 for a Directorate he pointed out what has remained the key problem of NATO: If the Atlantic Alliance is to retain any vitality, it requires a common foreign policy—or at least an agreed range of divergence. In its absence, the attempt to devise a common military strategy is likely to prove futile. As long as the Alliance cannot agree even on a common trade policy toward the East, it will be impossible to convince the Allies to relinquish their freedom of action over decisions affecting their very survival. Lord Avon and Dean Acheson have come to the same conclusion. The time seems ripe to create a political body at the highest level for concerting the policies of the nations bordering the North Atlantic.

Organizational devices should never be confused with substantive solutions. Nevertheless the following outline could serve as an illustration of a desirable direction if not as a detailed blueprint for action. The political body could be constituted as an Executive Committee of the NATO Council. It could be composed of six members: five permanent members (the United States, Great Britain, France, the Federal Republic and Italy) and one rotating member representing the smaller NATO countries. The rotating member could be elected by a vote of the NATO Council from which the permanent members are excluded, thus protecting the rights of the smaller countries. The

Allies would agree to accept a two-thirds vote as binding with escape clauses to be described. In order to give this Executive Committee appropriate status, membership should be no lower than Deputy Foreign Ministers meeting at least bi-monthly. In the interval between meetings, the NATO Ambassadors could act as deputies.

The Executive Committee should formulate common Atlantic purposes and define the limits of autonomous action where interests diverge. It should give political guidance for the military arrangements described in the previous chapters. It should be the political authority for the proposed Allied Nuclear Force. It should be charged with developing a common strategic doctrine.

As long as the Alliance is composed of sovereign states, the delegation of authority will clearly have to be limited. Each Ally, whether or not a member of the Executive Committee, would have to be given the right to appeal its decisions to the NATO Council, where a two-thirds majority would carry. Each Ally should have the right, for an interim period at least, to refuse to be bound by such a vote. However, it should be required to make a formal declaration to that effect within a given time. A negative vote either in the Executive Committee or in the NATO Council would not be taken as an indication of non-compliance. Instead, a formal notification that a country refuses to carry out the common decision would be required. The purpose of separating the two stages would be to enable the Allies to record their disagreement and yet to carry out the majority's decision for the sake of unity.

Within this framework, the European countries could, if they wished, form a closer association. For example, the Western European Union might well be given responsibility for the European component of the Allied Nuclear Force and, indeed, the European contribution to joint NATO plans. As Europe gains structure, the Executive Committee could draw nearer to the "twin pillars" concept. But Atlantic partnership, in this approach, could become operative even if European unity were delayed.

Atlantic partnership and increased European cohesion thus could be pursued simultaneously, with no advance commitment to giving priority to either course. An Atlantic Community could thus develop on a two-pronged basis.

Conceivably such a policy could end the sterile debate over the relative benefits of integration and coordination. It might heal a rift that, if continued, is bound to hazard everything that has been painfully built up over fifteen years. It would leave the internal evolution of Europe to the European countries and concentrate our efforts where we can be most constructive: in the elaboration of Atlantic relationships.

This requires that we become clear about the notion of Europe as a Third Force which is used so often in a pejorative sense in our discussions. In the sense of being powerful Europe is bound to be a Third Force, partly because we ourselves have made it so. Whether Europe will use its strength for a narrow or a wider conception depends in large part on the ability of leaders on both sides of the Atlantic to develop common purposes and a structure to give them effect. We can best counteract Third Force tendencies based on a form of neutrality by conducting ourselves so that most of our Allies will always consider the advantages of an Atlantic partnership greater than those which could be gained by a more parochial approach.

For this purpose steadiness and reliability are more important assets than an erratic quest for ever-more refined formulas. Confidence presupposes that the leaders of other countries can gear their actions to ours over a period of time. The United States should use its ingenuity to forge a variety of Atlantic institutions not only in the political realm but also in the spheres of economics, scholarship and the arts.

But institutions based on present concepts of national sovereignty are not enough. The West requires a larger goal: the constitution of an Atlantic Commonwealth in which all the peoples bordering the North Atlantic can fulfill their aspirations. Clearly, it will not come quickly;

many intermediate stages must be traversed before it can be reached. It is not too early, however, to prepare ourselves now for this step beyond the nation-state.

A FINAL WORD

When the Atlantic Alliance was founded in 1949, no one would have thought it possible that within fifteen years its pervasive problem would turn out to be the growing strength and self-confidence of Europe. In the face of what was believed to be the imminent threat of Soviet aggression, it would have seemed absurd to predict that fissures would open because the fear of Communist invasion had largely vanished. When Europe dreaded the return of America's traditional isolationism, it would have been incredible that some day our Allies would feel so confident of our support that they would consider it safe to disagree with our policies or even to oppose them.

In a way, then, many of the difficulties in the Atlantic Alliance could be a source of pride for the United States. They are the result of the success of policies ushered in by the Marshall Plan and consistently pursued through four postwar administrations. The West today is less imperiled by outside pressures than by a tendency to consume its own substance.

Yet it is easy to draw too much comfort from this. History is the tale of civilizations that sought their future in their past. There are no plateaus in international affairs; what is not a stepping stone soon becomes the beginning of a decline. Succeeding generations will not be able to draw comfort from the fact that an unmet challenge was produced by great achievement.

In the life of societies and international systems there comes a time when the question arises whether all the possibilities of innovation inherent in a given structure have been exhausted. At this point, symptoms are taken for causes; immediate problems absorb the attention that should be devoted to determining their significance. Events are not shaped by a concept of the future; the present becomes all-intrusive. However impressive such a structure may still appear to outsiders, it has passed its zenith. It will grow ever more rigid and, in time, irrelevant.

The West today confronts such a challenge. It has had centuries of great achievements punctuated by catastrophic upheaval. Its propensity for disaster has been high; but heretofore each tragedy was followed by a new burst of creativity. Are the stresses of today a sign of consolidation or the first symptoms of decay? Will they lead to renewal or to disintegration?

For a while longer the West can continue along familiar routes. The traditional machinery of the Atlantic Alliance is well designed to produce the appearance of amity. But if the Alliance continues to confuse form and substance, energy will increasingly have to be spent in reconciling illusion with reality. Each nation will be thrown on its own resources and will emphasize policies that magnify divisions. At each previous critical juncture the West—though with much travail—found political forms adequate for its needs. It made the transition from feudalism to the nation-state. Its challenge now is whether it can move from the nation-state to a larger community and draw from this effort the strength for another period of innovation.

Its ability to master this problem will largely determine whether the West can remain relevant to the rest of the world. Confronted by turmoil and hatred in the former colonial areas, the West desperately searches for means to demonstrate its good faith to its erstwhile subjects. But every satisfied demand spawns new pressures. The inward insecurity produced by centuries of subordination is not allayed by dealing with its manifestations any more than a tidal wave is understood by studying the surface of the ocean. In many of the new nations, popularity is unattainable partly because of the memory of colonial rule, partly because these nations often do not know what they really want. Their greatest need is a sense of purpose. But this can be conveyed only by example, not by preachments or

by efforts to ingratiate that compound the new nations'
sense of insecurity with our own.

What the West can mean to others depends therefore
in great part on what it means to itself. In the heyday of
colonialism, Western political forms were widely imitated.
The leaders of independence movements fought their op-
pressors in the name of principles they had acquired from
them. The reason was that for all the wrongs it committed,
the West appeared dynamic, creative and vital. If the
West is still to contribute to the rest of the world, it will
have to begin by demonstrating in its internal relationships that its wellsprings of creativity have not run dry.

The opportunity is great. The dynamic periods of Western history occurred when unity was forged from diversity.
This is the task once again. The struggles for prestige and
influence can be salutary if at some point they lead to a
heightened sense of community. Conversely, fifty years
from now no one will care who was "right" with respect
to the issues that form the headlines of the day if in the
process the West has torn itself to pieces.

The challenge is whether the difference in perspective
between the two sides of the Atlantic, which is at the heart
of many disagreements, can be turned into a source of
strength. Our idealism and impetuosity would gain depth
if leavened by the European sense of tragedy. And the
European consciousness of history could recover dynamism if bolstered by our hopefulness.

The deepest question before the West may thus be what
kind of vision it has of its future. With the growth of bureaucracy and expertise on both sides of the Atlantic, there
is a danger of becoming mired by the prudent, the tactical
or the expedient. Problems that are recognized are treated
with considerable adeptness. But many problems are not
recognized. The solution of immediate issues has priority
over the shaping of the future. The expert has a vested
interest in the existing framework; doing the familiar very
well has, after all, made him an expert. His weakness is
that he may confuse creativity with a projection of the

present into the future. He respects "facts" and considers them something to be adjusted to, perhaps to be manipulated, but not to be transcended.

In the decades ahead, the West will have to lift its sights. When technique becomes exalted over purpose, men become the victims of their complexities. They forget that every great achievement in every field was a vision before it became a reality. Both sides of the Atlantic would do well to keep in mind that there are two kinds of realists: those who use facts and those who create them. The West requires nothing so much as men able to create their own reality.

It has become fashionable to compare the disagreements of the West with rifts in the Communist world. But this comparison fails to do justice to the possibilities of the Atlantic area. In the Communist world schisms are inevitable and unbridgeable. Western societies have been more fortunate. Their evolution has been richer because at their best they have managed to relate diversity to community. Free from the shackles of a doctrine of historical inevitability, the nations of the West can render a great service by demonstrating that whatever meaning history has is derived from the convictions and purpose of the generation which shapes it.

INDEX

THE ATLANTIC
POLICY STUDIES

In 1963, on the basis of a grant from the Ford Foundation, the Council on Foreign Relations undertook a program of twelve major studies of the future of the Atlantic Community, known as the Atlantic Policy Studies. Henry A. Kissinger's reappraisal of the Atlantic Alliance, which appears in this volume, is the first of these studies. Dr. Kissinger's study is the outgrowth of a series of lectures on the control of nuclear weapons and attendant political problems of the Alliance, given at the Council on Foreign Relations in March, 1964.

The Atlantic Policy Studies were undertaken out of a conviction that a searching examination of United States relations with, and policies toward, Western Europe is urgently needed. The studies are an attempt to come to grips with basic questions about the future of America's Atlantic relations.

The studies are policy-oriented, seeking not only to describe and forecast but also to prescribe. Each of the twelve studies is the responsibility of its author, but will consider its special problems in the light of the general aim of the program as a whole. The program is under the guidance of a Steering Committee, of which Charles M. Spofford is the chairman.

The Atlantic Policy Studies are divided into four broad categories, dealing respectively with the external environment of the West; with problems of military strength and organization; with economic relations among the Atlantic countries and between them and less developed countries; and with Atlantic political relations.

Two studies of the Atlantic world's external environment have been commissioned and will be published as part of the series. One, by Zbigniew K. Brzezinski of Columbia University, considers the relations between the West, the Soviet Union and Eastern Europe. A second, by Theodore Geiger of the National Planning Association, examines the nature of the great transformation now going on throughout Asia, Africa and Latin America, and its implications for the future of relations with the Western world. A book by Hedley Bull of London University will examine further the military political problems of the Alliance in the areas of nuclear weapons, arms control, and strategic doctrine.

Economic problems both within the Atlantic area and between the Atlantic nations and the rest of the world are examined in four separate studies. One, by John O. Coppock of Stanford University, considers the principal problems of agricultural policy and trade within the Atlantic area. A second by Richard N. Cooper of Yale University examines international financial arrangements and monetary institutions among the Atlantic nations, and prescribes policies for the future in this area. Trade arrangements and economic integration within the Atlantic Community are the subject of a third economic study, by Bela Balassa of Yale University, in collaboration with a group of economists from the United States, Europe, Canada and Japan. John Pincus of the RAND Corporation has undertaken a study of economic relations, trade and aid, between the industrial nations and the less developed countries.

Political relations among the Atlantic nations are the subject of four studies. Miriam Camps of Chatham House and the Council on Foreign Relations is preparing a volume on the future of European unity. Hans Speier of the RAND Corporation and the Council on Foreign Relations has undertaken a study of the implications of German foreign policy for the United States. Stanley Hoffmann of Harvard University will give a series of lectures at the Council in the spring of 1965, which will review the principal constraints, particularly the domestic constraints, on United States action in Atlantic affairs. His lectures will be published as a volume in the Atlantic Policy Series. A fourth political volume, by the Director of the Atlantic Policy Studies, will be addressed to the question of the future shape of political relations among the Atlantic countries.

Harold van B. Cleveland
Director, Atlantic Policy Studies
Council on Foreign Relations

COUNCIL ON FOREIGN RELATIONS